THIRD EDITION

GRAMMAR IN CONTEXT

INSTRUCTOR'S MANUAL & TESTS

WITH ANSWER KEYS
FOR TESTS & BOOKS **1**, **2**, AND **3**

SANDRA N. ELBAUM

HEINLE & HEINLE

THOMSON LEARNING

United States · Australia · Canada · Mexico · Singapore · Spain · United Kingdom

Vice President, Editorial Director ESL/EFL: Nancy Leonhardt
Production Editor: Michael Burggren
Marketing Manager: Charlotte Sturdy
Manufacturing Coordinator: Mary Beth Hennebury
Composition: Modern Graphics, Inc.

For permission to use material in this text, contact us:

web   www.thomsonrights.com
fax   1-800-730-2215
phone   1-800-730-2214

Heinle & Heinle Publishers
20 Park Plaza
Boston, MA 02116

UK/EUROPE/MIDDLE EAST:
Thomson Learning
Berkshire House
168-173 High Holborn
London, WC1V 7AA, United Kingdom

AUSTRALIA/NEW ZEALAND:
Nelson/Thomson Learning
102 Dodds Street
South Melbourne
Victoria 3205 Australia

CANADA:
Nelson/Thomson Learning
1120 Birchmount Road
Scarborough, Ontario
Canada M1K 5G4

LATIN AMERICA:
Thomson Learning
Seneca, 53
Colonia Polanco
11560 México D.F. México

ASIA (excluding Japan):
Thomson Learning
60 Albert Street #15-01
Albert Complex
Singapore 189969

JAPAN:
Thomson Learning
Palaceside Building, 5F
1-1-1 Hitotsubashi, Chiyoda-ku
Tokyo 100 0003, Japan

SPAIN:
Thomson Learning
Calle Magallanes, 25
28015-Madrid, España

Printed in Canada
1 2 3 4 5 6 7 8 9   05 04 03 02 01

CONTENTS

TESTS AND TEST ANSWERS

CONTENTS

TESTS AND TEST ANSWERS

BOOK 3

BOOK 3

STUDENT BOOK ANSWER KEYS

BOOK 1

BOOK 2

BOOK 3

BOOK **1** / LESSON **ONE** / TEST

Part I Find the mistakes with the underlined words, and correct them. Not every sentence has a mistake. If the sentence is correct, write **C**.

EXAMPLES: *Those*
~~That~~ teachers are intelligent.

We're <u>not</u> hungry. *C*

1. <u>The teacher she</u> is nice.
2. They <u>aren't</u> happy.
3. <u>I from</u> Mexico.
4. <u>Is</u> cold today.
5. <u>My sister's</u> not a nurse.
6. <u>Los Angeles's</u> in California.
7. <u>This shoes</u> are brown.
8. <u>I'm not</u> an actor.
9. My books are new. <u>Its</u> expensive.
10. My parents are in <u>U.S.</u>
11. The U.S. <u>is a</u> rich country.
12. The teacher <u>is'nt</u> here today.
13. Mr. <u>Kane's</u> my English teacher.
14. Los Angeles is <u>a</u> American city.
15. China and Russia are <u>a</u> big countries.
16. My grandfather is <u>an</u> old man.
17. He's sixty <u>years old.</u>
18. Chicago and New York are <u>bigs.</u>
19. <u>Your</u> the best student in the class.
20. C
21. Is your brother in the U.S.? Yes, <u>he's.</u>
22. My <u>watch's</u> new.
23. Where <u>is</u> your parents now?
24. <u>It's</u> not hot today.
25. <u>The teacher in</u> the classroom now.

Part 2 Find the mistakes with word order, and correct them. Not every sentence has a mistake. If the sentence is correct, write **C**.

EXAMPLES: *are you*
Where ~~you are~~ from?

What's your last name? *C*

1. Is very strong my father.
2. You're a teacher very good.
3. Mr. Kane is a very nice teacher.
4. Where your teacher is from?
5. What kind of book is this?
6. I'm 5'9" tall. How are you tall?
7. Is at home your father?
8. Why you are late?

Part 3 Write a contraction. If it is not possible to make a contraction, put an **x** in the blank.

EXAMPLES: she is ___she's___

English is ___x___

1. he is _____
2. those are _____
3. I am not _____
4. Chicago is _____
5. Paris is _____
6. you are _____

7. they are not _____
8. that is _____
9. where is _____
10. who are _____
11. which is _____
12. what is _____

Part 4 Read the conversation between two students. They are talking about their classes and teachers. Fill in the blanks to complete the conversation. (Not all blanks need a word. Write 0 if no word is necessary.)

A. Hi, Alicia. How ___are you___ ?

B. I'm fine. I _____ on my way to class.
   (1)

A. Where _____ ?
   (2)

B. My classroom _____ on the third floor.
   (3)

A. _____ ?
   (4)

B. No. My class _____ very big. _____ small.
   (5)   (6)

A. _____ ?
   (7)

B. My teacher's name _____ Mr. Sands.
   (8)

A. _____ a good teacher?
   (9)

B. Yes. He _____ a very good teacher. But he's _____ very strict.
   (10)   (11)

A. _____ ?
   (12)

B. He _____ about 25 years _____ .
   (13)   (14)

A. _____ in the same class?
   (15)

B. No. My brother and I _____ in the same class. He's in a level three class. I _____
   (16)   (17)

   in a level two class. By the way, what time _____ ?
                                                (18)

A. _____ 4:58.
   (19)

B. I'm sorry. I can't talk to you now. I'm in a hurry.

A. Why _____ in a hurry?
   ₍₂₀₎

B. Because my class starts in two minutes. In _____ U.S., classes start on time. See
   ₍₂₁₎
   you later.

Part 5 Fill in the blanks with the correct preposition.

EXAMPLES: The book is ___*on*___ the table.

My brother lives ___*in*___ San Francisco.

1. The plant is _____ the corner.

2. The empty seat is _____ the two passengers.

3. The TV is _____ the students.

4. The picture is _____ the window.

5. The newspaper is _____ the table.

6. My apartment is _____ 1539 Washington Avenue.

7. The hospital is _____ Wilson Avenue.

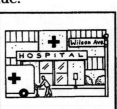

8. The sign is _____ the blackboard.

LESSON **TWO** / TEST

Part I   Find the mistakes with the underlined words, and correct them. Not every sentence has a mistake. If the sentence is correct, write **C**. Change British forms to American forms.

EXAMPLES: <u>I'm not</u> have a computer. *I don't*

Where <u>do your parents live</u>?   *C*

1. <u>How spell</u> "tomorrow"?

2. How many states <u>does the U.S. have</u>?

3. Why <u>you don't</u> work on Fridays?

4. I <u>no own</u> a bicycle.

5. My brother <u>watches</u> TV every night.

6. Where <u>does your sister live</u>?

7. How much <u>costs a phone call</u> to your hometown?

8. My sister <u>doesn't lives</u> near me.

9. My sister <u>studies</u> very hard every day.

10. California <u>doesn't have</u> a cold climate.

11. Where <u>you work</u>?

12. <u>I'm not speak</u> Spanish very well.

13. <u>How say</u> "tomorrow" in Spanish?

14. She <u>hasn't</u> a cell phone.

15. I <u>knowing</u> your teacher very well.

16. My family <u>live</u> in Guatemala.

17. How many children <u>your brother has</u>?

18. The teacher <u>uses</u> good grammar.

19. What <u>means</u> "LA"?

20. <u>Are you want</u> a sandwich for lunch?

21. Why <u>doesn't the classroom have</u> a TV?

22. Does your apartment have air-conditioning? Yes, it <u>is</u>.

23. When <u>does your math class begins</u>?

24. This classroom <u>doesn't have</u> carpeting.

Part 2   Write the *-s* form of the following verbs. Use correct spelling.

EXAMPLE: make _*makes*_

1. worry _____

2. stay _____

3. fix _____

4. go _____

5. wish _____

6. kiss _____

7. watch _____

8. see _____

Part 3 Fill in the first blank with the affirmative of the verb in parentheses ( ).
Then write the negative of this verb.

EXAMPLES: The President ___*lives*___ in the White House.
(live)

The Vice-President ___*doesn't live*___ in the White House.
(live)

The White House ___*is*___ in Washington, D.C.
(be)

It ___*isn't*___ in New York.
(be)

1. The Governor of California _____ in Sacramento.
(work)

The Governor of California _____ in Los Angeles.

2. Congress _____ the laws.
(make)

The President _____ the laws.

3. England _____ a royal family.
(have)

The U.S. _____ a royal family.

4. California and New York _____ a large population.
(have)

Alaska and Wyoming _____ a large population.

5. The University of Illinois _____ a state university
(be)

The University of Chicago _____ a state university. It's a private university.

6. You _____ your native language perfectly.
(know)

You _____ English perfectly.

Part 4 Read each statement. Then write a *yes/no* question about the words in
parentheses ( ). Make any necessary changes. Write a short answer. Some
answers are in parentheses ( ).

EXAMPLES: Maryland is a state (Washington, D.C.) (no)

___*Is Washington, D.C. a state? No, it isn't.*___

Alaska has a cold climate. (Florida) (no)

___*Does Florida have a cold climate? No, it doesn't.*___

1. McDonald's is a popular American restaurant. (Burger King) (yes)

_____

2. Americans like fast food. (good service) (yes)

_____

3. Japan and Korea are small countries. (Canada) (no)

_____

4. The governor lives in the state capital. (the president) (no)

_____

5. You know about the U.S. (Canada)

_____

6. The teacher speaks English well. (you)

_____

Part 5 Read each statement. Then write a *wh-* question about the words in parentheses ( ). You don't need to answer.

EXAMPLES: Mexico has 30 states. (How many/the U.S.)

_____ *How many states does the U.S. have?* _____

Puerto Rico isn't a state. (Why)

_____ *Why isn't Puerto Rico a state?* _____

1. You spell "government" G-O-V-E-R-N-M-E-N-T. (How/"senator")

_____

2. The Governor lives in the state capital. (Where/the President)

_____

3. Americans like baseball. (Why/Americans)

_____

4. A secretary works in an office. (Where/a homemaker)

_____

5. "Physician" means doctor. (What/"pharmacy")

_____

6. Bananas cost 59¢ a pound. (How much/apples)

_____

7. The school isn't open on Christmas Day. (Why/the school)

_____

8. Americans don't like taxes. (Why/Americans)

_____

Part 6 Read this conversation. Fill in the blanks with the missing words.

A. ___*Does*___ your daughter _____ with you?
   _(example)   (1)

B. Oh, no. She _____ live with me. She _____ 30 years old. She _____ in
         (2)   (3)   (4)
   Washington, DC.

A. _____ married?
     (5)

B. No. She's single.

A. Why _____ with you?
       (6)

B. She doesn't live with me because she's very independent. Besides, she wants to live in
   Washington. She _____ want to live with me in New York.
        (7)

A. _____ you _____ your daughter in Washington?
    (8)   (9)

B. Yes, I _____. I visit her once a year, and she _____ me once or
       (10)   (11)
   twice a year, for holidays. It doesn't cost much to fly to Washington.

A. How much _____?
          (12)

B. Sometimes it's less than $100.

A. What's your daughter's name?

B. Her name is Jillian.

A. How _____?
      (13)

B. J-I-L-L-I-A-N

A. _____ a good job?
     (14)

B. Yes, she has a very good job.

A. Where _____?
      (15)

B. She works for the U.S. government, in the department of commerce.

A. What _____?
      (16)

B. Commerce means business. I'm very proud of my daughter.

A. Why _____ proud of her?
       (17)

B. Because she _____ responsible, educated, and kind.
         (18)

LESSON **THREE** / TEST

Part 1   Find the mistakes with the underlined words, and correct them. Not every sentence has a mistake. If the sentence is correct, write **C**.

EXAMPLES: *There are*
~~There's~~ many Mexican students in my class.

I have a new computer. <u>It's</u> a very fast computer.*C*

1. I like <u>the dogs</u> because they are friendly animals.

2. Some <u>people are</u> very lucky.

3. <u>There are</u> a lot of dirty dishes in the kitchen sink.

4. <u>Are</u> two elevators in my building.

5. How many <u>sister's</u> do you have?

6. My friend has <u>the</u> new car. Do you want to see it?

7. Where are your parents? <u>They're</u> at home now.

8. <u>There's the Statue of Liberty</u> in New York.

9. How many letters <u>there are</u> in the English alphabet? <u>Have</u> 26 letters in the English alphabet.

10. What kind of letters are A, E, I, O, U? <u>They're</u> vowels.

11. <u>There's</u> washers and dryers in the basement.

12. My best friend has <u>a</u> nice husband and two great kids.

13. Do you have <u>a pencil</u> for the test?

14. <u>There are</u> 50 stars on the American flag.

15. <u>It's</u> a mistake on your homework paper.

Part 2   Write the plural form for each noun.

EXAMPLES: day ___*days*___   dish ___*dishes*___

tax _____   penny _____   dollar _____

tomato _____   radio _____   city _____

foot _____   leaf _____   boy _____

woman _____   match _____   tooth _____

dog _____   month _____   child _____

pie _____   class _____   man _____

Part 3 Fill in the blanks with *there, is, are, it, they,* or a combination of two words.

I live in Chicago, Illinois. ___*It's*___ a big city. _____ many interesting things
_(example)   ₍₁₎

to do and places to visit in Chicago. For example, _____ many museums.
                                                    ₍₂₎

_____ an art museum downtown. _____ free on Tuesdays.
₍₃₎   ₍₄₎

_____ has famous paintings from all over the world. _____
₍₅₎   ₍₆₎

also a big and wonderful science museum. _____ very popular, especially with
                                          ₍₇₎

children. I take my children there twice a year, and _____ love it.
                                                      ₍₈₎

Part 4 Fill in the blanks with *the, a, an, some, any,* or ∅ for no article.

A. There are ___*some*___ Spanish-speaking students in my class.
              _(example)

B. Are there _____ Asian students in your class?
             ₍₁₎

A. Yes. There's _____ man from China.
                ₍₂₎

B. Are you friends with _____ man from China?
                        ₍₃₎

A. Not really.

B. But you speak _____ same language.
                 ₍₄₎

A. No, we don't. I speak Mandarin, and he speaks Cantonese.

B. Do you have _____ English-Mandarin dictionary?
               ₍₅₎

A. Yes, I do. But a dictionary doesn't help me all the time. I go to movies, but sometimes

    I don't understand everything. I still have _____ problems with the language.
                                                ₍₆₎

B. Do you like _____ American movies?
               ₍₇₎

A. Yes. I do.

LESSON **FOUR** / TEST

Part 1   Find the mistakes with underlined words, and correct them. Not every sentence has a mistake. If the sentence is correct, write **C**.

EXAMPLES: I ~~go often~~ *often go* to the zoo.

She <u>usually takes</u> the train to work.*C*

1. <u>Never he</u> studies on Sunday.

2. Mother's Day <u>always is</u> in May.

3. I <u>seldom drink</u> coffee at night.

4. It <u>snows rarely</u> in April.

5. <u>Do you ever</u> speak English at home? Yes, I <u>ever</u> do.

6. <u>Ever do you watch</u> TV in the morning? No, <u>I never do</u>.

7. <u>How often</u> does the teacher give a teset? She gives a test <u>once a week</u>.

8. <u>She every day calls</u> her mother.

9. <u>Every other day we</u> read a story in class.

10. <u>Sometimes we</u> write a composition in class.

11. He never <u>doesn't work</u> on Sundays.

12. I <u>sometimes go</u> to the library after school.

Part 2   Complete the following statements and questions.

EXAMPLES: Is the college ever closed on Labor Day? Yes, it ___*always*___ is.

It is ___*usually*___ hot in August.

1. How _____ does your husband get a haircut? He gets a haircut once a month.

2. Do you _____ speak English with your family? No, I _____ do.

3. Is the college ever open on Sundays? No, it never _____.

4. Do you visit your cousins often? No. I only visit my cousins _____ in a while.

5. Do you ever write the answers in your book.? No, I never _____.

Part 3   Fill in the blanks with the correct preposition.

EXAMPLE: There is an election ___*in*___ 2004, 2008, 2012.

1. Christmas is _____ December.

2. Christmas is _____ December 25.

3. Do you have a class _____ Monday?

4. My class begins _____ 9 o'clock.

5. I usually watch TV _____ the evening.

6. Do you ever drink tea _____ the morning?

7. Do you ever take a nap[1] _____ the afternoon?

8. I usually sleep _____ 11 P.M. _____ 7 A.M.

9. I like to read _____ night.

10. Do you like to ski _____ the winter?

[1] *Take a nap* means to sleep for a short time in the day.

LESSON **FIVE** / TEST

Part I   Find the mistakes with the underlined words, and correct them. Not every
sentence has a mistake. If the sentence is correct, write **C**.

EXAMPLES: Who <u>live</u> in the White House?   *s* ^

My <u>children's</u> names are Mary and Sue.   *C*

1. <u>My sister and me</u> always take a walk on Sundays.

2. Whose coat <u>is that</u>?

3. <u>Its</u> hot today.

4. <u>Your</u> late today.

5. Where's <u>your</u> jacket?

6. My brother loves <u>his</u> wife very much.

7. My sister loves <u>his</u> husband very much.

8. I don't have <u>mine</u> dictionary with me today.

9. If you don't have your dictionary, you can borrow <u>mine</u>.

10. My parents aren't here. <u>They're</u> in California.

11. <u>Me and my friend</u> like to go fishing on Saturdays.

12. My <u>brother's</u> name is Peter. He doesn't like <u>him</u> name.

13. <u>The your</u> name is hard to pronounce.

14. Who <u>does know</u> the correct answer?

15. Who <u>have</u> a red pen?

16. <u>Whose</u> your English teacher?

17. <u>House my parents</u> is not very big.

18. <u>The school's name</u> is King College.

19. My computer is five years old. <u>Its</u> memory is small.

20. My father lives in Mexico. <u>His</u> a lawyer.

Part 2 Choose the correct word to complete these sentences.

> **EXAMPLE:** I have one brother. _____ married.
> a. His (b.) He's c. He d. Him

1. _____ 10:45 P.M. now.
   a. It   b. It's   c. Its   d. Is

2. In your country, do married women use _____ own last names?
   a. hers   b. theirs   c. their   d. they're

3. What is _____?
   a. her husband's name   c. the name his husband
   b. his husband's name   d. the name her husband

4. My brothers and sisters live in the U.S. _____ parents live in Korea.
   a. Us   b. We   c. Our   d. Ours

5. _____ name is Sofia Lopez-Garcia.
   a. I'm   b. Me   c. My   d. Mine

6. Please call _____ Sofia.
   a. me   b. my   c. mine   d. I

7. How many _____ do you have?
   a. cousin   b. cousins'   c. cousin's   d. cousins

8. My parents live in Toronto. _____ happy there.
   a. They're   b. They   c. There   d. Their

9. You didn't bring your dictionary today. You can use _____.
   a. my   b. I'm   c. mine   d. me

10. _____ is Jackson College.
    a. The name of my college   c. The name my college's
    b. My college's name   d. My the college's name

11. _____ the President of your country?
    a. Whom   b. Whose   c. Who   d. Who's

12. _____ knows the answer?
    a. Whom   b. Who   c. Whose   d. Who's

13. Who _____ baseball?
    a. does like   b. does likes   c. likes   d. like

14. _____
    a. Who's coat is that?   c. Who's is that coat?
    b. Whose coat is that?   d. Whose is that coat?

15. Her _____ problems are difficult.
    a. parent   b. parent's   c. parents'   d. parents

Part 3 Fill in the blanks with possessive forms and subject and object pronouns. Add apostrophes where necessary.

EXAMPLES: In the U.S., a son often uses ____*his*____ father's name. I have a friend,

Charles Bartlett. His father_*'s*_ name is also Charles Bartlett, but his father is Charles Bartlett Senior and my friend is Charlet Bartlett Junior.

Charles _____ wife is pregnant now, and if they have a son, _____ want to
(1)   (2)

name _____ Charles the third. If they have a daughter, they want to name _____
(3)   (4)

Mary Elizabeth.

Like many Americans, Charles has a nickname. _____ nickname is Chuck. Everyone
(5)

calls _____ by that name. _____ wife, Sue, calls him Chucky. Sue uses _____
(6)   (7)   (8)

husband _____ last name. Charles also has a middle name, Robert, but he only uses
(9)

_____ when he signs official documents.
(10)

LESSON **SIX** / TEST

Part 1   Find the mistakes with the underlined words, and correct them. Not every sentence has a mistake. Change sentences that use British English to American English. If the sentence is correct, write **C**.

EXAMPLES: Do you ~~liking~~ *like* New York City?

What is the teacher talking about now? *C*

I ~~haven't~~ *don't have* a cat.

1. She's not sleeping now. She's watching TV.

2. What does she wants?

3. How often does your mother visit you?

4. Why she isn't using her car today?

5. What are you thinking about now?

6. They're having a beautiful house.

7. The President is wearing a blue tie today.

8. Do they have a new car?

9. I'm always drink coffee in the morning.

10. My brother live in New Jersey.

11. What is your sister doing now? She's talking on the phone.

12. What kind of job your father has?

Part 2   Two students meet at the beach. Fill in the blanks with the correct form of the verb in parentheses ( ). Use the simple present or the present continuous.

A.   Hi. I see that you _____*are reading*_____ a book. What book _____?
(read)   (1. read)

B.   It's for my history class. I _____ for a test now. The teacher _____
(2. study)   (3. give)

us a test every other Friday. I _____ to study outdoors. What _____
(4. like)   (5. you/do)

here?

A. I _____ to get a suntan.
   (6. try)

B. Why _____ to get a suntan? Don't you _____ that the sun is bad for
   (7. you/try)   (8. know)
   your skin?

A. I usually _____ to have a suntan. I _____ that a suntan _____ good.
   (9. like)   (10. think)   (11. look)

B. I don't agree. I always _____ in the shade.
   (12. sit)

Part 3 Fill in the blanks with the negative form of the underlined words.

   EXAMPLE: I'm studying for a history test. I _*'m not studying*_____ for an
   English test.

1. He's reading a book. He _____ a magazine.

2. He likes history. He _____ math.

3. The test is on Friday. It _____ today.

4. I always sit in the shade. I _____ in the sun.

Part 4 Read each statement. Then write a *yes/no* question about the words in
   parentheses ( ). Write a short answer with the word given.

   EXAMPLE: The book is long. (good) (yes)

   _*Is the book good?*   *Yes, it is.*_____

1. He likes math. (history) (no)

   _____

2. He is sitting in the park. (in the sun) (yes)

   _____

3. The teacher gives tests. (quizzes) (no)

   _____

4. The day is hot. (sunny) (yes)

   _____

Part 5 Read each statement. Then write a question with the words in ( ). An answer is not necessary.

> EXAMPLE: He's sitting in the sun. (why)
>
> _Why is he sitting in the sun?_

1. He's reading a book. (what kind of book)

_____

2. He doesn't like the shade. (why)

_____

3. The teacher gives a test every week. (why)

_____

4. His friend isn't sitting in the sun. (why)

_____

NAME_____

LESSON **SEVEN** / TEST

Part 1   Find the mistakes with the underlined words, and correct them. Not every sentence has a mistake. If the sentence is correct, write **C.**

EXAMPLE: Where will you ~~be go~~ on your honeymoon?

<u>Will you send</u> me a postcard?   *C*

1. I <u>will going</u> to buy a wedding present for my cousin.

2. I have to leave now. <u>I'll see</u> you later.

3. When I <u>will be</u> in Bermuda, <u>I'll send</u> you a postcard.

4. Why <u>you aren't going to watch</u> the movie with us tomorrow?

5. I <u>going to buy</u> a new house soon.

6. When <u>will you be</u> back from your trip?

7. If you <u>don't eat</u> breakfast now, you <u>will hungry</u> later.

8. He'll buy a car when he <u>finds</u> a job.

9. When <u>we will have</u> a test?

10. Why <u>the teacher isn't going to be</u> here tomorrow?

Part 2   Fill in the blanks with the simple present, the present continuous, or the future tense of the verb in parentheses ( ). Use the affirmative form.

EXAMPLES: I ___*like*___ my profession.
   (like)

   This semester I ___*am studying*___ advanced programming.
   (study)

1. I _____ a lot of experience with computers.
   (have)

2. I _____ for a job now.
   (look)

3. I _____ the newspaper next Sunday.
   (buy)

4. When I _____ a job, I _____ a car.
   (find)   (buy)

5. Little by little, my English _____ .
   (improve)

18   **BOOK I**/ LESSON **SEVEN**/ TEST

Part 3   Fill in the blanks with the negative form of the underlined verbs.

        EXAMPLES: It<u>'s</u> easy to find a low-paying job. It ___*isn't*___ easy to find a good job.

                         Some jobs <u>offer</u> good benefits. Some jobs ___*don't offer*___ good benefits.

1. I <u>want</u> to find a good job. I _____ to work in a factory.

2. <u>I'm going to ask</u> my counselor for advice. I _____ my friends.

3. Some workers <u>are losing</u> their jobs. Computer repairers _____ their jobs.

4. Some jobs <u>will increase</u> in the future. Jobs for factory workers _____ in the future.

5. My counselor <u>has</u> information about jobs in the U.S. She _____ information about jobs in other countries.

Part 4   Read each statement. Write a *yes/no* question with the words in parentheses ( ). Write a short answer with the word in parentheses ( ).

        EXAMPLES: My father works in a bank. (your mother) (no)

                         Does your mother work in a bank?   No, she doesn't.

                         I'm looking for a job. (you) (yes)

                         Are you looking for a job?   Yes, I am.

1. My father has a good job. (your mother) (yes)

   _____

2. I'm preparing for the future. (you) (yes)

   _____

3. The counselor will give you information about jobs. (about apartments) (no)

   _____

4. Your brother is studying to be a programmer. (your sister) (no)

   _____

5. Her son is going to study medicine. (her daughter) (no)

   _____

Part 5   Read each statement. Then write a *wh-* question with the words in parentheses ( ). An answer is not necessary.

EXAMPLES: Linda is unemployed. (why/she)

Why is she unemployed?

She doesn't want to work on Saturdays. (what days/she)

What days does she want to work?

1. Linda is going to visit her counselor. (when/she)

_____

2. She needs information about jobs. (why/she)

_____

3. She doesn't want to work at home. (why/she)

_____

4. She is looking for a new job. (what kind of job/she)

_____

5. Someone will help her. (who)

_____

LESSON **EIGHT** / TEST

Part 1   Find the mistakes with the underlined words, and correct them. Not every sentence has a mistake. If the sentence is correct, write **C**.

EXAMPLES: Lindbergh <u>flied</u> across the Atlantic Ocean in 1927.
flew

Lindbergh <u>was</u> a pilot for the U.S. Mail Service.*C*

1. The Wright Brothers <u>invented</u> the airplane.

2. Lindbergh and Earhart <u>was</u> aviators.

3. Lindbergh <u>born</u> in 1902.

4. Lindbergh wanted to <u>won</u> a prize.

5. Earhart <u>didn't returned</u> from her last trip.

6. Earhart <u>had</u> 39 years old when she disappeared.

7. What <u>did the teacher say</u>?

8. When <u>arrived your father</u>?

9. When <u>Goddard died</u>?

10. Why <u>was</u> you late?

11. Who <u>invented</u> the rocket?

12. Why <u>weren't you</u> here yesterday?

13. Did you <u>saw</u> the accident?

14. What <u>happened</u> on December 17, 1903?

Part 2   Write the past tense of each verb.

EXAMPLES: see ____*saw*____   look ___*looked*___

1. worry _____   6. know _____

2. take _____   7. feel _____

3. go _____   8. find _____

4. put _____   9. speak _____

5. sit _____   10. talk _____

11. eat _____   14. stop _____

12. sleep _____   15. destroy _____

13. hear _____

Part 3   Fill in the blanks with the negative form of the underlined verb.

EXAMPLE: The Wright Brothers <u>invented</u> the airplane. They _____*didn't invent*_____ the telephone.

1. Amelia Earhart and Charles Lindberg <u>were</u> aviators. They _____ inventors.

2. Lindbergh <u>flew</u> to Paris. He _____ to Rome.

3. Earhart's plane <u>disappeared</u>. Lindbergh's plane _____ .

4. Wilbur Wright <u>died</u> young. Orville Wright _____ young.

5. The Wright brothers <u>were</u> interested in airplanes. They _____ interested in rockets.

Part 4   Read each statement. Write a *yes/no* question about the words in parentheses ( ). Write a short answer with the word in parentheses ( ).

EXAMPLE: Lindbergh learned to fly. (Earhart) (yes)

   Did Earhart learn to fly?   Yes, she did. _____

1. Lindbergh loved to fly. (Earhart) (yes)

   _____

2. Lindbergh became famous. (Earhart) (yes)

   _____

3. Goddard studied physics. (aviation) (no)

   _____

4. Goddard was born in the U.S. (in California) (no)

   _____

5. Apollo 11 went to the moon. (Goddard's rockets) (no)

   _____

Part 5   Write a *wh-* question about the words in parentheses ( ). It is not necessary to answer the questions.

     EXAMPLES: The Wright Brothers were famous. (why/they)

         Why were they famous?

         Lindbergh went to Paris. (where/Earhart)

         Where did Earhart go?

1. The Wright Brothers invented something. (what/they)

2. The Wright Brothers were born in the U.S. (when/they)

3. Earhart went to Ireland. (why/she)

4. Lindbergh won a prize. (what kind of prize/he)

5. Americans loved Lindbergh. (why/they)

6. People laughed at Goddard. (why)

7. Someone laughed at Goddard. (who)

8. The reporter wrote something about Goddard. (what)

9. The President heard something about Goddard. (what)

10. Gagarin was the first man in space. (who/first woman)

LESSON **NINE** / TEST

Part I   Find the mistakes with the underlined words, and correct them. Not every sentence has a mistake. If the sentence is correct, write **C**.

EXAMPLE: She <u>must to leave</u> early.

She <u>needs to leave</u> early.   *C*

1. She wanted <u>to went</u> to the museum.

2. It <u>might rain</u> tomorrow.

3. <u>I happy to be</u> in the U.S.

4. <u>He's afraid speak</u> English.

5. <u>Is important to own</u> a car.

6. She <u>can't English speak</u>.

7. He <u>doesn't have to cook</u> dinner.

8. They <u>shouldn't to watch</u> TV.

9. Please be here at six o'clock. <u>Not be</u> late.

10. He <u>likes play</u> tennis.

11. <u>Don't talk</u> so loud. I'm trying <u>to study</u>.

12. <u>Let's go</u> for a walk. <u>Let's not stay</u> inside.

13. You <u>should use</u> your dictionary <u>to check</u> your spelling.

14. Where <u>I can buy</u> used books?

15. I'm sorry <u>to leave</u> so soon.

16. You <u>must take</u> the final exam.

17. My father <u>can drives</u> very well.

18. <u>It's dangerous drive</u> when you're sleepy.

19. She uses a VCR <u>for record</u> her favorite TV shows.

20. She <u>shouldn't wearing</u> pants to her job interview.

21. He <u>needs to use</u> the phone.

22. I'm afraid <u>to go</u> out at night.

Part 2 Fill in the first blank with *to* or nothing ∅. Then complete the negative form in the second blank.

EXAMPLES: I'm afraid ___*to*___ walk alone at night. _*I'm not afraid to walk*_ alone during the day.

I can ___∅___ help you on Friday. I ___*can't*___ help you on Sunday.

1. I have _____ work on Fridays. I _____ work on Sundays.

2. You should _____ drive carefully. You _____ drive when you are sleepy.

3. She wants _____ leave now. She _____ stay.

4. It's necessary _____ study English. It _____ study French.

5. Let's _____ talk about grammar. _____ talk about our problems.

Part 3 Change each sentence to a question beginning with the word given.

EXAMPLES: I need to go to the post office.

Why _*do you need to go to the post office?*_

They should leave.

When _*should they leave?*_

1. She wants to go on vacation.

Where _____

2. He's afraid to speak English.

Why _____

3. He can't walk.

Why _____

4. He has to work.

When _____

5. It's important to have a driver's license.

Why _____

6. It isn't necessary to bring a dictionary.

   Why _____

7. She'd like to learn Spanish.

   When _____

Part 4   Decide if the sentences have the same meaning or different meanings.
Write **S** for same, **D** for different.

      EXAMPLES: Do you have to leave? / Would you like to leave?   *D*

                      Would you help me now? / Could you help me now?   *S*

1. May I help you? / Should I help you?

2. What would you like to do tonight? / What do you want to do tonight?

3. May I use your book? / Can I use your book?

4. It might rain tonight. / It may rain tonight.

5. I should leave now. / I must leave now.

6. Could you close the window? / Would you close the window?

7. She has to make an appointment with the doctor. / She must make an appointment with the doctor.

8. We will finish this lesson tomorrow. / We might finish this lesson tomorrow.

9. You don't have to park here. / You must not park here.

10. Before you buy shoes, you should try them on. / Before you buy shoes, you can try them on.

11. At my job, we don't have to wear a suit on Fridays. / At my job, we must not wear a suit on Fridays.

12. I may buy a new car soon. / I should buy a new car soon.

LESSON **TEN** / TEST

Part I   Find the mistakes with the underlined words, and correct them. Not every sentence has a mistake. If the sentence is correct, write **C**.

EXAMPLES: She drank three teas. *cups of*

Many people saw the accident.   *C*

1. The teacher gave me a lot of <u>informations</u>.

2. There was <u>a lot of snow</u> last winter.

3. She doesn't have <u>any</u> friends in the U.S.

4. I bought <u>five cartons milk</u>.

5. I <u>don't have no</u> coffee at home.

6. She bought <u>a new furniture</u>.

7. If I work hard and save, I will have <u>too much</u> money.

8. Your son can't drive because he's <u>too</u> young.

9. I can't find a good job because I don't have <u>an</u> experience.

10. She has <u>a few</u> questions about the lesson.

11. I have <u>much</u> trouble with my car.

12. There are <u>a tall mountains</u> near my hometown.

13. <u>A lot of boy</u> came to the baseball game.

14. In my country, there is <u>a lot of</u> unemployment. There isn't <u>a lot of</u> here.

15. He doesn't have <u>any</u> time to help you.

16. I don't have <u>any</u> computer. I use my brother's computer.

17. <u>How many nuts</u> did you eat?

18. I can't help you now. I'm <u>too much</u> tired.

19. If I have <u>a little of</u> free time, we can get together for lunch.

20. My mom gave me <u>some advice</u> about marriage.

Part 2 Fill in the blanks with an appropriate measurement of quantity. In some cases, more than one answer is possible.

EXAMPLE: a ___*slice (OR loaf)*___ of bread

1. a _____ of soup

2. a _____ of coffee

3. a _____ of soap

4. a _____ of water

5. a _____ of mail

6. a _____ of advice

7. an _____ of corn

LESSON **ELEVEN** / TEST

Part I   Find the mistakes with the underlined words, and correct them. Not every sentence has a mistake. If the sentence is correct, write **C**.

EXAMPLES: I'm not <u>finish</u> with my homework.   *ed*

The <u>tall man</u> put the box on the <u>high shelf</u>.   *C*

1. She looks great. She's <u>too</u> beautiful.

2. She has <u>a very good</u> job.

3. I bought some new books at the <u>books</u> store.

4. The bus driver drove <u>carefully</u>.

5. I can't help you now. I'm <u>too tire</u>.

6. Do you prefer a light breakfast or <u>a heavy</u>?

7. Put the small packages on the lower shelf. Put the large <u>ones</u> on the other shelf.

8. She can't go to college yet. She's <u>too much young</u>.

9. I <u>very</u> like my English class.

10. He is a very <u>careful</u> person.

11. He speaks English very <u>fluent</u>.

12. She dresses <u>well</u>.

13. I'm <u>worry</u> about my mother.

14. This sweater is old. That <u>one</u> is new.

15. You have <u>intelligents</u> children.

16. I'm <u>interest</u> in sports.

17. My sister sings <u>very beautifully</u>.

18. She sings very <u>good</u>.

Part 2   Find the mistakes in word order, and correct them. Not every sentence has a mistake. If the sentence is correct, write **C**.

EXAMPLES: He (very slowly) drives. ↵

He has a driver's license.   *C*

1.   He fast gave his speech.

2.   Mary is a person very intelligent.

3.   I am enough old to get married.

4.   She has enough experience to find a good job.

5.   He finished quickly the job.

6.   How many presents birthday did you receive?

Part 3   Fill in the blanks with the correct form, adjective or adverb, of the word in parentheses ( ).

EXAMPLES: Are you a ___*patient*___ person? Can you wait here
(patient)

___*patiently*___ ?
(patient)

1.   Some Americans speak English too _____ , and I can't understand them.
(quick)

2.   He checked his paper _____ before turning it in.
(careful)

3.   She is a very _____ person.
(sweet)

4.   She talks very _____ .
(sweet)

5.   Spanish is _____ for me. I learned Spanish very _____ .
(easy)   (easy)

6.   You drive too _____ . You should drive more _____ .
(fast)   (slow)

7.   Do you exercise _____ ?
(regular)

8.   He's a very _____ student.
(serious)

9.   Are you a _____ cook?
(good)

10.   I don't cook very _____ .
(good)

LESSON **TWELVE** / TEST

Part 1   Find the mistakes with the underlined words, and correct them. Not every sentence has a mistake. If the sentence is correct, write **C**.

EXAMPLES: An orange is ~~the~~ smaller than a grapefruit.

The Sears Tower is the tallest building in the U.S.   *C*

1. He is one of the oldest student in the college.

2. My mom is best cook in the world.

3. Texas is a bigger state.

4. I am thinner that my sister.

5. She speaks English more better than I do.

6. My neighbors are the noisiest people in the world.

7. I drive slowlier than you do.

8. He reads more books I do.

9. New York is one of the most big cities in the world.

10. San Francisco is one of the most beautiful cities in the world.

11. My the best friend lives in Boston.

12. Lesson One is easyer than Lesson Ten.

13. You are the funniest person in the class.

14. I'm much taller than my sister.

Part 2   Find the mistakes in word order, and correct them. Not every sentence has a mistake. If the sentence is correct, write **C**.

EXAMPLES: You ~~more~~ understand *more* than I do.

You are more intelligent than I am.   *C*

1. I more quickly type than my friend.

2. She has more money than I do.

3. He earlier woke up than I did.

4. I know more about geography than you do.

5. San Francisco is the most beautiful city in California.

6. You have more time than I do.

7. You are the most wonderful teacher in the world.

8. My brother is the person most intelligent in my family.

Part 3   Fill in the blanks with the comparative form or the superlative form of the word in parentheses ( ). Add *the* or *than* if necessary.

EXAMPLE: Texas is _____*bigger than*_____ California.

(big)

Alaska is _____*the biggest*_____ state in the U.S.

(big)

1. What is _____ way to call long distance?

(cheap)

2. My old computer was _____ my new computer.

(expensive)

3. My new computer is _____ my old computer.

(fast)

4. My brother drives _____ I do.

(well)

5. December 21 is _____ day of the year.

(short)

6. Book One is _____ Book Two.

(easy)

7. Mary is _____ girl in her class.

(popular)

8. Who is _____ basketball player in the world?

(good)

9. The book was interesting, but the movie was even _____ .

(interesting)

10. Bill had _____ grade on the test.

(bad)

LESSON **THIRTEEN** / TEST

Part I   Find the mistakes with the underlined words, and correct them. Not every sentence has a mistake. If the sentence is correct, write **C**.

EXAMPLES: There's a new coffee shop on Main Street, <u>isn't it</u>? *there*

You have an American car, <u>don't you</u>?   *C*

1. I like to play golf, and my best friend <u>too.</u>

2. I play golf on Saturdays, <u>but</u> my best friend doesn't.

3. Chicago isn't the capital of Illinois, is it? <u>Yes, it isn't.</u>

4. Chicago is a big city, <u>and</u> Springfield isn't.

5. You have a new computer, and I <u>do too.</u>

6. You aren't an American citizen, <u>do you</u>?

7. My father doesn't speak English well, and my uncle doesn't <u>too.</u>

8. You didn't come to class yesterday, <u>did</u> you?

9. This is an easy test, isn't <u>this</u>?

10. There are 20 students in this class, <u>aren't they</u>?

11. I don't have a bicycle, but my brother <u>does.</u>

12. The teacher explained the grammar clearly, <u>didn't the teacher</u>?

Part 2   This is a conversation between two students. Fill in the blanks with auxiliary verbs to complete this conversation. Use *either* and *too* when necessary.

A. Where are you from?

B. Mexico.

A. I _____*am too*_____. I come from Mexico City.
      (example)

B. I _____. I come from Guadalajara. But I lived in Mexico City while I was
         (1)

in college.

B. Where did you go to college?

A. The National University.

B. I _____ (2) . I went there from 1992 to 1994.

A. I was there from 1991 to 1993.

B. I didn't live near the university.

A. I _____ (3) . I lived far from the university, near the airport.

B. I _____ (4) . I lived only five minutes from the airport.

A. This is very interesting. We have a lot in common.

B. Yes, it is interesting, but I can't talk now.

A. I _____ (5) . I have a class in five minutes. I'd like to continue this conversation some other time.

B. I _____ (6) . Let's meet in the cafeteria at noon. I'll be free at that time.

A. Sorry. I _____ (7) . I have to go home and take care of my little sister.

Part 3 In this conversation, a counselor is trying to find out if her information about a student is correct. Add a tag question to each statement.

A. Your first language is Spanish, _____*isn't it?*_____ (example)

B. Yes, it is.

A. You didn't take the TOEFL, _____ (1)

B. No, I didn't.

A. Your major is math, _____ (2)

B. Yes, it is.

A. And you're planning to become a programmer, _____ (3)

B. No, I'm not. I want to be an engineer.

A. You don't have a scholarship, _____ (4)

B. No, I don't.

A. I have no more questions for you. Now you probably have some questions for

me, _____ (5)

B. Yes, I do. The tuition is a thousand dollars a semester, _____ (6)

A. Yes, it is.

B. And I can apply for a government loan, _____
(7)

A. Yes, you can.

B. This college doesn't have dormitories, _____
(8)

A. No, it doesn't.

LESSON **FOURTEEN** / TEST

Part I   Barbara, her husband, Mike, and their two children are on vacation now. Barbara is writing a letter to her friend Judy. Fill in the blanks with the correct tense of the verb in parentheses ( ) to complete this letter. Use the simple present, the present continuous, the future, or the simple past.

Dear Judy,

    We're in beautiful, sunny Hawaii now. When we ___*left*___ Boston two days ago, it
                                                      (leave)

_____ cold and snowy, but now I _____ in the warm sun. Honolulu is
(1. be)   (2. sit)

beautiful, and we all _____ it here. This week we _____ in a lovely hotel
                      (3. love)   (4. stay)

in Honolulu. Next week we _____ a trip to some of the other islands near
                          (5. take)

here.

    The hotel _____ a large swimming pool, tennis courts, and a golf course. Mike
              (6. have)

usually _____ up early and _____ tennis. I always _____ to sleep
        (7. get)   (8. play)   (9. like)

late. We _____ each other at about noon every day.
         (10. see)

    Last night, we _____ in a Hawaiian restaurant. Mike and I loved the food, but
                   (11. eat)

the children _____ it. Tomorrow we _____ in a Chinese restaurant.
             (12. hate)   (13. eat)

We _____ the children with a baby-sitter because they don't like Chinese food. They
   (14. leave)

can go to a fast-food restaurant.

    It is afternoon now, and I'm at the beach. The children aren't here. Mike _____
                                                                              (15. take)

them downtown this morning. They went shopping for souvenirs. They _____ me to
                                                                   (16. ask)

go with them, but I don't like to shop. That's all for now. I _____ you a postcard
                                                              (17. send)

next week. And I _____ you in Boston at the end of the month.
                 (18. see)

Take care,

Barbara

Part 2 Fill in the blanks with the negative form of the underlined verb.

> **EXAMPLES:** Barbara is writing a letter. She ____*isn't writing*____ a composition.
>
> She left Boston two days ago. She ____*didn't leave*____ Boston a week ago.

1. They went to Hawaii. They _____ to Puerto Rico.

2. They will go to other islands. They _____ to California.

3. Barbara and Mike see each other at noon. They _____ each other in the morning.

4. Mike likes to get up early. Barbara _____ to get up early.

5. Mike is shopping for souvenirs. Barbara _____ for souvenirs.

6. Barbara and Mike are going to eat Chinese food tomorrow. The children

   _____ Chinese food.

7. They should leave the children with a baby-sitter. They _____ take their children to the Chinese restaurant.

8. Barbara is in Hawaii. Judy _____ in Hawaii.

Part 3 Read each statement. Then write a *yes/no* question about the words in parentheses ( ). Write a short answer.

> **EXAMPLE:** It's cold in Boston. (in Hawaii)
>
> ___*Is it cold in Hawaii?   No, it isn't.*___

1. The hotel has tennis courts. (a swimming pool)

   _____

2. Barbara and Mike ate in a Hawaiian restaurant last night. (the children)

   _____

3. The children will eat at a fast-food restaurant tomorrow. (Barbara and Mike)

   _____

4. Barbara and Mike like Chinese food. (the children)

   _____

5. Barbara is writing a letter now. (Mike)

   _____

6. Mike went downtown. (the children)

_____

7. They are going to visit other islands. (the Virgin Islands)

_____

Part 4   Read each statement. Then write a *wh-* question about the words in parentheses ( ). An answer is not necessary.

EXAMPLES: They went to Hawaii. (why)

_*Why did they go to Hawaii?*_____

Boston is cold now. (how cold)

_*How cold is Boston now?*_____

1. Barbara is writing a letter now. (who . . . to OR to whom)

_____

2. Mike isn't sitting in the sun. (why)

_____

3. The children don't like Chinese food. (why)

_____

4. They'll visit other islands. (which islands)

_____

5. They are going to return to Boston. (when)

_____

6. Barbara likes to sleep late. (why)

_____

7. Someone went downtown. (who)

_____

8. Barbara and Mike go on a vacation. (how often)

_____

9. Barbara didn't go downtown. (why)

_____

10. They should leave the children with a baby-sitter. (why)

_____

BOOK **1** / LESSON **ONE** TEST / ANSWERS

Part 1

1. The teacher is nice.
2. C
3. I'm from Mexico.
4. It's cold today.
5. C
6. Los Angeles is in California.
7. These shoes are brown.
8. C
9. My books are new. They're expensive.
10. My parents are in the U.S.
11. C
12. The teacher isn't here today.
13. C
14. Los Angeles is an American city.
15. China and Russia are big countries.
16. C
17. C
18. Chicago and New York are big.
19. You're the best student in the class.
20. C.
21. Is your brother in the U.S.? Yes, he is.
22. My watch is new.
23. Where are your parents now?
24. C
25. The teacher is in the classroom now.

Part 2

1. My father is very strong.
2. You're a very good teacher.
3. C
4. Where is your teacher from?
5. C
6. I'm 5'9" tall. How tall are you?
7. Is your father at home?
8. Why are you late?

Part 3

1. he's
2. X
3. I'm not
4. Chicago's
5. X
6. you're
7. they're not OR they aren't
8. that's
9. where's
10. X
11. X
12. what's

Part 4

1. 'm
2. is your class(room)
3. is
4. Is your class big
5. isn't
6. It's
7. What's your teacher's name
8. is
9. Is he
10. 's
11. '
12. How old is he (your teacher/Mr. Kane)
13. 's
14. old
15. Are you and your brother
16. aren't
17. 'm
18. is it
19. It's
20. are you
21. the

Part 5

1. in
2. between
3. in front of
4. near/next to/by/beside
5. under/beneath
6. at
7. on
8. over/above

LESSON TWO

Part 1

1. <u>How do you spell</u> "tomorrow"?
2. C
3. Why <u>don't you</u> work on Fridays?
4. I <u>don't own</u> a bicycle.
5. C
6. C
7. How much <u>does a phone call cost</u> to your hometown?
8. My sister <u>doesn't live</u> near me.
9. C
10. C
11. Where <u>do you work</u>?
12. I <u>don't speak</u> Spanish very well.
13. <u>How do you say</u> "tomorrow" in Spanish?
14. She <u>doesn't have</u> a cell phone.
15. I <u>know</u> your teacher very well.
16. My family <u>lives</u> in Guatemala.
17. How many children <u>does your brother have</u>?
18. C
19. What <u>does "LA" mean</u>?
20. <u>Do you want</u> a sandwich for lunch?
21. C
22. Does your apartment have air-conditioning? Yes, it <u>does</u>.
23. When <u>does your math class begin</u>?
24. C

Part 2

1. worries
2. stays
3. fixes
4. goes
5. wishes
6. kisses
7. watches
8. sees

Part 3

1. works
   doesn't work
2. makes
   doesn't make
3. has
   doesn't have
4. have
   don't have
5. is
   isn't
6. know
   don't know

Part 4

1. Is Burger King a popular American restaurant? Yes, it is.
2. Do Americans like good service? Yes, they do.
3. Is Canada a small country? No, it isn't.
4. Does the President live in the state capital? No, he doesn't.
5. Do you know about Canada? Yes, I do. (OR No, I don't.)
6. Do you speak English well? No, I don't. (OR Yes, I do.)

Part 5

1. How do you spell "senator"?
2. Where does the President live?
3. Why do Americans (OR they) like baseball?
4. Where does a homemaker work?
5. What does "pharmacy" mean?
6. How much do apples cost? (OR How much are apples?)
7. Why isn't the school (OR it) open on Christmas Day?
8. Why don't Americans (OR they) like taxes?

Part 6

1. live
2. doesn't
3. is
4. lives
5. Is she
6. doesn't she live
7. doesn't
8. Do
9. visit
10. do
11. visits
12. does it cost (to fly to Washington)
13. do you spell Jillian
14. Does she have
15. does she work
16. does commerce mean
17. are you
18. is

LESSON THREE

Part 1

1. I like <u>dogs</u> because they are friendly animals.
2. C
3. C
4. <u>There are</u> two elevators in my building.
5. How many <u>sisters</u> do you have?
6. My friend has <u>a</u> new car. Do you want to see it?
7. C
8. <u>The Statue of Liberty is</u> in New York.

9. How many letters <u>are there</u> in the English alphabet? <u>There are</u> 26 letters in the English alphabet.
10. C
11. <u>There are</u> washers and dryers in the basement.
12. C
13. C
14. C
15. <u>There's</u> a mistake on your homework paper.

Part 2

taxes	pennies	dollars	women	matches	teeth
tomatoes	radios	cities	dogs	months	children
feet	leaves	boys	pies	classes	men

Part 3

1. There are
2. there are
3. There is (OR There's)
4. It is (OR It's)
5. It
6. There is (OR There's)
7. It is (OR It's)
8. they

Part 4

1. any
2. a
3. the
4. the
5. an
6. some
7. ∅

LESSON FOUR

Part 1

1. He <u>never</u> studies on Sunday.
2. Mother's Day <u>is always</u> in May.
3. C
4. It <u>rarely snows</u> in April.
5. C/Yes, I <u>sometimes</u> do. (OR *always, often, usually*)
6. <u>Do you ever</u> watch TV in the morning? No, I never do.

7. C
8. She calls her mother <u>every day</u>. (OR <u>Every day</u> she calls her mother.)
9. C
10. C
11. He never <u>works</u> on Sundays.
12. C

Part 2

1. often
2. ever
   never OR rarely OR seldom
3. is
4. once
5. do

Part 3

1. in
2. on
3. on
4. at
5. in
6. in
7. in
8. from/to
9. at
10. in/during

LESSON FIVE

Part 1

1. <u>My sister and I</u> always take a walk on Sundays.
2. C
3. <u>It's</u> hot today.
4. <u>You're</u> late today.
5. C
6. C
7. My sister loves <u>her</u> husband very much.
8. I don't have <u>my</u> dictionary with me today.
9. C
10. C
11. <u>My friend and I</u> like to go fishing on Saturdays.
12. C/He doesn't like <u>his</u> name.
13. <u>Your</u> name is hard to pronounce.
14. Who <u>knows</u> the correct answer?
15. Who <u>has</u> a red pen?
16. <u>Who's</u> your English teacher?
17. <u>My parents' house</u> is not very big.
18. <u>The name of the school</u> is King College.
19. C
20. My father lives in Mexico. <u>He's</u> a lawyer.

Part 2

1. b	4. c	7. d	10. a	12. b	14. b
2. c	5. c	8. a	11. d	13. c	15. c
3. a	6. a	9. c			

Part 3

1. ' (OR 's)	4. her	7. His	9. 's
2. they	5. His	8. her	10. it
3. him	6. him		

LESSON SIX

Part 1

1. C
2. What <u>does she want</u>?
3. C
4. Why <u>isn't she using</u> her car today?
5. C
6. <u>They have</u> a beautiful house.
7. C
8. C
9. I always <u>drink</u> coffee in the morning.
10. My brother <u>lives</u> in New Jersey.
11. What <u>is your sister doing</u> now? <u>She's talking</u> on the phone.
12. What kind of job <u>does your father have</u>?

Part 2

1. are you reading	4. like	7. are you trying	10. think
2. 'm studying	5. are you doing	8. know	11. looks
3. gives	6. 'm trying	9. like	12. sit

Part 3

1. isn't reading
2. doesn't like
3. isn't
4. don't sit OR never sit

Part 4

1. Does he like history? No, he doesn't.
2. Is he sitting in the sun? Yes, he is.
3. Does the teacher give quizzes? No, she/he doesn't.
4. Is it (the day) sunny? Yes, it is.

Part 5

1. What kind of book is he reading?
2. Why doesn't he like the shade?
3. Why does the teacher give a test every week?
4. Why isn't his friend sitting in the sun?

LESSON SEVEN

Part I

1. I <u>am going</u> to buy a wedding present for my cousin. OR I <u>will buy</u> . . .
2. C
3. When I <u>am</u> in Bermuda, . . .
4. Why <u>aren't you going to watch</u> the movie with us tomorrow?
5. I'm <u>going to buy</u> a new house soon.
6. C
7. If you <u>don't eat</u> breakfast now, you <u>will be hungry</u> later.
8. C
9. When <u>will we have</u> a test?
10. Why <u>isn't the teacher going to be</u> here tomorrow?

Part 2

1. have
2. am looking
3. will buy (OR am going to buy)
4. find/will buy (OR am going to buy)
5. is improving

Part 3

1. don't want
2. 'm not going to ask
3. aren't losing
4. won't increase
5. doesn't have

Part 4

1. Does your mother have a good job? Yes, she does.
2. Are you preparing for the future? Yes, I am.
3. Will the counselor give you information about apartments? No, he/she won't.
4. Is your sister studying to be a programmer? No, she isn't.
5. Is her daughter going to study medicine? No, she isn't.

Part 5

1. When is she going to visit her counselor?
2. Why does she need information about jobs?
3. Why doesn't she want to work at home?
4. What kind of job is she looking for?
5. Who will help her?

LESSON EIGHT

Part I

1. C
2. Lindbergh and Earhart <u>were</u> aviators.
3. Lindbergh <u>was</u> born in 1902.
4. Lindbergh wanted to <u>win</u> a prize.
5. Earhart <u>didn't return</u> from her last trip.
6. Earhart <u>was</u> 39 years old when she disappeared.
7. C
8. When <u>did your father arrive</u>?
9. When <u>did Goddard die</u>?
10. Why <u>were</u> you late?
11. C
12. C
13. Did you <u>see</u> the accident?
14. C

Part 2

1.	worried	5.	sat	9.	spoke	13.	heard
2.	took	6.	knew	10.	talked	14.	stopped
3.	went	7.	felt	11.	ate	15.	destroyed
4.	put	8.	found	12.	slept		

Part 3

1. weren't
2. didn't fly
3. didn't disappear
4. didn't die
5. weren't

Part 4

1. Did Earhart love to fly? Yes, she did.
2. Did Earhart become famous? Yes, she did.
3. Did Goddard study aviation? No, he didn't.
4. Was Goddard born in California? No, he wasn't.
5. Did Goddard's rockets go to the moon? No, they didn't.

Part 5

1. What did they invent?
2. When were they born?
3. Why did she go to Ireland?
4. What kind of prize did he win?
5. Why did they love Lindbergh (OR him)?
6. Why did they laugh at Goddard?
7. Who laughed at Goddard?
8. What did he write about Goddard?
9. What did the President hear about Goddard?
10. Who was the first woman in space?

LESSON NINE

Part 1

1. She wanted to go to the museum.
2. C
3. I am happy to be in the U.S.
4. He's afraid to speak English.
5. It is important to own a car.
6. She can't speak English.
7. C
8. They shouldn't watch TV.
9. Please be here at six o'clock. Don't be late.
10. He likes to play tennis.
11. C
12. C
13. C
14. Where can I buy used books?
15. C
16. C
17. My father can drive very well.
18. It's dangerous to drive when you're sleepy.
19. She uses a VCR to record her favorite TV shows.
20. She shouldn't wear pants to her job interview.
21. C
22. C

Part 2

1. to/don't have to
2. Ø/shouldn't
3. to/doesn't want to
4. to/isn't necessary to
5. Ø/Let's not
6. Ø/Don't be
7. must not use

Part 3

1. does she want to go (on vacation)?
2. is he afraid to speak English?
3. can't he walk?
4. does he have to work?
5. is it important to have a driver's license?
6. isn't it necessary to bring a dictionary?
7. would she like to learn Spanish?

Part 4

1.	D	3.	S	5.	D	7.	S	9.	D	11.	D
2.	S	4.	S	6.	S	8.	D	10.	D	12.	D

LESSON TEN

Part 1
1. The teacher gave me a lot of <u>information</u>.
2. C
3. C
4. I bought <u>five cartons of</u> milk.
5. I <u>don't have any</u> coffee at home. (OR I <u>have no</u> coffee at home.)
6. She bought <u>new furniture</u>.
7. If I work hard and save, I will have <u>a lot of</u> money.
8. C
9. I can't find a good job because I don't have <u>any</u> experience. (NOTE: *Any* can be omitted.)
10. C
11. I have <u>a lot of</u> trouble with my car.
12. There <u>are tall mountains</u> near my hometown.
13. <u>A lot of boys</u> came to the baseball game.
14. In my country, there is <u>a lot of</u> unemployment. There isn't <u>a lot</u> here.
15. C
16. I don't have <u>a</u> computer. I use my brother's computer.
17. C
18. I can't help you now. I'm <u>too</u> tired. (OR <u>much too</u> tired.)
19. If I have <u>a little</u> free time, we can get together for lunch.
20. C

Part 2
1. bowl (OR can OR pot)
2. cup of
3. bar
4. glass (OR pitcher)
5. piece
6. piece
7. ear

LESSON ELEVEN

Part 1
1. She looks great. She's <u>very</u> beautiful.
2. C
3. I bought some new books at the <u>book</u> store.
4. C
5. I can't help you now. I'm <u>too tired</u>.
6. Do you prefer a light breakfast or <u>a heavy one</u>?
7. C
8. <u>She</u> can't go to college yet. She's <u>too young</u>. (OR <u>much too young</u>.)
9. I like my English class <u>very much</u>.
10. C
11. He speaks English very <u>fluently</u>.
12. C
13. I'm <u>worried</u> about my mother.
14. C
15. You have <u>intelligent</u> children.
16. I'm <u>interested</u> in sports.
17. C
18. She sings very <u>well</u>.

Part 2
1. He gave his speech fast.
2. Mary is a very intelligent person.
3. I am old enough to get married.
4. C
5. He finished the job quickly. OR He quickly finished the job.
6. How many birthday presents did you receive?

Part 3
1. quickly
2. carefully
3. sweet
4. sweetly
5. easy/easily
6. fast/slowly
7. regularly
8. serious
9. good
10. well

LESSON TWELVE

Part 1

1. He is <u>one of the oldest students</u> in the college.
2. My mom is <u>the best</u> cook in the world.
3. Texas is a <u>big</u> state.
4. I am <u>thinner than</u> my sister.
5. She speaks English <u>better</u> than I do.
6. C
7. I drive <u>more slowly</u> than you do.
8. He reads <u>more books than I do</u>.
9. New York is <u>one of the biggest cities</u> in the world.
10. C
11. <u>My</u> best friend lives in Boston.
12. Lesson One is <u>easier than</u> Lesson Ten.
13. C
14. C

Part 2

1. I type more quickly than my friend.
2. C
3. He woke up earlier than I did.
4. C
5. C
6. C
7. C
8. My brother is the most intelligent person in my family.

Part 3

1. the cheapest
2. more expensive than
3. faster than
4. better than
5. the shortest
6. easier than
7. the most popular
8. the best
9. more interesting
10. the worst

LESSON THIRTEEN

Part 1

1. I like to play golf, and my best friend <u>does too</u>.
2. C
3. Chicago isn't the capital of Illinois, is it? <u>No, it isn't</u>.
4. Chicago is a big city, <u>but</u> Springfield isn't.
5. C
6. You aren't an American citizen, <u>are you</u>?
7. My father doesn't speak English well, and my uncle doesn't <u>either</u>.
8. C
9. This is an easy test, isn't <u>it</u>?
10. There are 20 students in this class, <u>aren't there</u>?
11. C
12. The teacher explained the grammar clearly, <u>didn't she</u> or <u>he</u>?

Part 2

1. don't
2. did too
3. didn't either
4. did too
5. can't either
6. would too
7. won't (be)

Part 3

1. did you?
2. isn't it?
3. aren't you?
4. do you?
5. don't you?
6. isn't it?
7. can't I?
8. does it?

LESSON FOURTEEN

Part 1

1. was
2. am sitting
3. love
4. are staying
5. are going to (OR will) take
6. has
7. gets
8. plays

9. like
10. see
11. ate
12. hated
13. are going to (OR will) eat

14. will (OR are going to) leave
15. took
16. asked
17. will send
18. will see

Part 2

1. didn't go
2. won't go

3. don't see
4. doesn't like

5. isn't shopping
6. aren't going to eat

7. shouldn't
8. isn't

Part 3

1. Does the hotel have a swimming pool? Yes, it does.
2. Did the children eat in a Hawaiian restaurant last night? Yes, they did.
3. Will Barbara and Mike eat at a fast-food restaurant tomorrow? No, they won't.

4. Do the children like Chinese food? No, they don't.
5. Is Mike writing a letter now? No, he isn't.
6. Did the children go downtown? Yes, they did.
7. Are they going to visit the Virgin Islands? No, they aren't.

Part 4

1. Who is she (OR Barbara) writing to? OR To whom is she (OR Barbara) writing?
2. Why isn't he (OR Mike) sitting in the sun?
3. Why don't the children (OR they) like Chinese food?
4. Which islands will they visit?
5. When are they going to return to Boston?

6. Why does she (OR Barbara) like to sleep late?
7. Who went downtown?
8. How often do they go on vacation?
9. Why didn't she (OR Barbara) go downtown?
10. Why should they leave the children with a baby-sitter?

NAME_____

BOOK 2 / LESSON ONE / TEST

Part 1 Find the mistakes in the following sentences, and correct them. Not every sentence has a mistake. If the sentence is correct, write **C**.

                       sometimes
  EXAMPLES: The teacher gives ~~sometimes~~ a hard test.
                        ^

                 Why <u>do you always work</u> late? *C*

1. Where <u>does your brother works</u>?

2. My father <u>don't have</u> a car.

3. Everyone in my family <u>speak</u> English.

4. The teacher <u>doesn't knows</u> the answer.

5. We <u>usually eat</u> at a restaurant on Sundays.

6. We <u>usually are</u> tired on Sundays.

7. <u>We all the time</u> get together on Sundays.

8. Does the teacher ever give homework on the weekends? Yes, <u>ever</u>.

9. <u>What often</u> do you call your mother?

10. I call my mother <u>once a week</u>.

11. <u>Sometimes</u> I drink tea at night.

12. <u>Never I drink</u> coffee at night.

13. What <u>means "insurance"</u>?

14. How much <u>costs insurance for your car</u>?

15. How <u>do you say</u> "insurance" in Spanish?

16. <u>How spell</u> your name?

17. Why <u>you don't have</u> a computer?

18. Where <u>lives your sister</u>?

19. I <u>don't American movies like</u>.

20. My brother <u>doesn't live</u> with me.

21. Some people <u>has</u> a very good life.

22. Are you hungry? Yes, I <u>do</u>.

23. Are you thirsty? Yes, <u>I'm</u>.

24. The <u>church's</u> on the corner of Main and Elm.

25. My sister <u>has 15 years</u>.

26. <u>Is</u> impossible to learn English in one month.

27. The hospital <u>located</u> on Maple Street.

28. Why <u>is the teacher</u> late?

29. Some students <u>aren,t</u> here today.

30. <u>I'm speak</u> Spanish well.

31. My family <u>lives</u> in Canada.

32. The President <u>he</u> lives in the White House.

33. I <u>amn't</u> interested in sports.

34. <u>Your</u> a very kind person.

Part 2   Write the negative form of the underlined verb.

   EXAMPLES: Oranges <u>grow</u> in a warm climate.

        They _____*don't grow*_____ in a cold climate.

        The U.S. <u>is</u> a big country.

        Taiwan _____*isn't*_____ a big country.

1. In the U.S., winter <u>begins</u> in December.

 It _____ in November.

2. English <u>has</u> a lot of irregular verbs in the past tense.

 It _____ a lot of irregular verbs in the present tense.

3. Brazil and Canada <u>are</u> big countries.

 Cuba and Haiti _____ big countries.

4. We <u>need</u> practice with English.

 We _____ practice with our own languages.

5. "Large" <u>means</u> big.

 "Long" _____ big.

Part 3   Read each statement. Then write a *yes/no* question about the words in parentheses. Write a short answer.

> **EXAMPLE:**   My sister has a dog. (a big dog) (yes)
>
> *Does she have a big dog?   Yes, she does.*

1. You like cats. (dogs) (yes)

   _____

2. Your dog is big. (friendly) (yes)

   _____

3. The children want a pet. (a bird) (no)

   _____

4. My cat sometimes sleeps on the sofa. (ever/in your bed) (yes/sometimes)

   _____

5. I buy special food for my dog. (meat) (no)

   _____

Part 4   Read each statement. Then write a *wh-* question about the words in parentheses ( ). An answer is not necessary.

> **EXAMPLES:**   February has 28 days. (How many/March)
>
> *How many days does March have?*
>
> Mexico is in North America. (where/Venezuela)
>
> *Where is Venezuela?*

1. Americans speak English. (What language/Peruvians)

   _____

2. The President works in Washington. (Where/the Governor)

   _____

3. The Vice-President doesn't live in the White House. (Why)

   _____

4. I come from Poland. (Where/you)

   _____

5. You pay your rent once a month. (How often/pay your gas bill)

   _____

6. Alex is 35 years old. (How old/his wife)

   _____

7. The U.S. has 50 states. (How many/Mexico)

   _____

8. You spell "Illinois" I-L-L-I-N-O-I- S. (How/spell/Florida)

   _____

9. "Vet" means animal doctor. (What/"pet"/mean)

   _____

10. You say "hello" in English. You say "hola" in Spanish. (How/say/ "hello"/ in Polish)

   _____

LESSON **TWO** / TEST

Part I   Find the mistakes with the underlined words, and correct them. Not every sentence has a mistake. If the sentence is correct, write **C**.

EXAMPLES: What kind of bicycle <u> you going to buy</u>? *are*

Are you wearing a watch today? *C*

1. Barbara <u>will going to buy</u> a new car.

2. When the movie <u>will be</u> over, everyone will go to my house.

3. When <u>will the movie be</u> over?

4. <u>I going to write</u> a letter tonight.

5. There <u>will be</u> a good program on TV next Saturday.

6. You can't carry that heavy box alone. <u>I help</u> you.

7. If I <u>am</u> tired, I won't go to the party tonight.

8. What <u>you going to do</u> tomorrow night?

9. <u>She's going to</u> Canada next week.

10. Why <u>he won't</u> tell me the answer?

11. <u>She's listening</u> to the radio now.

12. If I don't eat breakfast, I <u>will hungry</u> later.

13. Why <u>you aren't</u> working now?

14. <u>We taking</u> a test now.

15. <u>Are you hearing</u> the noise outside now?

16. My family <u>will be buy</u> a house next year.

17. When <u>are you going to</u> graduate?

18. When <u>will the teacher return</u> the tests?

Part 2 Mike (M) is talking to his friend Sam (S) on the phone. Fill in the blanks with the correct tense and form. Use the simple present, present continuous, and future.

S: Hello?

M: Hi, Sam. This is Mike.

S: Hi, Mike. How (be/you) _____*are you*_____?

(example)

M: Fine.

S: What _____ now?

(1. you/do)

M: I _____ a football game on TV now. _____

(2. watch)   (3. you/want)

to come over[1] and watch it with me?

S: I can't. I _____ to stay home now.

(4. need)

M: Why _____ to stay home?

(5. you/need)

S: I _____ care of the kids now. The baby is sick, and she _____

(6. take)   (7. need)

a lot of attention. She _____ quietly now. The other two

(8. sleep)

_____ a video game.

(9. play)

M: Where's your wife?

S: She's at the mall[2] now. She _____ for a new coat.

(10. shop)

M: What time _____ home?

(11. she/be)

S: Probably around 4 o'clock.

M: Why don't you come over when she _____ home? The game won't be

(12. get)

finished yet.

S: I can't. It's my turn to cook dinner. I _____ a spaghetti dinner tonight.

(13. make)

But I _____ enough tomato sauce. When Lisa _____ home, I

(14. not/have)   (15. come)

_____ to the supermarket and get some tomato sauce.

(16. go)

M: I _____ to the store as soon as the game _____ over. I

(17. go)   (18. be)

_____ some for you. I have to pass your house, so I _____

(19. get)   (20. deliver)

it to you on my way home.

S: That's very nice of you. I really appreciate it.

[1] *Come over* = come to my house.
[2] A *mall* = shopping center.

Part 3   Fill in the blanks with the negative form of the underlined verb.

EXAMPLE: Mike <u>is</u> at home. He ___*isn't*___ at work.

1.   Mike <u>is watching</u> a football game. He _____ a baseball game.

2.   Sam <u>needs</u> to stay home. Mike _____ to stay home.

3.   Sam's wife <u>is</u> at the mall. She _____ at home.

4.   She's <u>going to buy</u> a new coat. She _____ groceries.

5.   Mike <u>will go</u> to the supermarket later. He _____ to the library.

Part 4   Write a *yes/no* question about the words in parentheses. Then write a short answer.

EXAMPLE: Mike is at home. (Sam)
Is Sam at home?   Yes, he is.

1.   Sam's wife will come home soon. (at 3 o'clock)

_____

2.   Sam's wife is shopping. (for a coat)

_____

3.   Sam is taking care of his kids. (Mike)

_____

4.   Mike wants to watch a football game. (Sam)

_____

5.   Sam is going to cook tonight. (Sam's wife)

_____

Part 5   Write a *wh-* question about the words in parentheses. An answer is not necessary.

EXAMPLE: Mike wants to get together with Sam. (why)
Why does he want to get together with Sam?

1.   Sam is going to cook dinner. (why)

_____

2.   Mike will go to the store. (when)

_____

3. Sam doesn't want to leave the house. (why)

   _____

4. The baby needs a lot of attention. (why)

   _____

5. The children are playing a game. (what kind of game)

   _____

LESSON **THREE** / TEST

Part 1   Write the past form of the following verbs.

EXAMPLE: live __*lived*__   spend __*spent*__

1. see _____   11. let _____

2. worry _____   12. teach _____

3. take _____   13. eat _____

4. drive _____   14. give _____

5. cut _____   15. write _____

6. grow _____   16. understand _____

7. stand _____   17. talk _____

8. leave _____   18. read _____

9. run _____   19. drink _____

10. come _____   20. go _____

Part 2   Find the mistakes with the underlined words, and correct them. Not every sentence has a mistake. If the sentence is correct, write **C**.

EXAMPLES: My grandfather ~~was~~ died two years ago.

I <u>studied</u> German when I was a child.   *C*

1. I decided to <u>ate</u> in a restaurant last weekend.

2. I <u>didn't</u> tired after the football game yesterday.

3. <u>Were</u> a lot of people at Martin Luther King's funeral.

4. She <u>didn't went</u> to the museum yesterday.

5. Yesterday I <u>fell</u> down and broke my arm.

6. They <u>were see</u> the movie yesterday.

7. They <u>were born</u> in China.

8. They <u>were</u> hungry last night.

9. My father <u>use to tell</u> me stories when I was a child.

10. In my native country, <u>I'm used to live</u> with my parents and brothers and sisters. Now I live alone.

11. When <u>was your grandfather died</u>?

12. Why <u>you didn't come</u> to class yesterday?

13. Where <u>you bought</u> your new coat?

14. Did you <u>finish</u> your composition?

Part 3   Write the negative form of the underlined words.

   EXAMPLE: She <u>ate</u> the potatoes. She _____*didn't eat*_____ the meat.

1.   I <u>had</u> a dog when I was a child. I _____ a cat.

2.   She <u>drank</u> the water. She _____ the coffee.

3.   You <u>told</u> the truth. You _____ a lie.

4.   I <u>was</u> tired yesterday. I _____ sick.

5.   We <u>worked</u> on Saturday. We _____ on Sunday.

6.   He <u>felt</u> sick yesterday. He _____ well.

7.   She <u>put</u> the dishes in the cabinet. She _____ the glasses in the cabinet.

8.   The plane <u>arrived</u> late. It _____ on time.

Part 4   Write a question beginning with the word given. (An answer is not necessary.)

   EXAMPLE: Martin Luther King lived in the south.

   Where _____*did he live*_____?

1. King was born in 1929.

   Where _____

2. King fought for people's rights.

   Why _____

3. King got married in Georgia.

   To whom _____

4. Blacks and whites didn't sit together on a bus.

   Why _____

5. King wasn't happy with this situation.

Why _____

6. Blacks had to use separate washrooms.

When _____

7. King spoke in Washington, D.C.

What _____ about in Washington?

8. King went to jail many times.

Why _____

9. King said, "I have a dream."

When _____

10. King wanted something for all Americans.

What _____

Part 5   Write two sentences with *used to*, comparing life today with life 50 (or more) years ago. (You can use examples from the U.S. or from your native country.)

EXAMPLE: *Women used to stay home to raise a family. Now many women*

work outside the home.

1. _____

2. _____

LESSON **FOUR** / TEST

Part I   Find the mistakes with the underlined words, and correct them. Not every sentence has a mistake. If the sentence is correct, write **C**.

    EXAMPLES: The <u>childrens</u>ʹ toys are on the floor.

                The <u>teacher's</u> name is Mr. Hill. *C*

1. <u>Whose coat</u> is that?

2. <u>Whose</u> your math teacher?

3. I sometimes use <u>car my brother.</u>

4. Where is your <u>parent's house</u>?

5. Did they bring <u>theirs</u> books today?

6. What <u>happened</u> after everyone left the party?

7. Who <u>did close</u> the door last night?

8. Did you forget <u>you're</u> keys?

9. The teacher's name is Mr. Thompson, but I don't know <u>his</u> first name.

10. <u>It's</u> a beautiful day today.

11. Where did your brother meet <u>her</u> girlfriend?

12. If you don't have your book today, you can use <u>mine.</u>

13. Where did the students leave <u>they're</u> papers?

14. Did you find <u>you</u> gloves?

15. <u>Me and my best friend</u> went to see a movie last night.

16. She spoke to <u>my friend and me</u> about the problem.

17. <u>The my friend's</u> new car is very beautiful.

18. There are many new <u>book's</u> in the library.

19. We should buy <u>ourself</u> a nice present.

20. My <u>uncle's</u> best friend made a party for him.

21. Does your sister use <u>her husband's last name</u>?

22. Who <u>have</u> a watch?

23. A bird is building <u>its</u> nest in that tree.

24. Do you visit <u>yours</u> parents often?

25. Their team is wearing blue shirts. <u>Ours</u> is wearing yellow shirts.

Part 2   Choose the correct word to complete each sentence.

> **EXAMPLE:**   My sister got married in _____*c*_____ house.
> a. ours   b. our's   c. our   d. ours'

1. Did you enjoy _____?
   a. your sister's wedding   b. wedding your sister
   c. your sister's the wedding   d. the wedding your sister

2. _____ gifts are those?
   a. Who's   b. Who   c. Whom   d. Whose

3. They're the _____ gifts.
   a. newlywed   b. newlyweds   c. newlyweds'   d. newlywed's

4. My wedding was in a church. _____ was in a restaurant.
   a. Your's   b. You're   c. Your   d. Yours

5. My sister's bridesmaids wore pink dresses. _____ wore green dresses.
   a. My   b. Mine   c. Mine's   d. Mines

6. Look at those flowers. _____ so pretty.
   a. Its   b. It's   c. Their   d. They're

7. I like the flowers. Do you like _____?
   a. they   b. them   c. its   d. it

8. The bride's dress is white. _____ flowers are pink and white.
   a. Hers   b. Her's   c. She's   d. Her

9. The groom's name is Edward Miller. _____ mother's name is Elizabeth Miller.
   a. Her   b. His   c. Hers   d. Him

10. The bride and groom opened some gifts at the wedding, but they didn't open _____.
    a. us   b. our   c. ours   d. our's

11. What is _____?
    a. that church name   b. the name of that church
    c. the name that church   d. the name's that church

12. _____ took pictures at the wedding?
    a. Who   b. Whom   c. Whose   d. Who's

13. _____ that woman? She's the bride's grandmother.
   a. Who   b. Who's   c. Whose   d. Whos'

14. Who _____ the bride's dress?
   a. made   b. make   c. did make   d. is make

15. She made the dress _____ .
   a. self   b. oneself   c. herself   d. himself

Part 3   Fill in the blanks with *said* or *told*.

   EXAMPLES: She ____*said*____ , "Sit down."

   She ____*told*____ the truth.

1. She _____ the answer.

2. She _____ him the answer.

3. She _____ good-bye.

4. She _____ them to sit down.

5. She _____ us about her problem.

6. She _____ an interesting story.

7. She _____ me a secret.

8. She _____ , "My name is Barbara."

Part 4   Complete the question. Some of these questions ask about the subject. Some do not.

   EXAMPLES: Who ____*took*____ pictures at your sister's wedding?

   A professional photographer took pictures.

   How much ____*did the pictures cost?*____

   The pictures cost over $1000.

1. Where _____ married?
   My sister got married at St. Paul's Church.

2. Who(m) _____?
   She married Larry Franklin.

3. What kind of gift _____ to the bride and groom?
   I gave them towels.

4. Who _____ for the wedding?
   My parents paid for the wedding.

5. How many people _____ the wedding?
About 100 people attended the wedding.

6. Who _____ them a check for $500?
My grandparents gave them a check for $500.

7. Who _____ the bouquet?
The bride's best friend caught the bouquet.

8. What _____ to questions about love and respect?
The bride and groom answered "I do."

9. Where _____ on their honeymoon?
The newlyweds will go to Niagara Falls.

10. My brother-in-law's ring doesn't have a diamond.

Whose _____ a diamond?
My sister's ring has a diamond.

Part 5   Fill in the blanks with a reflexive pronoun.

   EXAMPLE: She bought _____*herself*_____ a beautiful ring.

1. I did the homework all by _____.

2. Did you watch the movie by _____ or did your brother watch it with you?

3. My sister learned to use a computer by _____.

4. My little sisters and brothers learned to speak English by _____.

5. All of you should make _____ comfortable.

6. My automatic coffee maker turns _____ on in the morning.

7. My uncle learned to drive by _____.

LESSON **FIVE** / TEST

Part I   Find the mistakes with the underlined words, and correct them. Not every sentence has a mistake. If the sentence is correct, write **C**.

> **EXAMPLES:**   In my class, there are three peoples from Italy.
>
> There's a lot of snow in the mountains.   *C*

1. There's the Statue of Liberty in New York.

2. Many Americans own a house.

3. Almost Americans have a television.

4. Childrens like to watch TV.

5. Are more women than men in the U.S.

6. Immigrants come to America because they want a freedom.

7. New York and Los Angeles are a big cities.

8. Los Angeles is one of the biggest city in the U.S.

9. How much students have the textbook?

10. How much money do you have?

11. I paid a lot of money for my textbooks, but I didn't pay a lot of for my tuition because I have a scholarship.

12. You need a lot of advices in order to plan your future.

13. My father has much education.

14. Do you have any informations about the nursing program?

15. The teacher doesn't have no time to help me today.

16. They're are almost two million Native Americans in the U.S.

17. He's lonely because he has very few friends.

18. Many place names in the U.S. are Indian words.

19. I want to be rich. I want to have too much money.

20. I can't help you today because I have a little time.

21. Every students want to learn.

66   **BOOK 2**/ LESSON **FIVE**/ TEST

22. I drank three <u>cups coffee</u> this morning.

23. If you spend <u>too much time</u> playing computer games, you won't have time for your homework.

Part 2 Fill in the blanks with the singular or plural form of the word in parentheses.

> **EXAMPLE:** I like different ___*kinds*___ of ___*music*___. I like popular ___*songs*___,
> (kind)   (music)   (song)
> but I don't like jazz.

1. She bought a lot of new _____ for her apartment. She bought
   (furniture)

   _____ , _____ , and _____ . She also bought
   (chair)   (lamp)   (bookshelf)

   new _____ and steak _____ .
   (dish)   (knife)

2. My parents gave me a lot of _____ . They told me to listen to all my
   (advice)

   _____ and do all my _____ .
   (teacher)   (homework)

3. I always eat a lot of _____ . I like _____ ,
   (fruit)   (cherry)

   _____ , _____ , _____ , and
   (grape)   (peach)   (strawberry)

   _____ .
   (pear)

4. She doesn't have much _____ because she has two _____ .
   (time)   (job)

   She leaves her two _____ with a babysitter.
   (child)

5. A lot of _____ don't have a job. There's a lot of _____ in
   (person)   (unemployment)

   some _____ .
   (city)

Part 3 Fill in the blanks with an appropriate measurement of quantity.

> **EXAMPLE:** I bought a ___*loaf*___ of bread.

1. I ate a _____ of soup.

2. Please give me a _____ of water.

3. I want to give you a _____ of advice.

4. I'm going to buy a _____ of milk.

5. You should eat three of four _____ of fruit a day.

Part 4   Choose the correct word to fill in the blank.

      EXAMPLES: My name is Kim Park. I come from Korea. I came to the U.S. because

                  I couldn't find _____*a*_____ good job in my country.
                  a. a   b. some   c. no   d. any

1. My uncle gave me _____. He told me to go to the U.S.
   a. an advice   b. some advice   c. some advices   d. any advice

2. I want to make _____ money in the U.S. and then return to Korea.
   a. a lot   b. much   c. many   d. a lot of

3. There are _____ job opportunities here.
   a. a lot   b. much   c. many   d. any

4. I studied English for many years in Korea. My English is almost perfect. I have _____ problems with English.
   a. any   b. no any   c. very little   d. very few

5. I would like to study computers, but I don't have _____ experience with computers.
   a. much   b. many   c. no   d. an

6. I have a full-time job, go to school at night, and take care of my family. I have _____ free time.
   a. a little   b. very little   c. a few   d. very few

7. I have _____ relatives in the U.S. They live in Minneapolis.
   a. any   b. a   c. several   d. much

8. My relatives gave me _____ help when I came here.
   a. a   b. some   c. several   d. any

LESSON **SIX** / TEST

Part 1   Find the mistakes with the underlined words, and correct them. Not every sentence has a mistake. If the sentence is correct, write **C**.

EXAMPLE: The book**s** store is closed on Sundays.

She can't help you this week because she has <u>too many</u> things to do.   *C*

1. My <u>license driver's</u> is going to expire next month.

2. She made a pot of <u>vegetables soup</u>.

3. He <u>late woke up</u> this morning.

4. I don't feel <u>well</u> today.

5. The Fourth of July is American <u>Independence Day</u>.

6. My sister is <u>marry</u> and has a <u>six-month-old</u> baby.

7. When their son graduated, they looked very <u>happily</u>.

8. I'm <u>too much tired</u> to help you today.

9. I need fresh tomatoes for the sauce. I don't like to use canned <u>ones</u>.

10. She wrote <u>carefully the composition</u>.

11. We had <u>a discussion very long</u> about a serious problem.

12. The meal was <u>too</u> delicious. I enjoyed all of it.

13. He's tired because he <u>hardly worked</u> on a long project.

14. She looked very <u>excited</u> on her wedding day.

15. I'm not <u>enough tall</u> to reach the highest shelf.

16. I don't have <u>enough time</u> to watch TV.

17. I <u>very</u> want to visit Paris.

18. She has two <u>beautifuls</u> daughters.

19. My old computer is very <u>slowly</u>.

20. Where is the bank <u>locate</u>?

Part 2   Fill in the blanks with the correct form, adjective or adverb, of the verb in parentheses.

EXAMPLES: She has a ___*beautiful*___ voice. She sings very ___*beautifully*___ .
(beautiful)   (beautiful)

1. Did you study _____ for the test?
(hard)

2. He types very _____ and _____ .
(quick)   (accurate)

3. He is a _____ driver. He drives very _____ .
(good)   (good)

4. My sister speaks English _____ .
(fluent)

5. It is _____ important to wear a seat belt.
(extreme)

6. She just found a job. She looks very _____ .
(happy)

7. He arrived to the meeting very _____ .
(late)

8. No one speaks English _____ .
(perfect)

9. As _____ , the teacher gave a quiz on Friday.
(usual)

10. Sometimes I feel very _____ on Sunday.
(lazy)

11. You were _____ _____ about the situation.
(absolute)   (right)

12. My neighbors are very _____ people.
(friendly)

13. You sound very _____ today.
(sad)

14. Some teenagers talk on the phone _____ .
(constant)

LESSON **SEVEN** / TEST

Part I   Find the mistakes with the underlined words, and correct them. Not every sentence has a mistake. If the sentence is correct, write **C**.

EXAMPLES: I bought my book two months ~~before~~ *ago*.

While the child <u>was playing</u>, he fell and got hurt.   *C*

1. <u>When</u> he retired, he moved to Florida.

2. After <u>drive</u> for eight hours, I was tired.

3. When <u>arrived the airplane</u>, I was at the airport.

4. She had her first child <u>until</u> she was 28 years old.

5. I was washing the dishes <u>while</u> I broke the glass.

6. He slept <u>during</u> 2 hours.

7. He slept <u>during</u> the movie.

8. I always take a bath before <u>going</u> to bed.

9. While they <u>were watch</u> TV, the phone rang.

10. He practiced driving <u>until</u> he got his driver's license.

11. I'm going to New York. I'll be back <u>in</u> two weeks.

12. I <u>was going to write</u> my composition, but I lost the topic.

13. He came to the U.S. three years <u>before.</u>

14. He studied music <u>for three years.</u>

15. When <u>the test ended,</u> the students left.

16. While Einstein was visiting the U.S., the Nazis <u>were taking</u> his home.

Part 2 Fill in the blanks with the simple past or the past continuous of the verb in parentheses ( ).

EXAMPLE: A little girl ___*was walking*___ (walk) through the forest to her grandmother's house when she ___*met*___ (meet) a hunter.

1. The hunter _____ (ask) the little girl where she _____ (go) .

2. "I'm going to my grandmother's house," the little girl _____ (say) .

3. While the girl _____ (talk) to the hunter, a wolf _____ (hide) behind a tree and _____ (listen) to their conversation.

4. When the wolf _____ (hear) the little girl's words, he _____ (run) quickly to grandmother's house.

5. The wolf _____ (put) on grandmother's nightgown and _____ (get) into her bed.

6. When the little girl _____ (open) the door to her grandmother's house, the wolf _____ (lie) in grandmother's bed.

7. Suddenly the wolf _____ (jump) out of bed and _____ (run) after the little girl.

8. While the wolf _____ (chase) the little girl, the hunter _____ (arrive) and _____ (shoot) the wolf.

Part 3 Choose the correct word to fill in the blanks.

EXAMPLE: ___*b*___ she gets married, she will live with her husband.
a. Whenever   b. When   c. While   d. Until

1. She will get married _____ three months.
   a. by   b. after   c. in   d. during

2. She will get married _____ she graduates from college.
   a. when   b. while   c. until   d. whenever

3. She will live with her parents _____ she gets married. Then she will live with her husband.
   a. until   b. whenever   c. while   d. when

4. She will work for her father _____ her summer vacation.
   a. for   b. during   c. by   d. at

5. She graduated from high school _____ .
   a. three years before   c. before three years
   b. three years ago   d. before three years ago

6. She studied biology _____ two years.
   a. during   b. by   c. at   d. for

7. She was studying in a biology class _____ she met her future husband.
   a. while   b. whenever   c. during   d. when

8. _____ she has a problem, she talks to her best friend.
   a. until   b. before   c. while   d. whenever

9. _____ we were watching the movie, we were eating popcorn.
   a. While   b. During   c. Whenever   d. Until

10. You have to return your library books _____ Friday
    a. for   b. until   c. by   d. from

LESSON **EIGHT** / TEST

Part 1   Find the mistakes with the underlined words, and correct them. Not every sentence has a mistake. If the sentence is correct, write **C**.

EXAMPLES: You must ~~to~~ wear a seat belt in a car.

You have to wear a seat belt in a car.   *C*

1. I have a test tomorrow. I got to study tonight.

2. We maybe will go to the zoo on Saturday.

3. The teacher can to help you later.

4. You should go to the doctor immediately.

5. If you don't pass the final exam, you will have to repeat the course.

6. Are we permitted use our dictionaries to write a composition?

7. You not supposed to talk during a test.

8. Where I can get information about registration?

9. What should we do about the problem?

10. Last week I can't came to class because I was sick.

11. Would you rather go to a movie or stay home?

12. I rather study in the morning than at night.

13. It's going to rain. You better take an umbrella.

14. The test is going to be at 8 o'clock. You'd better don't come late.

Part 2   Choose the correct words in parentheses to complete each sentence.

EXAMPLE: You (may, (must)) wear a seat belt during takeoff and landing of an airplane.

1. You (must not, don't have to) use cell phones when a plane takes off. It's against the law.

2. When she was younger, she (can, could) run a mile in 5 minutes.

3. (Could, Would) I borrow your pen for a few minutes?

4. You (are not supposed to, don't have to) park at a bus stop.

5. There are clouds in the sky. It (should, might) rain this afternoon.

6. We do not have permission to use our dictionaries during a test. We (don't have to, may not) use our dictionaries.

7. I'd like to ask you a favor. (Would, Should) you drive me to the airport?

8. If you leave the house, you (shouldn't, don't have to) leave the oven on.

9. You'd (better, rather) pay your rent on time, or you're going to have a problem with your landlord.

10. I'd (better, rather) live in Miami than in New York because Miami has a nicer climate.

11. You('ve got to, would) leave the building immediately! It's on fire!

12. It's getting dark outside. It (must, should) be late.

13. I (can't, may not) understand the teacher because she's talking too fast.

14. Children (shouldn't, must not) watch TV all day.

15. I heard you won a free trip to Hawaii. You (must, had better) be excited.

LESSON **NINE** / TEST

Part I   Find the mistakes with the underlined words, and correct them. Not every sentence has a mistake. If the sentence is correct, write **C**.

> **EXAMPLES:**   Have you ever ~~break~~ *broken* a window?
>
> We've always wanted to learn English.   *C*

1. Have you ever <u>seeing</u> a French movie?

2. How long <u>he has been studying</u> English?

3. <u>I've want</u> to become a pilot since I was a child.

4. How long <u>she has been</u> a teacher?

5. <u>I never been</u> a good student.

6. She has been working in a factory since she <u>has come</u> to the U.S.

7. <u>How long time has</u> the baby been sleeping?

8. <u>Have you met ever</u> the president of the college?

9. I <u>know</u> my best friend for many years.

10. Have you ever gone to the art museum? Yes, I <u>went</u> there last Saturday.

11. Have they eaten dinner <u>yet</u>?

12. Yes, they've eaten dinner <u>yet</u>.

13. The airplane <u>has just arrived</u>.

14. I <u>had have</u> my car for three months.

15. She <u>has been writing</u> a letter for 15 minutes.

16. <u>I've eating</u> pizza many times.

17. How long <u>are they</u> married?

18. He's been working <u>since</u> eight hours.

19. She<u>'s bought</u> her car 3 months ago.

20. <u>I've never gone</u> to a basketball game.

21. She<u>'s talk</u> to her brother many times about the problem.

22. We've <u>been going</u> to the zoo many times.

23. We've had a test on modals <u>already.</u>

24. When <u>have you found</u> your job?

Part 2 Fill in the blanks with the simple past, the present perfect, or the present perfect continuous tense of the verb in parentheses.

Conversation 1

A. _____*Have*_____ you ever _____*gone*_____ to California?
      (example: go)

B. Yes, I _____ .
                      (1.)

A. When _____ you _____ there?
                  (2. go)

B. I _____ there last summer.
        (3. go)

A. I _____ California, but I'd like to.
                (4. never/visit)

Conversation 2

A. I _____ a great movie last week.
              (1. see)

B. What _____ you _____?
                (2. see)

A. *Yesterday's Woman.*

B. I _____ that movie. I _____ time to go to the movies
            (3. never/see)   (4. not/have)

      since I _____ studying English.
                    (5. start)

Part 3 Fill in the blanks with the simple present, the simple past, the present perfect, or the present perfect continuous tense of the verb in parentheses.

A. I _____*went*_____ to your apartment yesterday, but I couldn't find you.
        (example: go)

B. I don't live on Foster Avenue anymore. I _____ a few months ago.
                                                          (1. move)

A. Why _____?
          (2. you/move)

B. Because my father _____ to the U.S. about three weeks ago, and I needed a bigger
                            (3. come)

      apartment.

A. Where do you live now?

B. We _____ on Peterson Avenue.
              (4. live)

A. You never mentioned it to me.

B. I _____ time to talk with my friends since my father _____ to the
    (5. have)   (6. come)
U.S.

A. _____ your father _____ a job yet?
    (7. find)

B. No. He _____ for a job for two weeks, but he _____ one
            (8. look)   (9. not/find)
yet.

LESSON **TEN** / TEST

Part I   Find the mistakes with the underlined words, and correct them. Not every sentence has a mistake. If the sentence is correct, write **C**.

EXAMPLES: I'm afraid ~~at~~ *of* walking alone at night.

She insisted <u>on helping</u> me.   *C*

1. I'm tired <u>to</u> working so hard.

2. All my life I've eaten fresh food. <u>I'm not used to eating</u> food that has chemicals.

3. <u>Learn</u> a new language is difficult.

4. She went <u>shopping</u> last Saturday.

5. You can learn English faster by <u>practice</u> with Americans.

6. When I was a teenager, I used to <u>watching</u> TV all Saturday.

7. I dream about <u>go</u> back to my country.

8. Do you enjoy <u>watching</u> a soccer game?

9. I want to practice <u>skating</u>.

10. I'm interested <u>on</u> learning French.

11. My wife doesn't like to cook, but I don't mind <u>cooking</u>.

12. <u>Don't having</u> a job makes me feel depressed.

13. I <u>wanted to called</u> you, but I lost your phone number.

14. <u>Is</u> important to help poor people.

15. She <u>forgot buy</u> sugar when she was at the store.

16. Do you want <u>that I help</u> you move on Saturday?

17. He uses a bicycle <u>for go</u> to work.

18. They <u>used to live</u> in an apartment. Now they have a house.

19. Is it necessary <u>to</u> you to use your dictionary every day?

20. Do you expect the teacher <u>to give</u> everyone an A?

21. It's important <u>for me to</u> visit my parents often.

22. I've always lived with my family. I can't <u>get used to live</u> alone.

Part 2 Fill in the blanks with the gerund or infinitive of the verb in parentheses. In some cases, either the gerund or the infinitive is possible.

EXAMPLES: It's important ___*to eat*___ a healthy diet.
(eat)

___*Eating*___ a healthy diet is important.
(eat)

1. I decided _____ to Mexico for vacation.
(go)

2. Do you want me _____ you with your homework?
(help)

3. _____ a seat belt in a car is against the law.
(not/wear)

4. _____ a house is a big decision.
(buy)

5. We went _____ yesterday.
(swim)

6. I often put off _____ my homework.
(do)

7. I dislike _____ the dishes.
(wash)

8. You should go to your counselor _____ advice about colleges.
(get)

9. I have to wear a suit to my new job. I'm not used to _____ a suit every day, and I don't like it.
(wear)

10. My cousins are coming to visit. I look forward to _____ them.
(see)

11. Are you interested in _____ to a football game with me?
(go)

12. She was happy _____ a job.
(find)

13. It's impossible _____ a foreign language in a month.
(learn)

14. She began _____ piano when she was five years old.
(play)

15. Now she has short hair. When she was younger, she used _____ long hair.
(have)

16. The teacher doesn't permit us _____ our dictionaries during a test.
(use)

17. He learned English quickly by _____ with American friends.
(talk)

18. I love _____ .
(dance)

LESSON **ELEVEN** / TEST

Part 1   Find the mistakes with the underlined words, and correct them. Not every sentence has a mistake. If the sentence is correct, write **C**.

EXAMPLES: The man <u>which</u> ~~which~~ *whom* you met is a very famous architect.

I can't understand <u>a word you are saying</u>.   *C*

1. <u>The book I'm reading</u> is about the life of Napoleon.

2. The student <u>whose</u> sitting in the back row speaks English well.

3. The chicken <u>that ate my husband</u> had very little salt in it.

4. <u>The man is very intelligent who gave a speech last night</u>.

5. People <u>who lives</u> in Alaska are used to cold winters.

6. I have a friend <u>her</u> son is an artist.

7. The woman <u>what</u> played the piano at the concert is very talented.

8. The mistake <u>that he made it</u> cost the company thousands of dollars.

9. I rented <u>a movie was</u> three hours long.

10. <u>Who has</u> the best composition will win a prize.

11. The man <u>whose apartment I'm renting</u> will be in Germany for a year.

12. The teacher <u>which helped</u> me at registration was very kind.

13. The actor <u>whom we saw</u> in a movie recently just died.

14. I have a friend <u>that don't have</u> a telephone.

Part 2   Fill in the blanks to complete the adjective clause.

EXAMPLE: You need a lot of help with your composition. The teacher can give you the help _____*you need.*_____

1. My car doesn't have air-conditioning. I want to buy a car _____ air-conditioning.

2. Mary made a great dinner. Everything was delicious. But I didn't like the dessert _____, so I didn't eat it.

3. I applied for a job as a computer programmer, but the company didn't hire me. The person _____ has much more experience than I do.

4. I'm trying to sell my car. I put an ad in the newspaper and a sign on my car. I got more responses from the ad _____ in the newspaper.

5. He was dating a woman with 2 small children. He decided to break up with her because he didn't want to marry a woman _____ are small.

6. I bought a used computer from a neighbor. The woman whose _____ wanted to buy a much more powerful computer.

7. My present teacher doesn't speak Spanish. The teacher _____ last semester was fluent in Spanish.

LESSON **TWELVE** / TEST

Part I Find the mistakes with the underlined words, and correct them. Not every
sentence has a mistake. If the sentence is correct, write **C**.

EXAMPLES: I am the talle~~r~~*st* person in my family.

New York is the largest city in the U.S. *C*

1. She's not the same age as her best friend.

2. She's younger that her best friend.

3. You speak English more better than your father.

4. He has money more than I do.

5. I ran the race more quickly than you did.

6. I don't look like my mother at all. She has blond hair and a round face. I have brown
    hair and a narrow face.

7. Who is most intelligent student in this class?

8. My the oldest cousin is married.

9. Does decaf coffee taste like regular coffee?

10. San Francisco is one of the most beautiful city in the U.S.

11. What is the higher mountain in the world?

12. She wrote the composition more carefully this time than she did before.

13. My grandmother isn't the same old as my grandfather.

14. Her daughter is a more beautiful girl.

15. Bob and his brother have completely different characters. They aren't alike at all.

16. I'm lazier than my sister.

17. California is most populated state in the U.S.

18. John is very smart, but his girlfriend is even smarter.

19. She answered the questions on the test quicklier than I did.

20. He better sings than I do.

Part 2   Fill in the blanks.

EXAMPLE: My vacation in Toronto cost less than $2000. It was not

as _____*expensive*_____ as my vacation in Paris.

1. An orange and a grapefruit are _____ shape.

2. An orange isn't the same _____ a grapefruit. An orange is smaller.

3. An orange doesn't _____ like grapefruit. An orange is sweeter.

4. My sister and her husband are both doctors. They have _____ level of education.

5. My sister is 35 years old. Her husband is 35 years old. They are the same _____.

6. My sister _____ like her husband in many ways. For example, they are both interested in science. They both like sports.

7. My sister and her husband are not the same height. Her husband is _____.

8. My sister is more talented than I am. I don't play the piano _____ well _____ she does.

9. My sister and I are twins. Even our mother is not sure who is who. We look

exactly _____ .

10. My grammar book cost me $30. My reading book cost me $45. These two books are

not the same _____ .

11. You need to finish this test as soon _____ .

12. Your photo ID doesn't look _____ you at all. You are much handsomer than your picture.

13. My new computer didn't cost as _____ as my old one.

14. I'm not as talented as my mother. My mother is much _____ than I am.

LESSON **THIRTEEN** / TEST

Part I   Find the mistakes with the underlined words, and correct them. Not every sentence has a mistake. If the sentence is correct, write **C**.

EXAMPLES: The thief _arrested_ by the police. *was*

A package <u>was left</u> near your front door.   *C*

1. The birthday presents <u>were opened never</u>.

2. My watch <u>repaired</u> last week.

3. When <u>was your car stolen</u>?

4. Most of the pizza <u>wasn't eating</u>.

5. The accident <u>was happened</u> at 5:35 a.m.

6. Many soldiers <u>were killed</u> during the war.

7. My grandparents <u>were died</u> when I was small.

8. Who <u>was elected</u> President in November, 2000?

9. When <u>did</u> the book written?

10. Library books <u>should returned</u> at the front desk.

11. All the students <u>were send</u> information about registration.

12. The dishes <u>have already been washed.</u>

13. A dictionary <u>can use</u> for the composition test.

14. Newspapers and magazines <u>can find</u> in the library.

15. The winner of the contest <u>will be notified</u> by mail.

Part 2   Change the sentences from active to passive voice. Do not mention the performer. (The performer is in parentheses.) Use the same tense as the underlined verb.

EXAMPLE: (Someone) <u>stole</u> my bicycle last week.

My bicycle was stolen last week.

1. (They) <u>don't deliver</u> the mail on Sundays.

2. (Someone) <u>built</u> the bridge in 1920.

    _____

3. (Someone) <u>has made</u> a new movie about the Vietnam War.

    _____

4. (They) <u>speak</u> Spanish in Mexico.

    _____

5. (They) <u>don't allow</u> teachers to hit children.

    _____

6. (Someone) <u>will put</u> your name on a waiting list.

    _____

7. (Someone) <u>should clean</u> the hall once a week.

    _____

8. (Someone) <u>locks</u> the doors every night.

    _____

Part 3   Change the sentences from passive to active voice. Use the same tense.

> **EXAMPLE:**   The door <u>was closed</u> by the janitor.
>
> _The janitor closed the door._

1. The dinner <u>was made</u> by my mother.

    _____

2. A new book <u>has been written</u> by the author.

    _____

3. The compositions <u>will be read</u> by the teacher.

    _____

4. When <u>was</u> the ice cream <u>eaten</u> by the children?

    _____

5. How many cars <u>have been sold</u> by the salesman?

    _____

6. The car <u>wasn't driven</u> by me.

_____

7. Textbooks <u>are sold</u> by the college bookstore.

_____

8. Your help <u>isn't needed</u> by us.

_____

Part 4 Fill in the blanks with the passive or active of the verb in parentheses. Use an appropriate tense.

EXAMPLES:　Some dirty dishes _____*were left*_____ in the sink.
(leave)

I _____*didn't wash*_____ the dishes last night.
(not/wash)

1. She _____ all day yesterday.
(work)

2. The babysitter _____ $7 an hour for watching her neighbors' children last night.
(pay)

3. I _____ to school every day.
(go)

4. We _____ a great movie last weekend.
(see)

5. The movie _____ in France.
(make)

6. Next week, a prize _____ for the best painting.
(give)

7. Nothing _____ to correct the problem.
(do)

8. The windows _____ last night.
(not/close)

9. The answer to the problem can't _____.
(find)

10. The baby's asleep now. She _____ for two hours.
(sleep)

LESSON **FOURTEEN** / TEST

Part I   Find the mistakes with the underlined words, and correct them. Not every sentence has a mistake. If the sentence is correct, write **C**.

EXAMPLES: Most of my friend live in Hawaii.   *s*

Do you have <u>any</u> credit cards?   *C*

1. <u>Many of women</u> work outside the home.

2. I'm busy now. Please come back some <u>another</u> time.

3. <u>Some his friends</u> live in Thailand.

4. I have <u>very little</u> gas in my car. I need to stop immediately at a gas station.

5. <u>Almost the students</u> in my class are from Mexico.

6. <u>Most Americans</u> own a car.

7. I don't have <u>any</u> American friends.

8. I don't have <u>a</u> time to help you.

9. <u>All children</u> need love.

10. <u>Some the students</u> in my class never say anything.

11. She has two brothers. One is a pharmacist, and <u>the other</u> is a doctor.

12. <u>There's the Eiffel Tower</u> in Paris.

13. Some students in my class speak Polish. <u>Another students</u> speak Spanish.

14. Brazil <u>is big</u> country.

15. I didn't buy a dictionary. Did you buy <u>it</u>?

16. I have two cousins. One of my cousins is married. <u>The other my</u> cousin is single.

Part 2   Fill in the blanks with *the, a, an, any,* or ∅ article. In some cases, more than one answer is possible.

A. You look upset today.

B. I am. I have ____*a*____ problem with my neighbor.
    (example)

A. What's _____ problem?
    (1.)

B. She has _____ dog, and it barks so much.
          (2.)

A. All _____ dogs bark.
         (3.)

B. I know. But this dog barks all the time. I can't even sleep at night.

A. Did you talk to _____ landlord about _____ problem?
                      (4.)   (5.)

B. Yes. He said that none of _____ people in my building have made _____
                               (6.)   (7.)
    complaints about this woman or her dog. He gave me _____ advice about how to
                                                        (8.)
    deal with this situation.

A. What was his advice?

B. He said that I should talk to _____ owner of the dog.
                                   (9.)

A. Did you talk to her?

B. Yes, I did. But she said that there is nothing she can do about it.

A. Maybe you need to move to _____ new apartment.
                              (10.)

B. That's probably _____ good idea. First I need to save _____ money, and then
                     (11.)   (12.)
    I'll be able to move.

Part 3 Fill in the blanks with *other*, *others*, *another*, *the other*, *the others*.

A. How many classes are you taking this semester?

B. Only two. One is algebra. _____*The other*_____ is biology.
                                  (example)

A. I'm taking three classes, and I have a lot of homework. I have to write three papers by
    next week. One is for my accounting class. _____ are for my English
                                                (1.)
    class. I need to use a computer. Do you know where I can find one?

B. There are two computers in the library. One is on the south end. _____ one is
                                                                      (2.)
    near the circulation desk. I'll go with you because I need one too.

(At the library)

A. Oh, no. Somebody is using them. I guess we'll have to come back _____ time.
                                                                     (3.)

B. Let's go to the second floor. There are eight _____ on the second floor.
                                                   (4.)

(On the second floor)

A. We're in luck. Only two are occupied. All of _____ computers are free.
                                                  (5.)

Part 4   Fill in the blanks with *one, some, any, it* or *them*.

A. I like your apartment.

B. I don't like _____*it*_____. I'm moving on Saturday.
             (example)

A. Can I help you with your move?

B. Maybe you can. I need a van. Do you have _____?
                                             (1.)

B. No, I don't. But my brother-in-law has _____. I can ask him if I can
                                               (2.)

    borrow _____.
          (3.)

A. I need some boxes too. Do you have _____?
                                        (4.)

B. Yes, I have _____. I can give _____ to you on Friday.
                (5.)   (6.)

LESSON **FIFTEEN** / TEST

Part I   Read this letter of complaint. Fill in the blanks with the correct form of the verb in parentheses ( ): simple present, present continuous, future, simple past, past continuous, present perfect, present perfect continuous, infinitive, or base form. In some cases, more than one answer is possible.

4088 Monticello Street
Cleveland Heights, Ohio 44199

Mr. James Rich
Rich Apartment Rentals
1946 W. Tully Drive
Cleveland, Ohio 44176

Dear Mr. Rich,

I ___*am*___ a tenant in your building on Monticello Street. I _____ in my apartment

(example: be)   (1. live)

for three months. Before I _____ in, you _____ to fix the freezer compartment

                            (2. move)   (3. promise)

of the refrigerator. So far you _____ anything about this problem. As a result, it

                                      (4. not/do)

is impossible for me _____ anything in the freezer. Last week, I _____ over

                          (5. keep)   (6. buy)

$50 of meat, and I had to _____ everything out a few days later. Because I can't keep

                          (7. throw)

anything in the freezer, I have to _____ for fresh meat every day. This is very

                                    (8. shop)

inconvenient for me.

I _____ another complaint. It's too dark in the hallways at night. It _____

          (9. have)   (10. get)

dark outside at about six o'clock, but the hall lights don't go on until seven o'clock. Last

night while I _____ upstairs, I _____ because I _____ a child's

                (11. walk)   (12. fall)   (13. not/see)

toy on the stairs. Luckily I _____ badly hurt. However, someday, someone

                          (14. not/be)

_____ hurt.

(15. get)

There is one more complaint. The lock on my back door _____. I

                                            (16. not/work)

_____ to use my key in that lock many times, but I can't _____ that door. I

(17. try)   (18. open)

feel that this is a dangerous situation. If there _____ a fire in my apartment, I

                                        (19. be)

_____ use my back door. I want you _____ this lock

(20. not/be able to)   (21. change)

immediately.

I _____ you this letter now because it is impossible _____ you by
(22. write)   (23. reach)

phone. I _____ you many times, but each time I got your answering machine. Last
(24. call)

week, I _____ ten messages on your machine. If you _____ care of these
(25. leave)   (26. not/take)

problems immediately, I _____ to the city. They _____ out an inspector
(27. complain)   (28. send)

to check these problems. If you _____ these problems, you _____
(29. not/fix)   (30. have)

to pay the city.

Sincerely,

Jean Simms

Part 2   Read each statement. Then change the underlined verb to the negative
form to fill in the blank.

EXAMPLES: Jean is angry. She ___*isn't*___ happy.

She can open the front door. She ___*can't*___ open the back door.

1. Jean's complaining about her freezer. She _____ about the rent.

2. She lives on Monticello Street. She _____ on Tully Drive.

3. She's tried to call Mr. Rich many times. She _____ to write to Mr. Rich
    many times.

4. Next time she'll complain to the city. She _____ to Mr. Rich again.

5. She can use her refrigerator. She _____ her freezer.

6. She was using the stairs last night. She _____ the elevator.

7. She's going to write a letter to the city. She _____ another letter to Mr.
    Rich.

8. She fell on the stairs. She _____ in her apartment.

Part 3   Read each statement. Then write a *wh-* question about the words in parentheses ( ). An answer is not necessary.

EXAMPLES: Jean spent a lot of money on meat. (how much)

How much money did she spend on meat?

Jean lives on Monticello Street. (how long)

How long has she lived on Monticello Street?

1. Jean has several complaints. (how many complaints)

_____

2. The hall light goes on late. (what time)

_____

3. Someone fell on the stairs. (who)

_____

4. Jean didn't see the toy on the stairs. (why)

_____

5. She fell on the stairs. (where/go/when/fall)

_____

6. Mr. Rich hasn't answered Jean's calls. (why)

_____

7. Her freezer is out-of-order. (how long) [BE CAREFUL! You need to change the tense.]

_____

8. She needs to shop every day. (why)

_____

9. She will write a letter to the city. (when)

_____

10. She's called Mr. Rich many times. (how many times)

_____

11. Mr. Rich should fix the lock. (why)

_____

12. She left messages on Mr. Rich's answering machine yesterday. (how many)

_____

Part 4 Find the mistakes with the underlined words, and correct them. Not every sentence has a mistake. If the sentence is correct, write **C**.

EXAMPLES: My brother live in Germany.   *s*

I don't have a cell phone.   *C*

1. Everybody love children.

2. Finding a job takes time.

3. My father speaks English well.

4. He doesn't know the answer.

5. You don't have time to cook tonight? Don't worry. I cook tonight.

6. I am knowing the names of all the other students.

7. When I will arrive at my hotel, I'll call you.

8. If you don't eat breakfast now, you will hungry later.

9. When will you be buy a new computer?

10. My uncle was found a job last week.

11. We drove to Miami last summer.

12. She graduated from high school two years ago.

13. I been working in a hotel for three months.

14. My brother is married. He is married for five years.

15. I have had my new car for two weeks.

16. Have you ever taking a biology course?

17. I didn't ate breakfast this morning.

18. I cooked dinner when the fire started in the kitchen.

19. I have never being in Paris.

20. My grandmother has 80 years old.

21. The car has already washed.

22. She uses a special notebook for make a list of new words.

23. I need talk with the manager right now.

24. They wanted to bought a new car, but they didn't have enough money.

25. He wanted that I help him with his project, but I was too busy.

26. It's impossible <u>to lose</u> your accent completely.

27. We<u>'ve got to</u> leave the building immediately. There's a fire.

28. You <u>aren't supposed to write</u> the test with a pencil.

29. I used a newspaper <u>to cover</u> the floor while I was painting the walls.

30. His parents <u>couldn't came</u> to the U.S. with him because they didn't get a visa.

31. I <u>don't can</u> cook very well.

32. You should <u>to look</u> for a better job.

33. The teacher <u>can't help</u> you yesterday because he was too busy.

34. Why <u>you didn't</u> call me last night?

35. How many students <u>did</u> the homework last night?

36. How many students <u>did go</u> to the party?

37. When <u>your best friend came</u> to the U.S.?

38. Why <u>you can't</u> come here tomorrow?

39. Who <u>needs</u> more help with this lesson?

40. Why <u>you didn't</u> open the present?

41. When <u>will eat dinner the guests</u>?

42. How many states <u>does the U.S. have</u>?

43. When <u>did</u> America discovered?

44. How often <u>the teacher gives</u> a test?

45. Did you <u>understood</u> the teacher's explanation?

46. <u>How spell</u> "occasion"?

47. What <u>means</u> "occasion"?

48. What <u>happened</u> after I left the party?

49. How much <u>cost your ticket to the U.S.</u>?

50. <u>How say</u> "potato" in your language?

Part 5   Find and correct the mistakes with missing words, extra words, double negatives, and word order. Not every sentence has a mistake. If the sentence is correct, write **C**.

                      know
EXAMPLES: I don't ^ anything <u>know</u> about your problem.

                     I sometimes bring my dictionary to class.   *C*

1. The teacher left when was over the class.

2. I didn't know anyone at the party.

3. I and my parents live in a small apartment.

4. After ended the war, my family left the country.

5. Once in a while, I drink a glass of tea.

6. The thief entered very quietly the apartment.

7. My father he lives in Mexico.

8. You should your seat belt wear.

9. My parents from time to time visit me.

10. It's very hard the last lesson in the book.

11. Are a lot of grapes in the bowl on the table.

12. My teacher very intelligent.

13. Is hard to learn another language well.

14. I didn't see nothing that the children did.

15. I took an umbrella with me because was raining this morning.

16. I am always happy to see you.

17. I speak always English with my roommate.

18. Bill came in quietly and took a seat in the back of the room.

19. My wife and I always take a walk in the morning.

20. We have visited never the art museum in this city.

21. My brother fifteen years old.

22. The dinner that prepared my mother was delicious.

23. I read every book that the teacher recommended.

24. I met my uncle at the airport when came to America.

BOOK 2 / LESSON ONE TEST / ANSWERS

Part 1

1. Where <u>does your brother work</u>?
2. My father <u>doesn't have</u> a car.
3. Everyone in my family <u>speaks</u> English.
4. The teacher <u>doesn't know</u> the answer.
5. C
6. We <u>are usually</u> tired on Sundays.
7. We <u>always</u> get together on Sundays. OR <u>All the time, we</u> get together on Sundays.
8. Does the teacher ever give homework on the weekends? Yes, <u>sometimes</u> (OR <u>usually</u> OR <u>always</u> OR <u>often</u>).
9. <u>How often</u> do you call your mother?
10. C
11. C
12. I <u>never drink</u> coffee at night.
13. What <u>does</u> "insurance" mean?
14. How much <u>does insurance for your car cost</u>?
15. C
16. <u>How do you</u> spell your name?
17. Why <u>don't you</u> have a computer?
18. Where <u>does your sister live</u>?
19. I <u>don't like American movies.</u>
20. C
21. Some people <u>have</u> a very good life.
22. Are you hungry? Yes, I <u>am</u>.
23. Are you thirsty? Yes, <u>I am</u>.
24. The <u>church</u> is on the corner of Main and Elm.
25. My sister <u>is 15 years (old)</u>.
26. <u>It's</u> impossible to learn English in one month.
27. The hospital <u>is located</u> on Maple Street.
28. C
29. Some students <u>aren't</u> here today.
30. <u>I speak</u> Spanish well.
31. C
32. The President lives in the White House.
33. I'm not interested in sports.
34. <u>You're</u> a very kind person.

Part 2

1. doesn't begin
2. doesn't have
3. aren't
4. don't need
5. doesn't mean

Part 3

1. Do you like cats? Yes, I do.
2. Is your dog friendly? Yes, he (OR she OR it) is.
3. Do they want a bird? No, they don't.
4. Does your cat ever sleep in your bed? Yes, he (OR she OR it) sometimes does.
5. Do you buy meat for your dog? No, I don't.

Part 4

1. What language do Peruvians speak?
2. Where does the Governor work?
3. Why doesn't the Vice-President (OR he) live in the White House?
4. Where do you come from? OR Where are you from?
5. How often do you pay your gas bill?
6. How old is Alex's (OR his) wife?
7. How many states does Mexico have?
8. How do you spell Florida?
9. What does "pet" mean?
10. How do you say "hello" in Polish?

LESSON TWO

Part 1

1. Barbara <u>is going to buy</u> a new car. (OR Barbara <u>will buy</u> a new car.)
2. When the movie <u>is</u> over, everyone will go to my house.
3. C
4. <u>I'm going to write</u> a letter tonight.
5. C
6. You can't carry that heavy box alone. <u>I'll help</u> you.
7. C
8. What <u>are you going to do</u> tomorrow night?
9. C
10. Why <u>won't he</u> tell me the answer?
11. C
12. If I don't eat breakfast, I <u>will be hungry</u> later.
13. Why <u>aren't you</u> working now?
14. <u>We're taking</u> a test now.
15. <u>Do you hear</u> the noise outside now?
16. My family <u>will buy</u> a house next year.
17. C
18. C

Part 2

1. are you doing
2. am ('m) watching
3. Do you want
4. need
5. do you need
6. am ('m) taking
7. needs
8. is ('s) sleeping
9. are playing
10. is ('s) shopping
11. will she be OR is she going to be
12. gets
13. am ('m) going to make (OR am making)
14. don't have
15. comes
16. will ('ll) go OR am ('m) going (to go)
17. am ('m) going (to go)
18. is
19. will ('ll) get
20. will ('ll) deliver

Part 3

1. isn't watching
2. doesn't need
3. isn't
4. isn't going to buy
5. won't go

Part 4

1. Will she come home at 3 o'clock? No, she won't.
2. Is she shopping for a coat? Yes, she is.
3. Is Mike taking care of his kids? No, he isn't.
4. Does Sam want to watch a football game? No, he doesn't.
5. Is Sam's wife going to cook tonight? No, she isn't.

Part 5

1. Why is he going to cook dinner?
2. When will he go to the store?
3. Why doesn't he want to leave the house?
4. Why does the baby need a lot of attention?
5. What kind of game are they playing?

LESSON THREE

Part 1

1. saw
2. worried
3. took
4. drove
5. cut
6. grew
7. stood
8. left
9. ran
10. came
11. let
12. taught
13. ate
14. gave
15. wrote
16. understood
17. talked
18. read
19. drank
20. went

Part 2

1. I decided to <u>eat</u> in a restaurant last weekend.
2. I <u>wasn't</u> tired after the football game yesterday.
3. <u>There were</u> a lot of people at Martin Luther King's funeral.
4. She <u>didn't go</u> to the museum yesterday.
5. C
6. They <u>saw</u> the movie yesterday.
7. C
8. C
9. My father <u>used to tell</u> me stories when I was a child.
10. In my native country, <u>I used to live</u> with my parents and brothers and sisters. Now I live alone.
11. When <u>did your grandfather die</u>?
12. Why <u>didn't you come</u> to class yesterday?
13. Where <u>did you buy</u> your new coat?
14. C

Part 3

1. didn't have
2. didn't drink
3. didn't tell
4. wasn't
5. didn't work
6. didn't feel
7. didn't put
8. didn't arrive

Part 4

1. Where was King (OR he) born?
2. Why did King (OR he) fight for people's rights?
3. To whom did King (OR he) get married?
4. Why didn't blacks and whites (OR they) sit together on a bus?
5. Why wasn't King (OR he) happy with this situation?
6. When did blacks (OR they) have to use separate washrooms?
7. What did King (OR he) speak about in Washington?
8. Why did King (OR he) go to jail many times?
9. When did King (OR he) say, "I have a dream"?
10. What did King (OR he) want for all Americans?

Part 5

Answers will vary. Sample answers:

1. People used to get married at a younger age.
2. People used to live in one place for a long time.

LESSON FOUR

Part 1

1. C
2. <u>Who's</u> your math teacher?
3. I sometimes use <u>my brother's car</u>.
4. Where is your <u>parents' house</u>?
5. Did they bring <u>their</u> books today?
6. C
7. Who <u>closed</u> the door last night?
8. Did you forget <u>your</u> keys?
9. C
10. C
11. Where did your brother meet <u>his</u> girlfriend?
12. C
13. Where did the students leave <u>their</u> papers?
14. Did you find <u>your</u> gloves?
15. <u>My best friend and I</u> went to see a movie last night.
16. C
17. <u>My friend's</u> new car is very beautiful.
18. There are many new <u>books</u> in the library.
19. We should buy <u>ourselves</u> a nice present.
20. C
21. C
22. Who <u>has</u> a watch?
23. C
24. Do you visit <u>your</u> parents often?
25. C

Part 2

1. a
2. d
3. c
4. d
5. b
6. d
7. b
8. d
9. b
10. c
11. b
12. a
13. b
14. a
15. c

Part 3

1. said
2. told
3. said
4. told
5. told
6. told
7. told
8. said

Part 4

1. did your sister get
2. did she marry
3. did you give
4. paid
5. attended
6. gave
7. caught
8. did the bride and groom answer
9. will the newlyweds go
10. ring has

Part 5

1. myself
2. yourself
3. herself
4. themselves
5. yourselves
6. itself
7. himself

LESSON FIVE

Part 1

1. <u>The Statue of Liberty is</u> in New York.
2. C
3. <u>Most</u> Americans have a television.
4. <u>Children</u> like to watch TV.
5. <u>There are</u> more women than men in the U.S.
6. Immigrants come to America because they want <u>freedom</u>.
7. New York and Los Angeles are <u>big cities</u>.
8. Los Angeles is one of the biggest <u>cities</u> in the U.S.
9. <u>How many</u> students have the textbook?
10. C
11. I paid a lot of money for my textbooks, but I didn't pay <u>a lot</u> for my tuition because I have a scholarship.
12. You need a lot of <u>advice</u> in order to plan your future.
13. My father has <u>a lot of</u> education.
14. Do you have any <u>information</u> about the nursing program?
15. The teacher doesn't have <u>any</u> time to help me today.
16. <u>There are</u> almost two million Native Americans in the U.S.
17. C
18. C
19. I want to be rich. I want to have <u>a lot of</u> money.
20. I can't help you today because I have <u>(very) little</u> time.
21. Every <u>student wants</u> to learn.
22. I drank three <u>cups of coffee</u> this morning.
23. C

Part 2

1. furniture, chairs, lamps, bookshelves, dishes, knives
2. advice, teachers, homework
3. fruit, cherries, grapes, peaches, strawberries, pears
4. time, jobs, children
5. people, unemployment, cities

Part 3

1. bowl
2. glass OR cup
3. piece
4. carton OR quart OR gallon
5. pieces

Part 4

1. b	3. c	5. a	7. c
2. d	4. d	6. b	8. b

LESSON SIX

Part 1

1. My <u>driver's license</u> is going to expire next month.
2. She made a pot of <u>vegetable soup</u>.
3. He <u>woke up late</u> this morning.
4. C
5. C
6. My sister is <u>married</u> and has a <u>six-month-old</u> baby.
7. When their son graduated, they looked very <u>happy</u>.
8. I'm <u>too tired</u> to help you today.
9. C
10. She wrote <u>the composition carefully</u>.
11. We had <u>a very long discussion</u> about a serious problem.
12. The meal was <u>very</u> delicious. I enjoyed all of it.
13. He's tired because he <u>worked hard</u> on a long project.
14. C
15. I'm not <u>tall enough</u> to reach the highest shelf.
16. C
17. I want to visit Paris <u>very much</u>.
18. She has two <u>beautiful</u> daughters.
19. My old computer is very <u>slow</u>.
20. Where is the bank <u>located</u>?

Part 2

1. hard	5. extremely	9. usual	12. friendly
2. quickly, accurately	6. happy	10. lazy	13. sad
3. good, well	7. late	11. absolutely, right	14. constantly
4. fluently	8. perfectly		

LESSON SEVEN

Part 1

1. C
2. After <u>driving</u> for eight hours, I was tired.
3. When <u>the airplane arrived</u>, I was at the airport.
4. She had her first child <u>when</u> she was 28 years old.
5. I was washing the dishes <u>when</u> I broke the glass.
6. He slept <u>for</u> 2 hours.
7. C
8. C
9. While they <u>were watching</u> TV, the phone rang.
10. C
11. C
12. C
13. He came to the U.S. three years <u>ago</u>.
14. C
15. C
16. While Einstein was visiting the U.S., the Nazis <u>took</u> his home.

Part 2

1. asked, was going
2. said
3. was talking, was hiding, listening
4. heard, ran
5. put, got
6. opened, was lying
7. jumped, ran
8. was chasing, arrived, shot

Part 3

1. c	3. a	5. b	7. d	9. a
2. a	4. b	6. d	8. d	10. c

LESSON EIGHT

Part 1

1. I have a test tomorrow. I've got to study tonight.
2. We may go to the zoo on Saturday. OR Maybe we will go to the zoo on Saturday.
3. The teacher can help you later.
4. C
5. C
6. Are we permitted to use our dictionaries to write a composition?
7. You're not supposed to talk during a test.
8. Where can I get information about registration?
9. C
10. Last week I couldn't come to class because I was sick.
11. C
12. I'd rather study in the morning than at night.
13. It's going to rain. You'd better take an umbrella.
14. The test is going to be at 8 o'clock. You'd better not come late.

Part 2

1. must not
2. could
3. Could
4. are not supposed to
5. might
6. may not
7. Would
8. shouldn't
9. better
10. rather
11. 've got to
12. must
13. can't
14. shouldn't
15. must

LESSON NINE

Part 1

1. Have you ever seen a French movie?
2. How long has he been studying English?
3. I've wanted to become a pilot since I was a child.
4. How long has she been a teacher?
5. I have never been a good student.
6. She has been working in a factory since she came to the U.S.
7. How long has the baby been sleeping?
8. Have you ever met the president of the college?
9. I've known my best friend for many years.
10. C
11. C
12. Yes, they've eaten dinner already.
13. C
14. I have had my car for three months.
15. C
16. I've eaten pizza many times.
17. How long have they been married?
18. He's been working for eight hours.
19. She bought her car 3 months ago.
20. C
21. She's talked to her brother many times about the problem.
22. We've gone to the zoo many times.
23. C
24. When did you find your job?

Part 2

Conversation 1

1. have
2. did . . . go
3. went
4. have ('ve) never visited

Conversation 2

1. saw
2. did . . . see
3. have ('ve) never seen
4. haven't had
5. started

Part 3

1. moved
2. did you move
3. came
4. live
5. haven't had
6. came
7. has . . . found
8. has been looking OR has looked
9. hasn't found

LESSON TEN

Part 1

1. I'm tired <u>of</u> working so hard.
2. C
3. <u>Learning</u> a new language is difficult.
4. C
5. You can learn English faster by <u>practicing</u> with Americans.
6. When I was a teenager, I used to <u>watching</u> TV all Saturday.
7. I dream about <u>going</u> back to my country.
8. C
9. C
10. I'm interested <u>in</u> learning French.
11. C
12. <u>Not having</u> a job makes me feel depressed.
13. I <u>wanted to call</u> you, but I lost your phone number.
14. <u>It's</u> important to help poor people.
15. She <u>forgot to buy</u> sugar when she was at the store.
16. Do you want <u>me to help</u> you move on Saturday?
17. He uses a bicycle <u>to go</u> to work.
18. C
19. Is it necessary <u>for</u> you to use your dictionary every day?
20. C
21. C
22. I've always lived with my family. I can't <u>get used to living</u> alone.

Part 2

1. to go
2. to help
3. Not wearing
4. Buying
5. swimming
6. doing
7. washing
8. to get
9. wearing
10. seeing
11. going
12. to find
13. to learn
14. to play (OR playing)
15. to have
16. to use
17. talking
18. to dance (OR dancing)

LESSON ELEVEN

Part 1

1. C
2. The student <u>who's</u> sitting in the back row speaks English well.
3. The chicken that <u>my husband ate</u> had very little salt in it.
4. <u>The man who gave a speech last night is very intelligent</u>.
5. People <u>who live</u> in Alaska are used to cold winters.
6. I have a friend <u>whose</u> son is an artist.
7. The woman <u>who</u> OR <u>that</u> played the piano at the concert is very talented.
8. The mistake <u>that he made</u> cost the company thousands of dollars.
9. I rented <u>a movie that</u> (OR <u>which</u>) <u>was</u> three hours long.
10. <u>The person</u> (OR <u>the student</u>) <u>who has</u> the best composition will win a prize.
11. C
12. The teacher <u>who</u> (OR <u>that</u>) <u>helped</u> me at registration was very kind.
13. C
14. I have a friend <u>that doesn't have</u> a telephone.

Part 2

1. that (which) has
2. (that/which) she made
3. (that/who/whom) they hired OR who was hired
4. (that/which) I put
5. whose children
6. computer I bought
7. (who/whom/that) I had

LESSON TWELVE

Part 1

1. C
2. She's <u>younger than</u> her best friend.
3. You speak English <u>better</u> than your father.
4. He has <u>more money</u> than I do.
5. C
6. C
7. Who is <u>the most intelligent</u> student in this class?
8. <u>My</u> oldest cousin is married.
9. C
10. San Francisco is one of <u>the most beautiful cities</u> in the U.S.
11. What is <u>the highest</u> mountain in the world?
12. C
13. My grandmother isn't <u>as old as</u> my grandfather. (OR <u>the same age as</u>)
14. Her daughter is a (very) <u>beautiful</u> girl.
15. C
16. C
17. California is <u>the most populated</u> state in the U.S.
18. C
19. She answered the questions on the test <u>more quickly</u> than I did.
20. He <u>sings better</u> than I do.

Part 2

1. the same
2. size as
3. taste
4. the same
5. age
6. is
7. taller OR shorter
8. as . . . as
9. alike
10. price
11. as possible
12. like
13. much
14. more talented

LESSON THIRTEEN

Part 1

1. The birthday presents <u>were never opened</u>.
2. My watch <u>was repaired</u> last week.
3. C
4. Most of the pizza <u>wasn't eaten</u>.
5. The accident <u>happened</u> at 5:35 a.m.
6. C
7. My grandparents <u>died</u> when I was small.
8. C
9. When <u>was</u> the book written?
10. Library books <u>should be returned</u> at the front desk.
11. All the students <u>were sent</u> information about registration.
12. C
13. A dictionary <u>can be used</u> for the composition test.
14. Newspapers and magazines <u>can be found</u> in the library.
15. C

Part 2

1. The mail isn't delivered on Sundays.
2. The bridge was built in 1920.
3. A new movie has been made about the Vietnam War.
4. Spanish is spoken in Mexico.
5. Teachers aren't allowed to hit children.
6. Your name will be put on a waiting list.
7. The hall should be cleaned once a week.
8. The doors are locked every night.

Part 3

1. My mother made the dinner.
2. The author has written a new book.
3. The teacher will read the compositions.
4. When did the children eat the ice cream?
5. How many cars has the salesman sold?
6. I didn't drive the car.
7. The college bookstore sells textbooks.
8. We don't need your help.

Part 4

1. worked
2. was paid
3. go
4. saw
5. was made
6. will be given
7. has been done (OR was done)
8. were not closed
9. be found
10. has been sleeping

LESSON FOURTEEN

Part 1

1. <u>Many women</u> work outside the home.
2. I'm busy now. Please come back some <u>other</u> time.
3. <u>Some of his friends</u> live in Thailand.
4. C
5. <u>Most of the students</u> in my class are from Mexico.
6. C
7. C
8. I don't have (<u>any</u>) time to help you.
9. C
10. <u>Some of the students</u> in my class never say anything.
11. C
12. <u>The Eiffel Tower is</u> in Paris.
13. Some students in my class speak Polish. <u>Other students</u> speak Spanish.
14. <u>Brazil is a big country.</u>
15. I didn't buy a dictionary. Did you buy <u>one</u>?
16. I have two cousins. One of my cousins is married. <u>My other</u> cousin is single.

Part 2

1. the
2. a
3. ∅
4. the
5. the
6. the
7. any OR ∅
8. some OR ∅
9. the
10. a
11. a
12. some OR ∅

Part 3

1. The others
2. The other
3. another
4. others
5. the other

Part 4

1. one
2. one
3. it
4. any
5. some
6. them

LESSON FIFTEEN

Part 1

1. have lived OR have been living
2. moved
3. promised
4. have not done
5. to keep
6. bought
7. throw
8. shop
9. have
10. gets
11. was walking
12. fell
13. didn't see
14. was not
15. will get
16. doesn't work (OR isn't working)
17. have tried
18. open
19. is
20. will not be able to
21. to change
22. am writing
23. to reach
24. have called
25. left
26. don't take
27. will complain
28. will send
29. don't fix
30. will have

Part 2

1. isn't complaining
2. doesn't live
3. hasn't tried
4. won't complain
5. can't use
6. wasn't using
7. isn't going to write
8. didn't fall

Part 3

1. How many complaints does Jean (OR she) have?
2. What time does the hall light (OR it) go on?
3. Who fell on the stairs?
4. Why didn't Jean (OR she) see the toy on the stairs?
5. Where was she going when she fell?
6. Why hasn't Mr. Rich (OR he) answered Jean's (OR her) calls?
7. How long has her freezer been out-of-order?
8. Why does she need to shop every day?
9. When will she write a letter to the city?
10. How many times has she called Mr. Rich?
11. Why should Mr. Rich (OR he) fix the lock (OR it)?
12. How many messages did she leave on Mr. Rich's (OR his) answering machine yesterday?

Part 4

1. Everybody <u>loves</u> children.
2. C
3. C
4. C
5. You don't have time to cook tonight? Don't worry. I'll <u>cook</u> tonight.
6. I <u>know</u> the names of all the other students.
7. When I <u>arrive</u> at my hotel, I'll call you.
8. If you don't eat breakfast now, you <u>will be hungry</u> later.
9. When <u>will you buy</u> a new computer?
10. My uncle <u>found</u> a job last week.
11. C
12. C
13. I've been <u>working</u> in a hotel for three months.
14. My brother is married. He <u>has been</u> married for five years.
15. C
16. Have you ever <u>taken</u> a biology course?
17. I <u>didn't eat</u> breakfast this morning.
18. I <u>was cooking</u> dinner when the fire started in the kitchen.
19. I have never <u>been</u> in Paris.
20. My grandmother <u>is 80 years old</u>.
21. The car has already <u>been washed</u>.
22. She uses a special notebook <u>to make</u> a list of new words.
23. I <u>need to talk</u> with the manager right now.
24. They <u>wanted to buy</u> a new car, but they didn't have enough money.
25. He wanted <u>me to help</u> him with his project, but I was too busy.
26. C
27. C
28. C
29. C
30. His parents <u>couldn't come</u> to the U.S. with him because they didn't get a visa.
31. I <u>can't</u> cook very well.
32. You should <u>look</u> for a better job.
33. The teacher <u>couldn't help</u> you yesterday because he was too busy.
34. Why <u>didn't you</u> call me last night?
35. C
36. How many students <u>went</u> to the party?
37. When <u>did your best friend come</u> to the U.S.?
38. Why <u>can't you</u> come here tomorrow?
39. C
40. Why <u>didn't you</u> open the present?
41. When <u>will the guests eat dinner</u>?
42. C
43. When <u>was</u> America discovered?
44. How often <u>does the teacher give</u> a test?
45. Did you <u>understand</u> the teacher's explanation?
46. <u>How do you spell</u> "occasion"?
47. What <u>does "occasion" mean</u>?
48. C
49. How much <u>did your ticket to the U.S. cost</u>?
50. <u>How do you say</u> "potato" in your language?

Part 5

1. The teacher left when the class was over.
2. C
3. My parents and I live in a small apartment.
4. After the war ended, my family left the country.
5. C
6. The thief entered the apartment very quietly.
7. My father lives in Mexico.
8. You should wear your seat belt.
9. My parents visit me from time to time.
10. The last lesson in the book is very hard.
11. There are a lot of grapes in the bowl on the table.
12. My teacher is very intelligent.
13. It's hard to learn another language well.
14. I didn't see anything that the children did.

15. I took an umbrella with me because it was raining this morning.
16. C
17. I always speak English with my roommate.
18. C
19. C
20. We have never visited the art museum in this city.

21. My brother is fifteen years old.
22. The dinner that my mother prepared was delicious.
23. C
24. I met my uncle at the airport when he came to America.

BOOK 3 / REVIEW LESSON / TEST

Part 1   Verbs

Find the mistakes with the underlined words, and correct them. Not every sentence has a mistake. If the sentence is correct, write **C**.

EXAMPLES: I ~~doesn't~~ *don't* like classical music.

Don't bother your father. He <u>is sleeping</u>.   *C*

1. If I <u>will have</u> free time tonight, <u>I'll help</u> you.

2. I <u>wanted call</u> you last night, but I didn't have your phone number.

3. My sister <u>didn't went</u> to the party last night.

4. She <u>doesn't likes</u> cold weather.

5. She <u>can drive</u> a car now.

6. People who live in the U.S. <u>has</u> a lot of freedom.

7. Everybody <u>need</u> to pay taxes.

8. Next year I <u>will be go</u> back to my country.

9. You <u>was</u> late to the meeting yesterday.

10. I <u>been</u> in the U.S. for two years.

11. She used a knife <u>for open</u> the package.

12. <u>I'm not able to help</u> you today.

13. My father <u>doesn't has</u> a job.

14. She <u>need</u> more time to finish the test.

15. Jack <u>was finished</u> his homework two hours ago.

16. I <u>finded</u> a good job yesterday.

17. Her grandfather <u>borned</u> in Puerto Rico.

18. The students <u>are taking</u> a test now.

19. They <u>have seeing</u> the movie three times.

20. I <u>been driving</u> for 4 hours, and I'm tired.

Part 2   Adjectives, Adverbs, and Noun Modifiers

Find the mistakes with the underlined words, and correct them. Not every sentence has a mistake. If the sentence is correct, write **C**.

EXAMPLES: She is a slow~~ly~~ driver.

He does his job <u>very well</u>.   *C*

1. She likes to travel <u>very much</u>.

2. I have a <u>hundred-dollars bill</u> in my pocket.

3. When she writes a composition, she is very <u>carefully</u>.

4. Does your father drive <u>good</u>?

5. Those papers over there are important. <u>This</u> papers here are not important.

6. It's <u>too much</u> cold to go out today. Let's stay inside.

7. I ate dinner very <u>fast</u>.

8. She's tired because she worked very <u>hardly</u>.

9. My husband doesn't drive, and I don't <u>too</u>.

10. My college <u>locate</u> on Wright and Green Streets.

11. I won the lottery. I'm <u>too</u> happy.

12. Mary has two <u>beautifuls</u> daughters.

13. You speak English very <u>clearly</u>.

14. Is your best friend <u>married</u>?

15. They're <u>too young</u> to get married. They're only 17 years old.

Part 3   Comparatives and Superlatives

Find the mistakes with the underlined words, and correct them. Not every sentence has a mistake. If the sentence is correct, write **C**.

EXAMPLES: I am not <u>as thin ~~than~~</u> I was 10 years ago.
                                                                              as

My husband and I aren't <u>the same nationality</u>.   *C*

1. He's not <u>as old as</u> his wife. His wife is older.

2. She drives <u>more faster than</u> her husband.

3. He speaks English <u>better his wife</u>.

4. <u>I'm look like</u> my father. We both have blue eyes and curly black hair.

5. An orange is <u>the same shape as</u> a grapefruit.

6. I can type <u>more quickly than</u> you can.

7. New York <u>is biggest</u> city in the U.S.

8. Alaska is the <u>larger</u> state in the U.S.

9. She is one of <u>the most beautiful girl</u> in the world.

10. <u>You're don't look like</u> your photo ID.

11. She is <u>more intelligent than</u> her brother.

12. Chicago is big, but Los Angeles is <u>bigger than</u>.

Part 4   Count and Noncount Nouns

Find the mistakes with the underlined words, and correct them. Not every sentence has a mistake. If the sentence is correct, write **C**.

EXAMPLES: I drank a <u>can˄soda</u>.   *of*

She has <u>a lot of</u> good friends.   *C*

1. <u>A lot students</u> at this college come from Mexico.

2. I need to buy 2 <u>pounds coffee</u>.

3. I drink a lot of coffee. Do you drink <u>a lot</u>?

4. Bill Gates is a billionaire. He has <u>much money</u>.

5. My mother gave me <u>a lot of advices</u> when I was a child.

6. I have <u>a couple of</u> suggestions for you.

7. There were <u>too many</u> people at the party. Everyone had a good time.

8. I can't go out to eat with you today because I have <u>a little</u> money.

9. I didn't put <u>any milk</u> in your coffee.

10. I put <u>a little of</u> sugar in my coffee.

11. She didn't know <u>nobody</u> at the party.

12. There was <u>a lot of snow</u> last winter.

Part 5 Nouns and Possessive Forms

Find the mistakes with the underlined words, and correct them. Not every sentence has a mistake. If the sentence is correct, write **C**.

EXAMPLES: Many peoples like to complain about the weather.

The dentist examined my teeth. *C*

1. Most of my friend live in Germany.

2. I saw two mice in the kitchen.

3. My neighbor's make a lot of noise.

4. Every students wants to pass the course.

5. Husband of my sister is a mailman.

6. My sister has 4 childrens.

7. My parents' house is not very big.

8. Two women came late to the meeting.

Part 6 Pronouns and Possessive Forms

Find the mistakes with the underlined words, and correct them. Not every sentence has a mistake. If the sentence is correct, write **C**.

EXAMPLES: I love my father. He's His a good man.

If you need a pen, you can use mine. *C*

1. My husband visits her mother once a week.

2. She wants that I help her find a job.

3. Those birds are beautiful. Do you see they?

4. I lost my dictionary. Can I borrow yours?

5. I can find my books, but they can't find theirs books.

6. I can't find my keys. Have you seen its?

7. Did you ever see a bird make its nest?

8. Whose coat is that?

9. I like you because your a very kind person.

10. Please say me what you want.

11. Do you want him to turn off the light when he leaves?

12. I don't know your brothers. What are there names?

Part 7 Sentences and Word Order

Find the mistakes with sentences and word order, and correct them. Not every sentence has a mistake. If the sentence is correct, write **C**.

EXAMPLES: I can't (the newspaper) read in English.

He sometimes takes the bus to work.   *C*

1. My parents they have a new car.

2. Me and my sister went to California for our vacation.

3. She has always wanted to visit Paris.

4. She always is late for class.

5. She always drinks coffee in the morning.

6. She ate dinner quickly.

7. I think your new house is beautiful. Especially I like your living room.

8. I maybe will buy a new car.

9. When came home her husband, she ate dinner.

10. I afraid to speak English by telephone.

11. Is necessary to have a textbook in this class.

12. I like to go to the park because are a lot of beautiful trees there.

13. She faster finished the homework than I did.

14. Never we watch TV in the morning.

15. They have wanted always to own a house.

16. He didn't drive to work because was snowing too hard.

17. Everything that said the doctor was helpful to me.

18. I don't want to take your pen. Just I want to borrow it for a few minutes.

19. My sister and I went to the movie together.

20. Your brother is not old enough to drive.

21. I have experience more than you do.

22. He works as a driver bus.

23. You type more quickly than I do.

24. Once in a while, we go to the theater.

Part 8   Question Formation

Find the mistakes with the underlined words, and correct them. Not every sentence has a mistake. If the sentence is correct, write **C**.

EXAMPLES: Where <u>does</u> your father lives?

How many people <u>saw</u> the movie?   *C*

1. Does your brother <u>speaks</u> English well?

2. When <u>were</u> you buy your car?

3. What <u>means "clever"</u>?

4. How <u>say "book"</u> in Spanish?

5. Why <u>you can't</u> open the door?

6. What kind of soup <u>did he eat</u>?

7. When <u>you wake up</u> every morning?

8. Who <u>took</u> my money?

9. What kind of car <u>drives your brother</u>?

10. When <u>will you</u> go shopping next week?

11. How <u>spell</u> your last name?

12. How much <u>costs coffee</u> this week?

LESSON **ONE** / TEST

Part I   Find the mistakes with the underlined words, and correct them. Not every sentence has a mistake. If the sentence is correct, write **C**.

EXAMPLES: Have you ever ~~being~~ *been* to New York?

He came to the U.S. 5 years ago.   *C*

1. He's eating pizza several times this week.

2. How much homework has the teacher given this semester?

3. I've had three cups of coffee today.

4. Have you eaten dinner yet? Yes, I've eaten dinner yet.

5. He loves New York. He's gone to New York many times.

6. I've met already your brother.

7. I've gone to London five years ago.

8. Your sister lives in the U.S. How long time has she been living in the U.S.?

9. We have had 2 tests since the semester has begun.

10. My mother lives in France now. She lives there for 2 years.

11. Has your brother ever worked in a hotel?

12. I left my country 5 years ago. When have you left your country?

13. Susan's married now. How long has she been married?

14. Lynn was married, but now she's divorced. How long has she been married?

15. Have you read any good books lately?

16. They have lived in Mexico three years.

17. Ever since I was a child, I have wanted to visit Paris.

18. I haven't seen my parents in 5 years.

19. I have a job in a restaurant now. I have been worked in a restaurant since 1995.

20. They <u>been studying</u> English all their lives.

21. She<u>'s wearing</u> glasses since she <u>was</u> a little girl.

22. <u>Have you ever study</u> biology?

Part 2 Fill in the blanks in the conversation below with the correct tense of the verb in parentheses ( ). Use the present perfect, present perfect continuous, or simple past.

Situation: Two women, Karen (K) and Lucy (L), meet by chance in a shopping mall.

L: Karen! I ____*haven't seen*____ you since high school.
(example: not/see)

K: Lucy! Yes. We _____ each other for five years. How are you? Tell me
(1. not/see)

about your life. What _____ lately?
(2. you/do)

L: Well, I _____ married three years ago. And I _____ a baby six months ago.
(3. get)[1] (4. have)

K: That's wonderful. _____ your high school sweetheart, Steve?
(5. you/marry)

L: Oh, no. I _____ Steve since we _____ . I _____
(6. not/see) (7. graduate) (8. marry)

Robert Kanter. You _____ him. How about you? What _____
(9. never/meet) (10. happen)

in your life lately?

K: I _____ from college last year. I _____ a degree in teaching
(11. graduate) (12. get)

from the University of Michigan.

L: That's great. I _____ a great respect for the teaching profession.
(13. always/have)

Where do you teach?

K: I _____ a teaching job yet. Teaching jobs are hard to find. I work in a
(14. not/find)

day-care center.

L: How long _____ there?
(15. work)

K: For about four months.

L: _____ any of our old high school friends lately?
(16. you/see)

K: I _____ touch with most of them over the years, but I _____ into[2]
(17. lose) (18. run)

Susana Bartlett at a party last month.

[1] When we use *get married*, we don't use an object: Lucy <u>got married</u> in church. <u>Did</u> Karen <u>get married</u> last year? When we use *marry*, we put an object after the verb: Lucy <u>married</u> Robert Kanter. <u>Did</u> Karen <u>marry</u> Greg?
[2] *Run into:* meet by chance

L: How is she? _____ Richard?
(19. she/marry)

K: Yes, but she _____ with him for only one year. Then they got divorced.
(20. stay)

L: That's too bad. What about you? Did you marry your old boyfriend, Greg?

K: No. I _____ Greg for four years. I _____ married.
(21. not/see)   (22. never/be)

L: Well, it was nice seeing you again. We really should keep in touch.

K: Yes. We really should. Bye

LESSON **TWO** / TEST

Part I   Find the mistakes with the underlined words, and correct them. Not every sentence has a mistake. If the sentence is correct, write **C**.

EXAMPLES: The thief _was_ arrested by the police this morning.

Newspapers <u>can be found</u> in the library.   *C*

1. My car <u>didn't made</u> in America. It <u>was made</u> in Japan.

2. Something terrible <u>was happened</u> last night.

3. My grandfather <u>was born</u> in Poland.

4. My grandfather <u>was died</u> in the U.S.

5. Many soldiers <u>were killed</u> in the war.

6. The President <u>saw</u> on TV last night by millions of Americans.

7. The directions for the test <u>are written</u> at the top of the page.

8. A hat <u>found</u> near the building.

9. When <u>did</u> Columbus <u>discover</u> America?

10. When <u>was</u> the telephone <u>invented</u>?

11. The test <u>will be returned</u> next week.

12. The child <u>should be watching</u> by his mother.

13. The patient <u>is being examined by</u> the doctor now.

14. She <u>has been taken</u> pain medication for 3 weeks.

15. The results of the test <u>will announced</u> tomorrow.

16. The store <u>opens</u> at 8 o'clock every day.

17. The birthday cake <u>was eating</u> by the children.

Part 2 Change the following sentences to the passive voice. Do not mention the performer. Use the same tense as the underlined verb.

EXAMPLES: Someone <u>stole</u> the money.

The money was stolen.

They <u>speak</u> English in many countries.

English is spoken in many countries.

1. Someone <u>left</u> a package in front of my house.

2. Who <u>will</u> we <u>elect</u> as the next president?

3. They <u>don't permit</u> dogs in this park.

4. When <u>did</u> they <u>build</u> this school?

5. You <u>can't use</u> a pencil for the test.

6. Someone <u>is painting</u> the apartment now.

7. Someone <u>has left</u> the keys in the door.

8. They <u>should choose</u> a new secretary.

9. Someone <u>is going to clean</u> the apartment.

10. Someone <u>has to lock</u> the door.

Part 3   Change from passive to active. Use the same tense as the underlined verb.

EXAMPLES: You <u>will be helped</u> by the teacher.

The teacher will help you.

The movie <u>has been seen</u> by millions of people.

Millions of people have seen the movie.

1. The car <u>will be driven</u> by my sister.

_____

2. The composition <u>wasn't written</u> by me.

_____

3. The house <u>is being cleaned</u> by my brothers.

_____

4. The car <u>was washed</u> by them.

_____

5. Your name <u>should be written</u> on the top of the page.

_____

6. The presents <u>weren't opened</u> by us.

_____

7. <u>Were</u> you <u>met</u> at the airport by your uncle?

_____

8. The classroom <u>is going to be opened</u> by the janitor.

_____

9. I <u>have been driven</u> to the airport many times by my uncle.

_____

10. A decision <u>should be made</u> by you soon.

_____

Part 4 Fill in the blanks with the passive or the active voice of the verb in parentheses. Use an appropriate tense.

> **EXAMPLE:** A few weeks ago, while I ___*was shopping*___ at the supermarket
> (shop)
> near my house, I ___*was robbed*___.
> (rob)

I was at the checkout counter, paying for my groceries. When I _____ my
(1. give)

change by the cashier, I _____ it in my purse. But I was careless and _____
(2. put)   (3. not/close)

my purse. As I _____ out of the store, I _____ a pull at my purse.
(4. walk)   (5. feel)

Suddenly, I _____ a man run past me. A woman who _____ next to
(6. see)   (7. walk)

me _____, "That man _____ your wallet!" I _____ back into the store
(8. say)   (9. steal)   (10. run)

and _____ the manager what happened. The manager _____ the police
(11. tell)   (12. call)

immediately. In the meantime, I saw the thief run to the train station nearby. A train arrived,

and he got on it. I thought, "Now he'll never _____." When the police
(13. catch)

_____, I told them, "My wallet _____. The thief got on the train just
(14. arrive)   (15. steal)

a few minutes ago, so he'll _____." "Don't worry," said the police officer.
(16. never/find)

"The train _____. We _____ the conductor, and he
(17. can/stop)   (18. can/radio)

_____ the train." A few minutes later, the train was back at the station and
(19. can/stop)

one of the officers got on the train and _____ the thief.
(20. catch)

Ever since that _____, I have been much more careful about putting my
(21. happen)

change away, closing my purse, and keeping it close to my side as I leave the supermarket.

Part 5 Find the mistakes with the underlined words, and correct them. Not every
sentence has a mistake. If the sentence is correct, write **C**.

1. Did you <u>get marry</u> in church?

2. <u>I tired</u> now. I'm going to sleep.

3. I come from a small town, so <u>I'm not use to</u> the traffic in this city.

4. Last night I saw a very <u>boring</u> movie.

5. My sister isn't <u>interesting</u> in sports.

6. After the big meal, I felt very <u>satisfy</u>.

7. Is your apartment <u>air-condition</u>?

8. My college <u>located</u> 3 miles from my house.

9. After I take my shower, I'm going to <u>get dress</u>.

10. It is a well <u>known</u> fact that women live longer than men.

11. The buses are crowded in the morning, but they <u>don't crowded</u> in the middle of the afternoon.

12. <u>Are</u> you <u>confused</u> about the passive voice?

Part 6 Fill in the blanks with the present participle or the past participle of the verb in parentheses.

A. How was your trip to the U.S.?

B. It was a ___*tiring*___ trip, but I'm ___*excited*___ to be here.
                (example: tire)   (example: excite)

A. How many hours did it take?

B. Ten hours. They showed a movie on flight, but it was not very _____,
                                                     (1. interest)

so I fell asleep.

A. Did you stop anywhere?

B. Yes, we stopped in Rome.

A. Rome is such an _____ city.
                      (2. interest)

B. I'm sure it is, but I was _____ because we were only there for two hours.
                         (3. disappoint)

We never left the airport.

A. That's too bad. It's _____ to be in Rome and not have a chance to see
                        (4. frustrate)

the city.

B. That's OK. I was too _____ to enjoy it anyway.
                (5. tire)

A. How was the flight?

B. I have no complaints. I was _____ with the service. But the airport here
                      (6. satisfy)

is very _____. I didn't know where to go to pick up my luggage.
      (7. confuse)

A. I know what you mean. I was _____ when I arrived here too.
                      (8. confuse)

LESSON **THREE** / TEST

Part I   Find the mistakes with the underlined words, and correct them. Not every sentence has a mistake. If the sentence is correct, write **C**. Do not change a correct sentence.

EXAMPLES: How many times <u>have you being</u> in California? *been*

I <u>worked</u> hard yesterday.   *C*

1. I have a great job. I <u>been working</u> at the same job for 10 years.

2. I heard a terrible noise outside. What <u>was happened</u>?

3. *Romeo and Juliet* <u>wrote</u> by Shakespeare.

4. She <u>has come</u> to the U.S. five years ago.

5. I got to the airport late yesterday. By the time I got there, my relatives <u>had already arrived</u>.

6. When her husband died, she <u>had been married</u> for 49 years.

7. My sister is a teacher. <u>She's been</u> a teacher for 12 years.

8. He was walking on ice <u>while</u> he fell.

9. He has been very depressed ever since he <u>has lost</u> his job.

10. I <u>thinking</u> about you when you called.

11. By the time we arrived at our vacation spot, we <u>had been filling</u> up the gas tank four times.

12. When he arrived in New York for the first time, he <u>has never been</u> in a big city before.

13. When we finished dinner, we <u>washed</u> the dishes.

14. She <u>went</u> shopping three times last month.

15. I came to class late. When I came to class, the teacher <u>has already given</u> the test, so I missed it.

16. Last month, we've <u>gone</u> to three parties.

17. I heard your friend is working in a restaurant now. How long <u>is he working</u> in the restaurant?

18. She <u>was cook</u> dinner when the fire started.

19. She <u>had already graduated</u> from college by the time she left her country.

20. When the accident happened, we <u>called</u> the police immediately.

21. They <u>were eaten</u> dinner when the phone rang.

22. She's from Cuba. When she arrived in Chicago in January, she <u>had never experienced</u> cold weather before.

23. When she heard the bad news, she <u>was starting</u> to cry.

24. I <u>was planning</u> to call you, but I couldn't find your phone number.

25. She was driving over the speed limit <u>when</u> the police officer stopped her.

Part 2   Fill in the blanks with the simple past, the past perfect, or the past perfect continuous of the verb in parentheses.

> **EXAMPLE:**   This is my first English class. When I ___*came*___ to the U.S.,
> (come)
> I ___*had never studied*___ English before.
> (never/study)

1. By the time Sam _____, he _____ for 45 years.
   (retire)   (work)

2. When the train _____ at the station, the passengers _____ on.
   (arrive)   (get)

3. My friend _____ ESL classes when she _____ in the U.S.
   (not/take)   (arrive)
   because she _____ English as a child.
   (already/study)

4. We _____ for ten hours by the time our plane _____ in New York.
   (fly)   (land)

5. She _____ a ticket because she _____ too fast on the highway.
   (get)   (drive)

6. When I _____ the news about my scholarship, I _____ for
   (receive)   (shout)
   joy.

7. When I _____ up, I _____ a cup of coffee.
   (wake)   (make)

8. By the time last semester _____, I _____ 10 compositions.
   (end)   (write)

9. She _____ in Germany for three years when she _____ a visa to come to
   (live)   (get)
   the U.S.

10. I _____ how the movie was going to end because I _____ it before.
    (know)   (already/see)

11. He was afraid to fly because he _____ on an airplane before.
    (never/be)

12. When she asked me about my father, she _____ bad because she didn't know that
    (feel)
    my father _____.
    (die)

Part 3   Fill in the blanks with one of the past tenses: simple past, past continuous, present perfect (continuous), or past perfect (continuous). In some cases more than one answer is possible.

A: Where _____*did you meet*_____ you wife?
(example: you/meet)

B: At a party. The night of the party I was sick with a cold, so I _____
(1. not/want)

to go. I _____ my friend and left him a message telling him not to pick
(2. call)

me up.

A: But you went anyway?

B: Yes. After I called him, I _____ to bed and _____ on the TV.
(3. go)   (4. turn)

I _____ TV when the doorbell _____. It was my friend.
(5. watch)   (6. ring)

A: Why _____ to your house?
(7. your friend/go)

B: He never got my message. By the time I _____ him, he _____ his
(8. call)   (9. already/leave)

house.

A: So what _____ next?
(10. happen)

B: We went to the party. I _____ alone on the sofa when suddenly a young
(11. sit)

woman _____ up to me and said, "I think we went to high school together. Isn't
(12. come)

your name Peter Glass? We were students at the same high school."

A: Do you mean that when you _____ each other at the party, you _____
(13. see)   (14. already/know)

each other?

B: Just a little. We really didn't know each other well in high school. We started to talk about our high school days. I liked her and asked her out on a date.

A: How long _____ when you decided to get married?
(15. you/date)

B: For about six months.

A: How long _____ married?
(16. you/be)

B: For about 12 years. We're very happy.

A: It's a good thing your friend never received the message on his answering machine.

B: I _____ about that many times.
(17. think)

LESSON **FOUR** / TEST

Part 1   In the following sentences, find the **grammar** mistakes with the underlined words, and correct them. Not every sentence has a mistake. If the sentence is correct, write **C**.

> **EXAMPLES:**   You must not ~~to~~ drink that water.
>
> I <u>don't have to work</u> on Fridays if I don't want to.   *C*

1. She <u>can't understand</u> the grammar explanation.

2. <u>You better study</u> hard for the test.

3. The students <u>not allowed to talk</u> during a test.

4. I'm sure that in five more years, you <u>will be able to</u> speak English much better.

5. <u>You'd better don't</u> ride your bike today. It's going to rain.

6. What <u>I should do</u> about my noisy neighbors?

7. Before I look for a new job, I <u>will have to</u> rewrite my résumé.

8. My father knows how to fix cars. He <u>cans help</u> you with your car problem.

9. You <u>should to visit</u> your sick neighbor.

10. I've <u>got to see</u> the doctor now. It's an emergency.

11. Her old car doesn't work very well. She <u>ought to buy</u> a new car.

12. We're <u>not permit</u> to talk during the test.

13. You <u>not supposed to</u> make noise in the library.

14. She <u>not able to work</u> today because she's sick.

15. Why <u>you can't go</u> to the party?

16. The teacher <u>can't helping</u> you now. He's busy.

Part 2   Read the pairs of sentences. If the sentences have a similar meaning, write **S**. If the sentences have a different meaning, write **D**.

> **EXAMPLES:**   You <u>have to</u> take the final exam./ You <u>must</u> take the final exam.   *S*
>
> I'm <u>not able to</u> drive. / I <u>must not</u> drive.   *D*

1. You <u>must not</u> open the door. / You <u>don't have to</u> open the door.

2. You <u>don't have to</u> buy a dictionary. / <u>It's not necessary to</u> buy a dictionary.

3. She <u>has to</u> go to the hospital. / She<u>'s got to</u> go to the hospital.

4. We <u>should</u> talk to the doctor. / We <u>must</u> talk to the doctor.

5. The child <u>is not supposed to</u> open the door. / The child <u>doesn't have to</u> open the door.

6. It <u>could</u> rain tomorrow. / It <u>might</u> rain tomorrow.

7. We<u>'re supposed to</u> mail the package. / We <u>might</u> mail the package.

8. You <u>can't</u> talk during the test. / You <u>are not allowed to</u> talk during the test.

9. You <u>should</u> study harder. / You <u>ought to</u> study harder.

10. You <u>may not</u> use your dictionary during the test. / You <u>are not allowed to</u> use your dictionary during the test.

11. You <u>don't have to</u> use public transportation. / You <u>shouldn't</u> use public transportation.

12. The girl always plays with her neighbor's dog. She <u>probably loves</u> dogs. / She <u>must</u> love dogs.

13. You <u>must</u> be hungry. / You <u>might</u> be hungry.

14. He <u>is able to</u> repair his car. / He <u>can</u> repair his car.

15. If you don't have a computer, you <u>could</u> use one in the library. / If you don't have a computer, you <u>can</u> use one in the library.

16. I <u>may</u> be absent next week. / I <u>might</u> be absent next week.

17. <u>I'm supposed to drive my grandmother to the doctor.</u> / <u>My grandmother is expecting me to drive her to the doctor.</u>

18. You<u>'re not supposed to</u> drive over 65 miles per hour on the highway. / You <u>must not</u> drive over 65 miles per hour on the highway.

19. You <u>shouldn't</u> talk now. / You <u>must not</u> talk now.

20. It's going to rain. You<u>'d better</u> take an umbrella. / You <u>should</u> take an umbrella.

Part 3   Fill in the blanks. Use *can, could, may, might, must, would, should, ought to, have to, be supposed to,* or *be able to* to refer to the present or future. The sentence in brackets [ ] will help you. (In some cases, more than one answer may be possible.)

A phone conversation between two students:

A: Hi. This is Julia. You were absent from class, so I thought you ___*must*___ be sick.
    _(example)

B: I'm not exactly sick, but my back hurts.

A: You _____(1.)_____ go to the doctor. [This is my advice.] A back problem _____(2.)_____ be serious. [This is possible.]

B: I did go to the doctor. She told me it _____(3.)_____ be a simple muscle strain or possibly something more serious. [There are two possibilities.]

A: What did she tell you to do?

B: She said I _____(4. not)_____ jog or play tennis for at least a month [The doctor advised me.]

A: I know how much you love to play tennis. It _____(5.)_____ be hard for you to go for a whole month without playing tennis. [It is probably hard for you.]

B: You're right. And I _____(6. not)_____ lift weights either. [The doctor expects me to follow her advice.]

A: Watch out. If you don't exercise, you _____(7.)_____ get fat. [This is possible.]

B: She also gave me a prescription for some medication, but it makes me sleepy. I _____(8. not)_____ concentrate. [I don't have the ability.]

A: Don't worry. You'll be better in no time.[1]

B: I hope so. The doctor told me that if I don't see some improvement in two weeks, I _____(9.)_____ come and see her again. [This is her advice.] I _____(10.)_____ need back surgery. [This is possible.]

A: Let's hope not.

B: By the way, please tell the teacher that I won't _____(11.)_____ attend the next class. [I can't attend the next class.]

A: I'll tell him. The teacher told me to tell you that you _____(12.)_____ do your homework even though you're absent. [This is your obligation.]

B: Doesn't the teacher realize that I _____(13.)_____ injure my back by pushing a pencil? [Maybe this will happen.]

[1] *In no time:* very soon

NAME_____

LESSON **FIVE** / TEST

Part I   Find the **grammar** mistakes with the underlined words, and correct them.
Not every sentence has a mistake. If the sentence is correct, write **C**.

EXAMPLES: I couldn't ~~did~~ *do* my laundry yesterday because I didn't have time.

I didn't go to the movies yesterday because I <u>had to study</u> for a test.   *C*

1. I got up late and missed my bus. I <u>should gotten</u> up earlier.

2. She <u>was supposed to call</u> the teacher to tell her that she <u>couldn't come</u> to class, but she lost the teacher's phone number.

3. Our son didn't get a scholarship, so we <u>had to paid</u> for his tuition.

4. Thanks for driving me to my job interview. I <u>couldn't have gotten</u> there without your help.

5. When you lost your last job, you <u>must feel</u> terrible.

6. You <u>should go</u> to the party with us last week. We had a great time.

7. I <u>could have took</u> the bus to work, but I decided to walk instead.

8. Your mother was so worried when you didn't call her last week. You <u>should had called</u> her.

9. I <u>can't found</u> my keys yesterday.

10. My friend couldn't go to the museum with me yesterday because she <u>had to work</u>.

11. He left the party without thanking the hosts. He <u>should has said</u> thank-you before leaving.

12. I can't find my glasses. I <u>might have left</u> them in my jacket pocket.

13. Why didn't you tell me that you moved last week? I <u>could have helped</u> you.

14. Jim was looking for a job all day yesterday. He looked so tired when he got home. He <u>must had</u> a hard day.

15. A lot of people left the movie before it was over. They <u>must not have liked</u> it.

16. I <u>couldn't answer</u> any questions in class today because I didn't study the material last night.

Part 2   Fill in the blanks with the correct form of an appropriate verb to use modals in the past.

> **EXAMPLE:**   I arrived at the appointment late. I should _____*have left*_____ my house earlier.

1. I didn't study English when I was a child. I should _____ it in elementary school.

2. I couldn't _____ to class last week because I had to work overtime. But I'll come to every class from now on.

3. Why are you doing your homework in class? You should _____ it at home.

4. Sometimes I have to leave class early. Last week, I had to _____ early because my son was sick.

5. I wonder why my friend is so late. I hope he didn't get lost. I've been waiting for over an hour. He might _____ lost.

6. You said you came to the U.S. on September 31. You couldn't _____ to the U.S. on September 31. September has only 30 days.

7. The little boy must _____ ice cream. He has ice cream all over his face.

8. When his dog was run over by a car last year, he must _____ terrible.

9. I couldn't _____ the tire by myself, so I asked my brother to help me change it.

10. The cookies you made were so delicious that I could _____ all of them. But I ate only two.

Part 3   Fill in the blanks with the past of the modal or expression in parentheses.

I had a terrible day yesterday. First, when I tried to start my car in the morning,

I ____*couldn't*____ . I _____ the lights on all night because my battery
   (example: can/not)   (1. must/leave)

was dead. I _____ the subway to work, but I really wanted to drive. I saw a
         (2. should/take)

neighbor of mine and asked if he could give me a jump start. He said he _____
                                                                         (3. can/not/stop)

because he was in a hurry. He said he _____ an important meeting and didn't
                                        (4. have to/attend)

want to be late. Then I stopped another neighbor. She _____ me either because
                                                        (5. can/not/help)

she didn't have jumper cables and neither did I. Then I stopped another neighbor. I said,
"Do you remember when I helped you push your car last winter?" He answered, "It

_____ me because I don't even have a car. It _____ my twin
   (6. can/be)   (7. must/be)

brother."

Finally I saw another neighbor leaving the house. I begged him to give me a jump. By this time I was getting desperate. I _____ like a crazy person because I was
(8. must/look)
so nervous. "Calm down," he said as he agreed to help me. He attached the cables from my car to his car, but when I started my car, my battery exploded. He _____
(9. must/attach)
the positive to the negative by mistake. He _____ hurt, but he was lucky to
(10. could/get)
be standing away from the car. I was stupid. I _____ the subway to work
(11. can/take)
and arrived on time, but because of my actions, I arrived three hours late.

LESSON **SIX** / TEST

Part I Find the mistakes with adjective clauses, and correct them. Not every sentence has a mistake. If the sentence is correct, write **C**.

EXAMPLES: I have a cousin <u>who live</u> in Montreal. *s*

The man <u>you met</u> at my house doesn't live in this city. *C*

1. A student <u>who's</u> TOEFL score is high may not have to take English as a Second Language courses.

2. Please return the book <u>that you borrowed it</u> last week.

3. Children <u>their</u> parents work often come home to an empty house.

4. <u>Who</u> has the best costume will win a prize.

5. There are some married men <u>who doesn't</u> use a wedding ring.

6. The person <u>who broke</u> the vase should pay for it.

7. I don't know the man <u>which</u> you are talking about.

8. He attends a college <u>what has</u> a good engineering department.

9. I never saw the movie <u>you are talking about</u>.

10. Jane bought <u>a building has</u> six apartments.

11. The building <u>is located on Maple Street that Jane bought</u>.

12. The building <u>that Jane lives</u> is very modern.

13. The car <u>that bought my brother</u> runs very well.

14. The teacher <u>with whom</u> I studied beginning grammar now teaches at a different college.

15. The store <u>where</u> I buy my groceries is open 24 hours a day.

16. I don't know <u>anyone can</u> help you with your problem.

17. The man <u>I met</u> at the meeting doesn't speak Spanish.

18. The driver <u>I hit his car</u> called the police.

Part 2 Fill in the blanks to complete the adjective clause.

EXAMPLE: I receive catalogs for children's toys and clothes. The company

that sends me these catalogs knows that I have small children.

1. Many companies have your name and address. Companies _____ often send you mail.

2. Many people's names are on a list. People _____ often receive mail that they didn't ask for.

3. I receive a lot of catalogs. The catalogs _____ have beautiful pictures of products.

4. I shop in a special store. The store _____ has food and products from my country.

5. I receive mail addressed to another person. The person whose _____ moved out of my building last year.

6. I received my first piece of mail a week after I came to the U.S. I'll never forget the

day _____ a letter with my name on it.

Part 3 Complete each statement. Every sentence should have an adjective clause.

EXAMPLE: The store ___ _where I bought my books_ ___ is closed on Sundays.

1. The computer _____ four years ago is slow. I need to buy a much faster computer.

2. I need to study in a place _____.

3. Everyone _____ agreed that it was a very good movie.

4. Can the teacher pronounce everyone's names? No. There are a few students

whose _____.

5. I love to ski. I'd like to live in a place _____ all year round.

6. He likes to read at night because it's a time _____.

7. I don't know anyone _____.

8. Children shouldn't talk to people _____.

Part 4   Combine each pair of sentences into one sentence. Use the words in parentheses to add a nonessential adjective clause to the first sentence.

        EXAMPLE: The U.S. attracts immigrants from all over the world. (Many people think it's the greatest country.)

                The U.S., which many people think is the greatest country,

                attracts immigrants from all over the world.

1.   John Kennedy Jr. was killed in an airplane crash. (He was the son of President Kennedy.)

2.   John Kennedy Jr. was not interested in being a politician. (His father was president.)

3.   Tim Berners-Lee invented the World Wide Web. (It has changed the way we communicate with each other.)

5.   I like to watch TV on Saturdays. (There are a lot of sports programs on TV then.)

6.   My sister took a vacation in Hawaii. (She met her future husband there.)

Part 5   Shorten the adjective clauses by crossing out unnecessary words.

        EXAMPLE: Puerto Rico, ~~which is~~ in the Caribbean, is an American territory.

1.   John Kennedy, who was the 35th American President, was killed in 1963.

2.   I can't understand the Spanish that is spoken in Puerto Rico.

3.   The Sears Tower, which is located in Chicago, is one of the tallest buildings in the U.S.

4.   Lake Superior, which is between the U.S. and Canada, is the largest lake in North America.

5.   The professor who is giving the lecture knows a lot about Latin America.

Part 6   Some of the following sentences need commas. Put them in. If the sentences don't need commas, write "**NC**" (no commas).

> **EXAMPLES:**   The best movie I have ever seen was *Titanic*.   *NC*
>
> My mother, whom you met at the party, is an engineer.

1. People who are under 18 can't vote in the U.S.

2. Many people like to have a picnic on the Fourth of July which is American Independence Day.

3. The new computer I bought has a very large memory.

4. The first computer which occupied a very large room was not very fast.

5. The teacher I had last semester didn't teach us about nonessential adjective clauses.

6. Professor Kaplan who always gives us a test at the end of a lesson believes that it's important for us to study for at least one hour a day.

7. My best friend whose name is Jackie is very fond of cats.

8. Did you see the movie that was on TV last night?

9. *Star Wars* which is a science fiction movie is one of the most popular movies of all times.

10. Steven Spielberg who directed many wonderful movies has won many awards.

LESSON **SEVEN** / TEST

Part I Find the mistakes with the underlined words, and correct them. Not every sentence has a mistake. If the sentence is correct, write **C**.

EXAMPLES: Are you tall enough ^ <u>reach</u> the top shelf? *to*

<u>To make</u> mistakes in English is natural.   *C*

1. The students stopped <u>talking</u> when the teacher entered the room.

2. She's afraid <u>of lose</u> her job.

3. He wrote his paper by hand instead of <u>use</u> a computer.

4. <u>Leaving</u> my country was very difficult for me.

5. I began <u>driving</u> when I was 18 years old.

6. When he was single, he <u>used to going</u> out with his friends on the weekends, but now he stays home with his wife and baby.

7. It's hard to <u>get used to living</u> in another country.

8. She blamed him <u>for break</u> the dish.

9. I had difficulty <u>sell</u> my car.

10. Do you <u>like to go shopping</u> for clothes?

11. I don't like <u>wearing</u> boots in the winter.

12. Do you enjoy <u>watching</u> French movies?

13. I'm worried about <u>don't passing</u> this course.

14. He spent a lot of time <u>to look</u> for a job.

15. I like <u>to eat</u> fish, but I've never gone <u>fishing</u>.

16. It's important <u>have</u> a good family.

17. <u>Is</u> necessary to eat fruits and vegetables.

18. <u>Takes</u> a lot of time <u>to learn</u> English.

19. Let's turn on the radio <u>for hear</u> the news.

20. He bought tickets <u>to go</u> to the basketball game.

21. I have always <u>wanted meet</u> your uncle.

22. <u>Buy</u> a house requires a good income.

23. Is it hard <u>to you to</u> work and study at the same time?

24. The teacher wants <u>we do</u> our homework every day.

25. My brother isn't old enough <u>to get</u> his driver's license.

26. I was in the shower and didn't hear the phone <u>ring</u>.

27. Can you see the children <u>to play</u> in the park now?

28. I didn't remember <u>to turn</u> off the headlights of my car last night, and this morning the battery was dead.

29. I found this old jacket in my closet, but I don't remember <u>to buy</u> it.

30. Did you have a hard time <u>getting</u> a visa?

31. It will cost <u>to me</u> $10,000 to finish my degree.

32. The doctor wanted <u>my father to eat</u> a healthier diet, so he stopped <u>to eat</u> meat completely.

33. You car needs <u>to be repaired</u>.

34. She got her son <u>do</u> his homework.

35. She made her son <u>do</u> his homework.

36. She persuaded her son <u>do</u> his homework.

37. She helped her son <u>do</u> his homework.

38. She had her son <u>wash</u> the dishes.

39. She <u>let</u> her son watch TV.

40. I come from a tropical climate. I <u>don't used to living</u> in a cold climate.

41. I don't like <u>being told</u> what to do.

42. <u>Not knowing</u> English well makes my life more difficult.

Part 2 Fill in the blanks with the gerund, infinitive, or base form of the verb in parentheses ( ). If you see a pronoun, change it to its correct form.

A. I'm very upset. I'm having a hard time ___*making*___ an important decision.
(example: make)

My parents want _____ college and find a job.
(1. I/quit)

B. But why?

A. My father is sick and hasn't been able to work, so I can't afford _____
(2. attend)

college anymore. I need _____ a job and _____ my family.
(3. find)   (4. help)

B. I'm sorry about your father. But I don't think you should quit college. _____
(5. have)
a good career in the U.S. is very important. It's hard _____ a good job
(6. find)
without a college education. Have you thought about _____ for a
(7. apply)
government loan?

A. But I'll have _____ back the loan with interest when I graduate.
(8. pay)

B. When you have a good job, it will be easy _____ it back.
(9. you/pay)

A. I don't know how _____ for a loan.
(10. apply)

B. You can have your counselor _____ you.
(11. help)

A. I don't have a counselor.

B. Of course you do. Don't you remember _____ him at registration?
(12. meet)

A. Do you mean Mr. Shapiro? I didn't know he was a counselor. He was very nice. He let
me _____ late because my father was in the hospital during the week of
(13. register)
registration. I really appreciate _____ me permission to register late.
(14. he/give)

B. I suggest _____ an appointment to talk with him. _____
(15. make)   (16. not/finish)
college would be a big mistake. You've always dreamed about _____ an
(17. become)
engineer. Don't give up on your dream.

Part 3 Fill in the blanks with the correct preposition.

EXAMPLES: He's not happy ___*about*___ his father's losing his job.

He plans ___*on*___ becoming an engineer.

1. He's grateful to his parents _____ giving him an education.

2. He has a reason _____ wanting to leave college.

3. He wants to succeed _____ becoming an engineer.

4. He's worried _____ his father's health.

5. Continuing his education depends _____ getting a government loan.

6. He cares _____ helping his father.

7. He's accustomed _____ helping his family.

8. He's talking with his friend _____ leaving college.

9. He's interested _____ getting a loan.

Part 4 Tell if these pairs of sentences mean about the same thing or if they have completely different meanings. Write *same* or *different*.

       EXAMPLE: I like to live alone.

                      I like living alone. _____*same*_____

1. He used to drive.

    He's used to driving. _____

2. I didn't remember to buy toothpaste.

    I don't remember buying toothpaste. _____

3. I enjoy skiing.

    I like to ski. _____

4. Finding a good job is difficult.

    It's difficult to find a good job. _____

5. I'm afraid of walking alone at night.

    I'm afraid to walk alone at night. _____

6. He stopped talking to his brother.

    He stopped to talk to his brother. _____

7. It's impossible to learn a foreign language in two months.

    To learn a foreign language in two months is impossible. _____

LESSON **EIGHT** / TEST

Part I   Find the mistakes with the underlined words, and correct them. Not every sentence has a mistake. If the sentence is correct, write **C**.

EXAMPLES: <u>Because of</u> I didn't come to class yesterday, I didn't know what the homework was.

<u>Ever since</u> she came to the U.S., she has been working as a babysitter.   *C*

1. Although he loves her, <u>but</u> he won't marry her.

2. <u>Even</u> I don't speak English well, Americans understand me anyway.

3. We came to the U.S. <u>so that we could have</u> a better life.

4. Because it rained, <u>so</u> we had to cancel our picnic.

5. Before <u>watch</u> TV, you have to do your homework.

6. I couldn't come to class for three weeks. <u>However,</u> I did all the homework.

7. He has <u>so bad</u> eyesight that he can't read the words in the telephone directory.

8. <u>Since</u> he bought a car, he has been taking trips to the country on the weekends.

9. I have voice mail. I can receive messages <u>even</u> I'm talking on the phone.

10. He was able to get a job right away <u>because of</u> his fluency in English.

11. I don't like my apartment for several reasons. First, it doesn't have air-conditioning. In addition, <u>small rooms</u>.

12. I didn't pass the test <u>in spite of</u> I studied very hard.

13. You can't enter the building <u>unless</u> you have an employee ID card.

14. Martha missed 10 classes this semester. She won't pass the course <u>even if</u> she passes the final exam.

15. Everyone understands me <u>in spite of</u> my accent.

16. <u>Since</u> the test is so long, the students are going to need extra time to finish it.

17. When she <u>will graduate,</u> she will move to San Francisco.

18. Before <u>going</u> to bed, she closed all the windows.

19. She quit her job <u>so that she can spend</u> more time with her children.

20. We are taking this course <u>so that</u> we want to improve our English.

21. My neighbors are making <u>so much</u> noise that we can't sleep.

22. If I <u>am</u> at the post office today, I'll mail your package for you.

23. She used a knife <u>for open</u> the package.

24. I use the Internet <u>to read</u> the daily news in my language.

25. <u>Ever since</u> she got married, she has had a lot of responsibilities.

26. My English class has <u>so much students that</u> there aren't even enough seats.

Part 2   Punctuate the following sentences. Some sentences are already complete and need no more punctuation.

> **EXAMPLES:**   After the party, Mary had to clean up the house.
>
> I'll watch the news tonight if I have time.   *C*

1. Whenever I have a problem I go to my parents for advice.

2. I go to my parents for advice whenever I have a problem.

3. He turned off the alarm clock because he wanted to sleep for one more hour however the phone woke him up anyway.

4. Even though it will take him four years to get his medical degree he will continue until he finishes it.

5. They moved to a suburb because there are better schools there.

6. I was so angry with my brother that I didn't speak to him for two weeks.

7. He was so tired that he fell asleep in class.

8. Very few people bought tickets to the concert as a result the concert was canceled.

Part 3   Fill in the blanks with an appropriate time word: *when, whenever, while, for, during, since, until.*

> **EXAMPLE:**   He has been living by himself ___*for*___ two years.

1. He has been living by himself _____ he was 19 years old.

2. He always works for his grandfather _____ his vacation.

3. He will get married _____ he graduates from college.

4. _____ I was traveling to the U.S., I was dreaming about my future life.

5. _____ I came to the U.S., I had never met any Americans before.

6. _____ several years, I lived with my grandparents.

7. _____ I don't know the meaning of a word, I look it up in the dictionary.

8. Last night, I had to work _____ midnight.

Part 4 Fill in the blanks with *because, because of, since, for, so that, in order to,* or *therefore.*

> **EXAMPLE:** I took a typing class ____*in order to*____ type my compositions faster.

1. I came to the U.S. _____ I could have a better life.

2. Women use makeup _____ improve their appearance.

3. _____ I didn't come to class yesterday, I missed the test.

4. My mother was sick yesterday, and I had to take her to the doctor. _____ , I couldn't come to class.

5. He bought an exercise machine _____ exercise at home.

6. _____ his recent surgery, he can't play tennis for a while.

7. _____ no one passed the test on the passive voice, the teacher is going to review the lesson.

8. She reads novels _____ enjoyment.

Part 5 Fill in the blanks with *even though, in spite of the fact, in spite of,* or *however.*

> **EXAMPLES:** ____*In spite of*____ her busy schedule, she always has time for her children.

1. _____ he's a small man, he's very strong.

2. I wanted to buy a new car last year. _____ , I lost my job and didn't have enough money.

3. The runner finished the race _____ his injured ankle.

4. We had a wonderful time at the picnic _____ that it rained a little.

5. _____ I didn't come to class yesterday, I did the homework.

Part 6 Fill in the blanks with *if*, *unless*, or *even if*.

      EXAMPLE: _____*If*_____ I have time this weekend, I'll see a movie.

1. Level Four is a prerequisite for Level Five. You can't go to Level Five _____ you pass Level Four.

2. _____ I pass this course, I'd like to repeat it for more practice.

3. _____ I go to the library this afternoon, I'll try to find an article about immigration.

4. You have to do the homework _____ you're absent. Absence is no excuse for not doing the homework.

5. I'd rather watch TV than study. However, I won't be able to pass this course _____ I study.

Part 7 Fill in the blanks with *so*, *so many*, *so much*, or *such*.

      EXAMPLE: I was _____*so*_____ hungry that I ate dinner without you.

1. I was _____ busy this morning that I didn't even answer the phone.

2. She has _____ responsibilities that she's going to have to drop out of school.

3. Bill Gates has _____ money that he would never be able to spend it all.

4. The child ate _____ candy that he got sick.

5. We had _____ a wonderful time at the party that we didn't want to go home.

6. It was _____ a good movie that we watched it two times.

Part 8 Complete each sentence.

      EXAMPLE: I didn't learn to speak English _____*until*_____ I was 25 years old.

1. I need a car to _____.

2. I need a car so that _____.

3. I need a car because _____.

4. She speaks English well. However, _____.

5. She got a job right away because she is very well qualified. She speaks English well.

   In addition, _____.

6. He doesn't speak English well. As a result, _____.

7. Since _____, many people from other countries want to come to the U.S.

8. Even though _____, I like this city.

9. I passed the test in spite of the fact that _____.

10. You shouldn't call the emergency phone number unless _____.

11. It was so hot yesterday that _____.

12. I had so many things to do yesterday that _____.

13. She is such a beautiful woman that _____.

14. Even if _____, he can't pass the course because he hasn't taken any of the tests.

15. _____ until he found a job.

LESSON **NINE** / TEST

Part I   Find the mistakes and correct them. Not every sentence has a mistake. If the sentence is correct, write **C**.

EXAMPLES: I don't know what ~~is~~ her name ^is^.

   I don't know where to go.   *C*

1. The teacher told me come to her office.

2. She can't decide she should buy a house or a condo.

3. He said, "I want to leave early."

4. He said me that he wanted to leave early.

5. He told me that he wanted to leave early.

6. He asked me whether I had seen that movie or not.

7. I don't know what do you want.

8. She knows what you have to leave early.

9. She doesn't know what she needs.

10. Before I found my job, I thought that I will never find a job.

11. Before I came to the U.S., I didn't know what my life will be like.

12. She said that she would give me the answer the following day, but she didn't.

13. Do you think this test is hard? Yes, I think so.

14. He told me not to sit in the front row.

15. She told me don't be late.

16. It's necessary that we be on time for the meeting.

17. Several students suggested that the teacher reviews modals.

18. I think so you are the best teacher in the world.

19. I can't decide what to do.

20. The teacher insists that we not talk during a test.

21. Do you think it's going to rain?

22. I don't know the teacher is here today or not.

23. I told to my friend that I didn't want to go to the party.

24. He told me that he would call me last night, but he forgot.

25. The President said to the committee, "We will look at the problem more carefully."

Part 2 Find the mistakes with **punctuation** in the following sentences, and correct them. If the sentence is correct, write **C**.

EXAMPLES: The candidate said, "I will improve medical care in this country."

He said, "Today is a beautiful day." *C*

1. She told me, that she had lost my phone number.

2. "Where are you going," asked the wolf.

3. "I'm going to my grandmother's house," said the little girl.

4. The teacher said, "My name is Jerry."

5. "What are you going to do later?" my mother asked me.

6. Can you tell me where the library is.

7. I don't know where the library is.

8. I told my friend that I didn't want to go to the museum with her.

9. I didn't realize, that you had already bought the book.

10. She didn't want anyone to know that she had gotten married.

Part 3 Fill in the blanks with an included question.

EXAMPLE: Where is the teacher?

Can you tell me ___*where the teacher is?*___

1. What's your neighbor's name?

Do you know _____

2. What kind of car does the teacher have?

I don't know _____

3. Did she break the glass?

   I don't know _____

4. Who broke the glass?

   I don't know _____

5. When were they here?

   Nobody knows _____

6. What does "physician" mean?

   I don't know _____

7. Are the children sleeping?

   Can you tell me _____

8. Where was the test given?

   I don't know _____

9. Has she ever eaten pizza?

   I'm not sure _____

10. Can I get a refund?

    Do you know _____

11. Where should I go?

    I don't know _____

12. How much did your car cost?

    Would you tell me _____

13. Did the teacher collect the homework?

    Can you tell me _____

14. Will we have a test next Friday?

    I'm not sure _____

Part 4   Change the following sentences to reported speech. Follow the rule of sequence of tenses.

   EXAMPLE: He said, "I am late."

   He said that he was late.

1. He said, "I can understand your point of view."

2. He said, "You will always be my friend."

3. He said, "I didn't have enough sleep last night."

4. He said to us, "Don't be late."

5. He said to me, "Call me."

6. He said to his children, "You must turn off the TV and go to bed."

7. He said to his boss, "I won't be able to work tomorrow."

8. He said to his wife, "You don't need to cook dinner."

9. He said to his aunt, "I've lost your new phone number."

10. He said to me, "Buy me some stamps while you're at the post office."

11. He asked me, "Do you need my help?"

12. He asked me, "What do you want?"

13. He asked me, "What time is it?"

_____

14. He asked me, "Have you seen the movie?"

_____

15. He asked me, "Did you wash your hands before dinner?"

_____

16. He asked me, "How's your mother?"

_____

17. He asked me, "Do you have a headache?"

_____

18. He asked us, "Who knows the answer to my question?"

_____

19. He asked us, "Can you lend me some money?"

_____

20. He asked her, "When did you make your decision?"

_____

LESSON **TEN** / TEST

Part I Find the mistakes with the underlined words, and correct them. Not every sentence has a mistake. If the sentence is correct, write **C**.

EXAMPLES: What ~~will~~ *would* you do if you didn't have a car?

I would use public transportation if I <u>didn't have</u> a car. *C*

1. I wish I <u>can fly</u> like a bird.

2. I'm not rich. If I <u>were</u> rich, I'd help all my friends and relatives.

3. She <u>will help</u> you if she had more time, but she's too busy.

4. If we <u>could speak</u> English perfectly, we wouldn't be in this class.

5. He doesn't make a lot of money. If he <u>will make</u> a lot of money, he'd buy a house.

6. I love to send email to my friends. If I <u>didn't have</u> a computer, I wouldn't be able to send email to my friends.

7. I would move to a different apartment if I <u>will be</u> you.

8. If she didn't have small children, she<u>'d have</u> more free time.

9. If he <u>were</u> older, people would respect him more.

10. I don't have a cell phone. If I <u>would be have</u> a cell phone, I could call you from my car.

11. If you had told me about the problem last Saturday, I <u>might have been</u> able to help you.

12. He was driving too fast and got a ticket. If he <u>hadn't been driving</u> so fast, he wouldn't have gotten a ticket.

13. She was wearing her seat belt when the accident happened. Luckily she wasn't hurt. If she hadn't been wearing her seat belt, she <u>might got</u> hurt.

14. If I <u>would be</u> a child again, I would choose a different career.

15. Your vacation sounds wonderful. I wish I <u>have gone</u> with you.

16. We got a postcard from our relatives on vacation in Hawaii. They wrote, "We wish you <u>are</u> here."

17. If you <u>have been</u> at the concert, you would have enjoyed it.

18. She wouldn't sell her dog even if you <u>paid</u> her a million dollars.

19. I didn't study English in my country. I wish I <u>had studied</u> it then.

20. Too bad you weren't here when my brother was visiting. If you had met him, you <u>would found</u> many things in common with him.

Part 2   Choose the correct words to fill in the blank.

EXAMPLE: If I were the teacher, I _____*b*_____ so much homework.
a. didn't give   c. hadn't given
b. wouldn't give   d. won't give

1. If I _____ you, I'd buy a new car.
a. am   b. will be   c. would be   d. were

2. If it rains tomorrow, we _____ the picnic.
a. will cancel   b. would cancel   c. were cancel   d. would have canceled

3. I didn't remember his name. If I had remembered his name, I _____ him to you.
a. would introduce   b. will introduce   c. had introduced   d. would have introduced

4. If I won the lottery, I _____ my job.
a. would quit   b. will quit   c. had quit   d. would have quit

5. It's raining now. If it _____ now, I'd go for a bike ride.
a. didn't rain   b. weren't raining   c. won't rain   d. hadn't been raining

6. He didn't see the accident, so he couldn't give the police any information about it. He would have given the police information if he _____ the accident.
a. sees   b. will see   c. had seen   d. would see

7. My brother might come here next month. If he _____, he will live with me until he finds an apartment.
a. will come   b. would come   c. came   d. comes

8. I didn't shop yesterday because I didn't have time. If I _____ time yesterday, I would have bought groceries.
a. had   b. had had   c. would have   d. have had

9. I can't help you know. I would help you if I _____.
a. could   b. can   c. could have   d. would be able to

10. If I had been born in the U.S., I _____ in this English class now.
a. hadn't been   b. won't be   c. wouldn't be   d. wouldn't have been

11. If she _____ perfect English, her life in the U.S. would be easier.
a. spoke   b. had spoken   c. speaks   d. would speak

12. I have a car. If I _____ a car, I would have to use public transportation every day.
a. don't have   b. haven't had   c. didn't have   d. hadn't had

13. She _____ him if he were the last man on earth.
a. won't marry   b. didn't marry   c. hadn't married   d. wouldn't marry

14. If he had stopped at the red light, he _____ that car.
    a. didn't hit   b. wouldn't have hit   c. wouldn't hit   d. hadn't hit

15. He took the wrong bus and arrived late to the meeting. If he _____ the wrong bus, he would have arrived on time.
    a. didn't take   b. hadn't taken   c. wouldn't have taken   d. wouldn't take

16. If you _____ my brother like I know my brother, you wouldn't distrust him.
    a. knew   b. know   c. would know   d. will know

17. I can't speak spanish. I wish I _____ Spanish.
    a. can speak   b. had spoken   c. could speak   d. could have spoken

18. Those people are making so much noise. I wish they _____ quiet.
    a. will be   b. would be   c. are   d. would have been

19. Nobody told me about the party last night. I wish someone _____ me.
    a. would tell   b. told   c. had told   d. have told

20. I don't have much free time. I wish I _____ more free itme.
    a. had had   b. had   c. would have had   d. will have

BOOK 3 / REVIEW LESSON / TEST / ANSWERS

Part 1
1. If I <u>have</u> free time tonight, I'll help you.
2. I <u>wanted to call</u> you last night, but I didn't have your phone number.
3. My sister <u>didn't go</u> to the party last night.
4. She <u>doesn't like</u> cold weather.
5. C
6. People who live in the U.S. <u>have</u> a lot of freedom.
7. Everybody <u>needs</u> to pay taxes.
8. Next year I <u>will go</u> back to my country.
9. You <u>were</u> late to the meeting yesterday.
10. I <u>have been</u> in the U.S. for two years.
11. She used a knife <u>to open</u> the package.
12. C
13. My father <u>doesn't have</u> a job.
14. She <u>needs</u> more time to finish the test.
15. Jack <u>finished</u> his homework two hours ago.
16. I <u>found</u> a good job yesterday.
17. Her grandfather <u>was born</u> in Puerto Rico.
18. C
19. They <u>have seen</u> the movie three times.
20. I <u>have been driving</u> for 4 hours, and I'm tired.

Part 2
1. C
2. I have a <u>hundred-dollar bill</u> in my pocket.
3. When she writes a composition, she is very <u>careful</u>.
4. Does your father drive <u>well</u>?
5. Those papers over there are important. <u>These</u> papers here are not important.
6. It's <u>too</u> cold to go out today. Let's stay inside.
7. C
8. She's tired because she worked very <u>hard</u>.
9. My husband doesn't drive, and I don't <u>either</u>.
10. My college <u>is located</u> on Wright and Green Streets.
11. I won the lottery. I'm <u>very</u> happy.
12. Mary has two <u>beautiful</u> daughters.
13. C
14. C
15. C

Part 3
1. C
2. She drives <u>faster than</u> her husband.
3. He speaks English <u>better than his wife</u>.
4. I <u>look like</u> my father. We both have blue eyes and curly black hair.
5. C
6. C
7. New York <u>is the biggest</u> city in the U.S.
8. Alaska is the <u>largest</u> state in the U.S.
9. She is one of <u>the most beautiful girls</u> in the world.
10. <u>You don't look like</u> your photo ID.
11. C
12. Chicago is big, but Los Angeles is <u>bigger</u>.

Part 4
1. <u>A lot of students</u> at this college come from Mexico.
2. I need to buy 2 <u>pounds of coffee</u>.
3. C
4. Bill Gates is a billionaire. He has <u>a lot of money</u>.
5. My mother gave me <u>a lot of advice</u> when I was a child.
6. C
7. There were <u>many</u> (OR <u>a lot of</u>) people at the party. Everyone had a good time.
8. I can't go out to eat with you today because I have <u>(very) little</u> money.
9. C
10. I put <u>a little</u> sugar in my coffee.
11. She didn't know <u>anybody</u> at the party.
12. C

Part 5

1. Most of my <u>friends</u> live in Germany.
2. C
3. My <u>neighbors</u> make a lot of noise.
4. Every <u>student</u> wants to pass the course.
5. <u>My sister's husband</u> is a mailman.
6. My sister has 4 <u>children</u>.
7. C
8. C

Part 6

1. My husband visits <u>his mother</u> once a week.
2. She <u>wants me to help</u> her find a job.
3. Those birds are beautiful. Do you see <u>them</u>?
4. C
5. I can find my books, but they can't find <u>their</u> <u>books (OR theirs)</u>.
6. I can't find my keys. Have you seen <u>them</u>?
7. C
8. C
9. I like you because <u>you're</u> a very kind person.
10. Please <u>tell me</u> what you want.
11. C
12. I don't know your brothers. What are <u>their</u> names?

Part 7

1. My parents have a new car.
2. My sister and I went to California for our vacation.
3. C
4. She is always late for class.
5. C
6. C
7. I think your new house is beautiful. I especially like your living room.
8. Maybe I will buy a new car. (OR I may buy a new car.)
9. When her husband came home, she ate dinner.
10. I am afraid to speak English by telephone.
11. It's necessary to have a textbook in this class.
12. I like to go to the park because there are a lot of beautiful trees there.
13. She finished the homework faster than I did.
14. We never watch TV in the morning.
15. They have always wanted to own a house.
16. He didn't drive to work because it was snowing too hard.
17. Everything that the doctor said was helpful to me.
18. I don't want to take your pen. I just want to borrow it for a few minutes.
19. C
20. C
21. I have more experience than you do.
22. He works as a bus driver.
23. C
24. C

Part 8

1. Does your brother <u>speak</u> English well?
2. When <u>did</u> you buy your car?
3. What <u>does</u> "clever" mean?
4. How <u>do you say "book"</u> in Spanish?
5. Why <u>can't you</u> open the door?
6. C
7. When <u>do you wake up</u> every morning?
8. C
9. What kind of car <u>does your brother drive</u>?
10. C
11. How <u>do you spell</u> your last name?
12. How much <u>does coffee cost</u> this week?

LESSON ONE

Part 1

1. He's <u>eaten</u> pizza several times this week.
2. C
3. C
4. Have you eaten dinner yet? Yes, <u>I've eaten dinner</u> <u>already</u>.
5. C
6. <u>I've already met</u> your brother. (OR I've met your brother already.)
7. I <u>went</u> to London five years ago.
8. Your sister lives in the U.S. <u>How long has she</u> <u>been living</u> in the U.S.?
9. We have had 2 tests since the semester <u>began</u>.

10. My mother lives in France now. She <u>has lived</u> (OR <u>has been living</u>) there for 2 years.
11. C
12. I left my country 5 years ago. When <u>did you leave</u> your country?
13. C
14. Lynn was married, but now she's divorced. How long <u>was she</u> married?
15. C
16. They have lived in Mexico <u>for three years</u>.

17. C
18. C
19. I have a job in a restaurant now. I <u>have been working</u> (OR I <u>have worked</u>) in a restaurant since 1995.
20. They <u>have been studying</u> English all their lives.
21. She's <u>been wearing</u> glasses since she was a little girl.
22. <u>Have you ever studied</u> biology?

Part 2

1. haven't seen
2. have you been doing
3. got
4. had
5. Did you marry
6. haven't seen
7. graduated
8. married
9. have never met
10. has been happening
11. graduated

12. got
13. have always had
14. haven't found
15. have you been working OR have you worked
16. Have you seen
17. have lost
18. ran
19. Did she marry
20. stayed
21. haven't seen
22. have never been

LESSON TWO

Part 1

1. My car <u>wasn't made</u> in America. It was made in Japan.
2. Something terrible <u>happened</u> last night.
3. C
4. My grandfather <u>died</u> in the U.S.
5. C
6. The President <u>was seen</u> on TV last night by millions of Americans.
7. C
8. A hat <u>was found</u> near the building.

9. C
10. C
11. C
12. The child <u>should be watched</u> by his mother.
13. C
14. She <u>has been taking</u> pain medication for 3 weeks.
15. The results of the test <u>will be announced</u> tomorrow.
16. C
17. The birthday cake <u>was eaten</u> by the children.

Part 2

1. A package was left in front of my house.
2. Who will be elected as the next president?
3. Dogs are not permitted in this park.
4. When was this school built?
5. A pencil can't be used for the test.

6. The apartment is being painted now.
7. The keys have been left in the door.
8. A new secretary should be chosen.
9. The apartment is going to be cleaned.
10. The door has to be locked.

Part 3

1. My sister will drive the car.
2. I didn't write the composition.
3. My brothers are cleaning the house.
4. They washed the car.
5. You should write your name on the top of the page.

6. We didn't open the presents.
7. Did your uncle meet you at the airport?
8. The janitor is going to open the classroom.
9. My uncle has driven me to the airport many times.
10. You should make a decision soon.

Part 4

1. was given	7. was walking	13. be caught	18. can radio
2. put	8. said	14. arrived	19. can stop
3. didn't close	9. stole	15. was stolen	20. caught
4. was walking	10. ran	16. never be found	21. happened
5. felt	11. told	17. can be stopped	
6. saw	12. called		

Part 5

1. Did you <u>get married</u> in church?
2. <u>I'm tired</u> now. I'm going to sleep.
3. I come from a small town, so <u>I'm not used to</u> the traffic in this city.
4. C
5. My sister isn't <u>interested</u> in sports.
6. After the big meal, I felt very <u>satisfied</u>.
7. Is your apartment <u>air-conditioned</u>?
8. My college <u>is located</u> 3 miles from my house.
9. After I take my shower, I'm going to <u>get dressed</u>.
10. C
11. The buses are crowded in the morning, but they <u>aren't crowded</u> in the middle of the afternoon.
12. C

Part 6

1. interesting	3. disappointed	5. tired	7. confusing
2. interesting	4. frustrating	6. satisfied	8. confused

LESSON THREE

Part 1

1. I have a great job. I <u>have been working</u> at the same job for 10 years.
2. I heard a terrible noise outside. What <u>happened</u>?
3. *Romeo and Juliet* <u>was written</u> by Shakespeare.
4. She <u>came</u> to the U.S. five years ago.
5. C
6. C
7. C
8. He was walking on ice <u>when</u> he fell.
9. He has been very depressed ever since he <u>lost</u> his job.
10. I <u>was thinking</u> about you when you called.
11. By the time we arrived at our vacation spot, we <u>had filled</u> up the gas tank four times.
12. When he arrived in New York for the first time, he <u>had never been</u> in a big city before.
13. C
14. C
15. I came to class late. When I came to class, the teacher <u>had already given</u> the test, so I missed it.
16. Last month, we <u>went</u> to three parties.
17. I heard your friend is working in a restaurant now. How long <u>has he been working</u> in the restaurant?
18. She <u>was cooking</u> dinner when the fire started.
19. C
20. C
21. They <u>were eating</u> dinner when the phone rang.
22. C
23. When she heard the bad news, she <u>started</u> to cry.
24. C
25. C

Part 2

1. retired/had been working OR had worked
2. arrived/got
3. didn't take/arrived/had already studied
4. had been flying/landed
5. got/had been driving
6. received/shouted
7. woke/made
8. ended/had written
9. had been living/got
10. knew/had already seen
11. had never been
12. felt/had died

Part 3

1. didn't want
2. called
3. went
4. turned
5. was watching
6. rang
7. did your friend go
8. called
9. had already left
10. happened
11. was sitting
12. came
13. saw
14. had already known
15. had you been dating
OR were you dating
16. have you been
17. have thought

LESSON FOUR

Part 1

1. C
2. You'd better study hard for the test.
3. The students are not allowed to talk during a test.
4. C
5. You'd better not ride your bike today. It's going to rain.
6. What should I do about my noisy neighbors?
7. C
8. My father knows how to fix cars. He can help you with your car problem.
9. You should visit your sick neighbor.
10. C
11. C
12. We're not permitted to talk during the test.
13. You are not supposed to make noise in the library.
14. She is not able to work today because she's sick.
15. Why can't you go to the party?
16. The teacher can't help you now. He's busy.

Part 2

1. D
2. S
3. S
4. D
5. D
6. S
7. D
8. S
9. S
10. S
11. D
12. S
13. D
14. S
15. S
16. S
17. S
18. S
19. D
20. S

Part 3

1. should OR ought to
2. could OR might OR may
3. could OR might OR may
4. shouldn't
5. must
6. shouldn't OR am not supposed to
7. could OR might OR may
8. can't OR am not able to
9. should OR ought to
10. may OR might
11. would
12. be able to
13. must OR should OR are supposed to
14. could OR might OR may

LESSON FIVE

Part 1

1. I got up late and missed my bus. I should have gotten up earlier.
2. C
3. Our son didn't get a scholarship, so we had to pay for his tuition.
4. C
5. When you lost your last job, you must have felt terrible.
6. You should have gone to the party with us last week. We had a great time.
7. I could have taken the bus to work, but I decided to walk instead.
8. Your mother was so worried when you didn't call her last week. You should have called her.
9. I couldn't find my keys yesterday.
10. C

11. He left the party without thanking the hosts. He <u>should have said</u> thank-you before leaving.
12. C
13. C
14. Jim was looking for a job all day yesterday. He looked so tired when he got home. He <u>must have had</u> a hard day.
15. C
16. C

Part 2

1. have studied
2. come
3. have done
4. leave
5. have gotten
6. have come
7. have eaten
8. have felt
9. change
10. have eaten

Part 3

1. must have left
2. should have taken
3. couldn't stop
4. had to attend
5. couldn't help
6. couldn't have been
7. must have been
8. must have looked
9. must have attached
10. could have gotten
11. could have taken

LESSON SIX

Part 1

1. A student <u>whose</u> TOEFL score is high may not have to take English as a Second Language courses.
2. Please return the book <u>that you borrowed</u> last week.
3. Children <u>whose</u> parents work often come home to an empty house.
4. <u>The person who</u> has the best costume will win a prize. (OR The child who . . .)
5. There are some married men <u>who don't</u> use a wedding ring.
6. C
7. I don't know the man <u>whom</u> (OR <u>who</u> OR <u>that</u> OR ∅) you are talking about.
8. He attends a college <u>that has</u> a good engineering department.
9. C
10. Jane bought <u>a building that has</u> six apartments.
11. The building <u>that Jane bought</u> is located on Maple Street.
12. The building <u>where Jane lives</u> is very modern. OR The building <u>that Jane lives in</u> is very modern.
13. The car <u>that my brother bought</u> runs very well.
14. C
15. C
16. I don't know <u>anyone who</u> (OR <u>that</u>) can help you with your problem.
17. C
18. The driver <u>whose car I hit</u> called the police.

Part 2

1. that have your name and address
2. whose names are on a list
3. (that) I receive
4. where I shop
5. mail I receive
6. (when) I received

Part 3

1. I bought
2. that is quiet OR where I have total quiet (answers will vary)
3. who saw the movie
4. names the teacher can't pronounce
5. where I can ski
6. when the house is quiet OR when everyone is asleep (answers will vary)
7. who lives in Paris OR who doesn't own a TV (answers will vary)
8. they don't know (answers will vary)

Part 4

1. John Kennedy Jr., who was the son of President Kennedy, was killed in an airplane crash.
2. John Kennedy Jr., whose father was president, was not interested in being a politician.
3. Tim Berners-Lee invented the World Wide Web, which has changed the way we communicate with each other.
5. I like to watch TV on Saturdays, when there are a lot of sports programs on.
6. My sister took a vacation in Hawaii, where she met her future husband.

Part 5

1. John Kennedy, the 35th American President, was killed in 1963.
2. I can't understand the Spanish spoken in Puerto Rico.
3. The Sears Tower, located in Chicago, is one of the tallest buildings in the U.S.
4. Lake Superior, between the U.S. and Canada, is the largest lake in North America.
5. The professor giving the lecture knows a lot about Latin America.

Part 6

1. NC
2. Many people like to have a picnic on the Fourth of July , which is American Independence Day.
3. NC
4. The first computer , which occupied a very large room , was not very fast.
5. NC
6. Professor Kaplan , who always gives us a test at the end of a lesson , believes that it's important for us to study for at least one hour a day.
7. My best friend , whose name is Jackie , is very fond of cats.
8. NC
9. *Star Wars* , which is a science fiction movie , is one of the most popular movies of all times.
10. Steven Spielberg , who directed many wonderful movies , has won many awards.

LESSON SEVEN

Part 1

1. C
2. She's afraid of losing her job.
3. He wrote his paper by hand instead of using a computer.
4. C
5. C
6. When he was single, he used to go out with his friends on the weekends, but now he stays home with his wife and baby.
7. C
8. She blamed him for breaking the dish.
9. I had difficulty selling my car.
10. C
11. C
12. C
13. I'm worried about not passing this course.
14. He spent a lot of time looking for a job.
15. C
16. It's important to have a good family.
17. It's necessary to eat fruits and vegetables.
18. It takes a lot of time to learn English.
19. Let's turn on the radio to hear the news.
20. C
21. I have always wanted to meet your uncle.
22. Buying a house requires a good income. OR To buy . . .
23. Is it hard for you to work and study at the same time?
24. The teacher wants us to do our homework every day.
25. C
26. C
27. Can you see the children playing in the park now?
28. C
29. I found this old jacket in my closet, but I don't remember buying it.
30. C

31. It will cost <u>me</u> $10,000 to finish my degree.
32. The doctor wanted my father to eat a healthier diet, so he stopped <u>eating</u> meat completely.
33. C
34. She got her son <u>to do</u> his homework.
35. C
36. She persuaded her son <u>to do</u> his homework.

37. C
38. C
39. C
40. I come from a tropical climate. <u>I'm not used to living</u> in a cold climate.
41. C
42. C

Part 2

1. me to quit
2. to attend
3. to find
4. help
5. Having
6. to find

7. applying
8. to pay
9. for you to pay
10. to apply
11. help

12. meeting
13. register
14. his (OR him in informal English) giving

15. making
16. Not finishing
17. becoming

Part 3

1. for
2. for
3. in (OR at)

4. about
5. on
6. about

7. to
8. about

9. in

Part 4

1. different
2. different

3. same
4. same

5. same
6. different

7. same

LESSON EIGHT

Part 1

1. Although he loves her, he won't marry her.
2. <u>Even though</u> I don't speak English well, Americans understand me anyway.
3. C
4. Because it rained, we had to cancel our picnic.
5. Before <u>watching</u> TV, you have to do your homework.
6. C
7. He has <u>such bad</u> eyesight that he can't read the words in the telephone directory.
8. C
9. I have voice mail. I can receive messages <u>even if</u> I'm talking on the phone.
10. C
11. I don't like my apartment for several reasons. First, it doesn't have air-conditioning. In addition, <u>the rooms are small</u>.
12. I didn't pass the test <u>in spite of the fact that</u> I studied very hard.

13. C
14. C
15. C
16. C
17. When she <u>graduates</u>, she will move to San Francisco.
18. C
19. She quit her job <u>so that she could spend</u> more time with her children.
20. We are taking this course <u>because</u> we want to improve our English.
21. C
22. C
23. She used a knife <u>to open</u> the package.
24. C
25. C
26. My English class has <u>so many students that</u> there aren't even enough seats.

Part 2

1. Whenever I have a problem, I go to my parents for advice.
2. C
3. He turned off the alarm clock because he wanted to sleep for one more hour. However, the phone woke him up anyway.
4. Even though it will take him four years to get his medical degree, he will continue until he finishes it.
5. C
6. C
7. C
8. Very few people bought tickets to the concert. As a result, the concert was canceled.

Part 3

1. since
2. during
3. when
4. While (OR When)
5. When
6. For
7. Whenever (OR When)
8. until

Part 4

1. so that
2. (in order) to
3. Since (OR Because)
4. Therefore
5. (in order) to
6. Because of
7. Since (OR Because)
8. for

Part 5

1. Even though
2. However
3. in spite of
4. in spite of the fact
5. Even though

Part 6

1. unless
2. Even if
3. If
4. even if
5. unless

Part 7

1. so
2. so many
3. so much
4. so much
5. such a
6. such a

Part 8

Answers will vary

1. drive to work
2. I can drive to work
3. my job is far from my house
4. she can't find a job
5. she has good computer skills
6. he's having a hard time finding a job
7. the U.S. is a democracy
8. there's a lot of crime here
9. I didn't study
10. it's an emergency
11. we didn't want to go out
12. I didn't have time to read the newspaper
13. everyone looks at her
14. he passes the final exam
15. He couldn't buy a car

LESSON NINE

Part 1

1. The teacher told me <u>to come</u> to her office.
2. She can't <u>decide if she</u> should buy a house or a condo.
3. C
4. He <u>told</u> me that he wanted to leave early.
5. He told me <u>that he wanted to leave</u> early.
6. C
7. I don't know <u>what you want</u>.
8. She knows <u>that</u> you have to leave early.
9. C
10. Before I found my job, I thought that I <u>would</u> never <u>find</u> a job.
11. Before I came to the U.S., I didn't know what my life <u>would be</u> like.
12. C
13. C
14. C
15. She told me <u>not to</u> be late.

16. C
17. Several students suggested <u>that the teacher review</u> modals.
18. I <u>think you</u> are the best teacher in the world.
19. C
20. C
21. C

22. I don't know <u>if</u> (OR <u>whether</u>) <u>the teacher is</u> here today or not.
23. I <u>told</u> my friend that I didn't want to go to the party.
24. C
25. C

Part 2

1. She told me that she had lost my phone number.
2. "Where are you going?" asked the wolf.
3. C
4. The teacher said, "My name is Jerry."
5. C
6. Can you tell me where the library is?

7. C
8. C
9. I didn't realize that you had already bought the book.
10. C

Part 3

1. what your neighbor's name is?
2. what kind of car the teacher has.
3. if (OR whether) she broke the glass (or not).
4. who broke the glass.
5. when they were here.
6. what "physician" means.
7. if (OR whether) the children are sleeping (or not)?
8. where the test was given.

9. if (OR whether) she has ever eaten pizza (or not).
10. if (OR whether) I can get a refund (or not)?
11. where I should go. (OR where to go.)
12. how much your car cost?
13. if (OR whether) the teacher collected the homework (or not)?
14. if (OR whether) we will have a test next Friday (or not)?

Part 4

1. He said that he could understand my point of view.
2. He said that I would always be his friend.
3. He said that he hadn't had enough sleep the night before.
4. He told us not to be late.
5. He told me to call him.
6. He told his children that they had to turn off the TV and go to bed.
7. He told his boss that he wouldn't be able to work the next day.
8. He told his wife that she didn't need to cook dinner.
9. He told his aunt that he had lost her new phone number.

10. He told me to buy him some stamps while I was at the post office.
11. He asked me if I needed his help.
12. He asked me what I wanted.
13. He asked me what time it was.
14. He asked me if I had seen the movie.
15. He asked me if I had washed my hands before dinner.
16. He asked me how my mother was.
17. He asked me if I had a headache.
18. He asked us who knew the answer to his question.
19. He asked us if we could lend him some money.
20. He asked her when she had made her decision.

LESSON TEN

Part I

1. I wish I <u>could fly</u> like a bird.
2. C
3. She <u>would help</u> you if she had more time, but she's too busy.
4. C

5. He doesn't make a lot of money. If he <u>made</u> a lot of money, he'd buy a house.
6. C
7. I would move to a different apartment if I <u>were</u> you.

8. C

9. C

10. I don't have a cell phone. If I <u>had</u> a cell phone, I could call you from my car.

11. C

12. C

13. She was wearing her seat belt when the accident happened. Luckily she wasn't hurt. If she hadn't been wearing her seat belt, she <u>might have gotten</u> hurt.

14. If I <u>were</u> a child again, I would choose a different career.

15. Your vacation sounds wonderful. I wish I <u>had gone</u> with you.

16. We got a postcard from our relatives on vacation in Hawaii. They wrote, "We wish you <u>were</u> here."

17. If you <u>had been</u> at the concert, you would have enjoyed it.

18. C

19. C

20. Too bad you weren't here when my brother was visiting. If you had met him, you <u>would have found</u> many things in common with him.

Part 2

1. d	5. b	9. a	13. d	16. a	19. c
2. a	6. c	10. c	14. b	17. c	20. b
3. d	7. d	11. a	15. b	18. b	
4. a	8. b	12. c			

BOOK 1 / ANSWER KEY

LESSON ONE

Exercise 1
1. is
2. are
3. are
4. is
5. are
6. is
7. are
8. am

Exercise 2
Answers will vary, but some possible answers are:
1. east
2. city
3. island
4. 3:00
5. cloudy
6. 55
7. New York

Exercise 3
1. San Francisco is beautiful.
2. Texas is a big state.
3. It is hot today.
4. The teacher is from New York.
5. My brother is 25 years old.
6. Canada is a big country.
7. The students are in the classroom.
8. The map is on page 3.
9. My parents are German.
10. I am a student.

Exercise 4
1. It
2. It
3. They
4. I
5. It
6. It
7. They
8. We
9. It
10. They

Exercise 5
Answers will vary, but some possible answers are:
1. Boston
2. Vermont and New Hampshire
3. My teachers
4. The White House
5. Spanish
6. English
7. The U.S. and Canada
8. We
9. It
10. We

Exercise 6
1. are; 're
2. is; 's
3. is; 's; 's
4. are
5. is; 's
6. is; are
7. is; are; 's; is
8. are; 're
9. is; 're
10. are; 're

Exercise 7
1. I
2. 's
3. 's
4. is
5. He's
6. is
7. It's
8. are
9. 're
10. are
11. 's
12. She's
13. are
14. 're
15. is
16. 're
17. You're
18. 'm

Exercise 8
Answers will vary, but some possible answers are:
1. Roses are
2. Apartments in New York are
3. Public transportation's
4. My shoes are
5. Politicians are
6. My brother's
7. California and Texas are
8. My friends are
9. English is
10. San Francisco's
11. Harvard University's
12. My children are

Exercise 9
Answers will vary, but some possible answers are:
1. is tired.
2. is noisy.
3. is old.
4. is rainy.
5. are friendly.
6. is interesting.

Exercise 10
Answers will vary, but some possible answers are:
1. Canada is a country.
2. Alaska is a state.
3. Blue is a color.
4. Wednesday is a weekday.
5. Christmas is a holiday.
6. Saturday and Sunday are weekend days.
7. The Pacific and the Atlantic are Oceans.
8. White and green are colors.
9. January and February are the first two months of the year.
10. California and Illinois are states.

Exercise 11
1. August is a hot month.
2. Puerto Rico is a beautiful island.

3. Toyota is a big company.
4. I'm a good student.
5. Los Angeles and Chicago are American cities.
6. John is a popular name.

Exercise 12

1. is a
2. are
3. are
4. is an
5. are
6. is an
7. are
8. are

Exercise 13

Answers will vary, but some possible answers are:

1. My dentist is a
2. Marta's a
3. Microsoft is a
4. A car is an
5. Fall is a
6. Thanksgiving is an
7. June, July, and August are
8. Portugal and Belgium are
9. Peru and Brazil are
10. Tokyo and Sao Paulo are
11. Madonna and Michael Jackson are
12. Cadillacs and Fords are

Exercise 14

Answers will vary, but some possible answers are:

1. The Museum of Natural History is an
2. The Empire State Building is a
3. Macy's and Bloomingdale's are
4. April and May are
5. Central Park is a
6. The Stage Deli
7. Fifth Avenue and Broadway are
8. Columbia is a
9. Hell's Kitchen is a
10. The Twin Towers are

Exercise 15

Answers will vary, but some possible answers are:

1. Mexico City is
2. Professional basketball players are
3. Theater tickets are
4. French is
5. Good health is
6. Soccer is
7. A large apartment is
8. Sanchez is
9. Tahiti is

Exercise 16

Answers will vary, but some possible answers are:

1. is on the second floor.
2. is above the chalkboard.
3. is near the door.
4. is in the corner.
5. is on the wall.

6. is behind the desk.
7. am near the window.
8. are on my desk.
9. is on the first floor.
10. is next to the fire station.
11. is across from our classroom.
12. are in the classroom.

Exercise 17

1. These are
2. This is
3. These are
4. Those are
5. This is
6. Those are
7. That is
8. That is

Exercise 18

1. We're not; We aren't
2. It isn't; It's not
3. I'm not
4. They aren't; They're not
5. You're not' You aren't
6. We aren't; We're not

Exercise 19

1. isn't
2. is; 's
3. aren't
4. are
5. isn't
6. 's
7. aren't
8. isn't
9. are
10. is; isn't

Exercise 20

Answers will vary.

Exercise 21

Answers will vary, but some possible answers are:

1. 'm not
2. 'm
3. is
4. aren't
5. are
6. aren't
7. isn't
8. are
9. aren't
10. is
11. isn't
12. is
13. isn't
14. is
15. isn't
16. is

Exercise 22

1. They aren't states.
2. I'm not from the U.S.
3. Cuba isn't a big country.
4. Maryland and Delaware aren't big states.
5. We aren't in the library.
6. You're not a math teacher.
7. Springfield isn't a big city.
8. Miami isn't in Illinois.
9. July and August aren't cold months.
10. I'm not American.

Exercise 23

Answers will vary, but some possible answers are:

1. 'm not
2. 'm
3. 'm
4. is

5. 's
6. 's
7. 's
8. 's
9. aren't

10. aren't
11. 're
12. 'm
13. is
14. 's

Exercise 24

1. Yes, it is.
2. Yes, they are.
3. Yes, it is.
4. No, it isn't.

5. No, it isn't.
6. Yes, it is.
7. Yes, it is.
8. No, it isn't.

Exercise 25

Answers will vary, but some possible answers are:

1. No, it isn't. It's small.
2. No, it isn't. Korean is.
3. Yes, it is.
4. No, I'm not. I'm from Asia.
5. No, I'm not.
6. Yes, I am.
7. No, they're not.
8. Yes, it is.
9. No, you're not.
10. No, we aren't.
11. No, we aren't.

Exercise 26

Answers will vary, but some possible answers are:

1. A. Is this school near your house?
   B. No, it isn't.
2. A. Is it near public transportation?
   B. Yes, it is.
3. A. Is the cafeteria on this floor?
   B. No, it isn't.
4. A. Is it open now?
   B. No, it isn't.
5. A. Is the library in this building?
   B. Yes, it is.
6. A. Is it closed now?
   B. No, it isn't.
7. A. Is this course free?
   B. Yes, it is.
8. A. Are the textbooks free?
   B. No, they aren't.
9. A. Is the teacher strict?
   B. No, he isn't.
10. A. Is this room clean?
    B. Yes, it is.
11. A. Is it big?
    B. No, it isn't.
12. A. Is the chalkboard black?
    B. Yes, it is.

Exercise 27

Answers will vary, but some possible answers are:

1. A. Are you from Asia?
   B. No, I'm not. I'm from South America.
2. A. Are you a new student?
   B. Yes, I am.

3. A. Is your country big?
   B. Yes, it is.
4. A. Are you from the capital city?
   B. No, I'm not, but I'm from the biggest city.
5. A. Are you an immigrant?
   B. No, I'm not.
6. A. Are you happy in the U.S.?
   B. Yes, I am.
7. A. Is baseball popular in your country?
   B. No, it isn't. Soccer is.
8. A. Are American cars popular in your country?
   B. No, they aren't. Japanese cars are popular.
9. A. Are teachers strict in your country?
   B. Yes, they are.
10. A. Is education free in your country?
    B. Yes, it is.

Exercise 28

1. A. Are American teachers rich?
   B. No, they aren't.
2. A. Is a high school education free?
   B. Yes, it is.
3. A. Is a college education free?
   B. No, it isn't.
4. A. Are college books free?
   B. No, they aren't.
5. A. Is medical care free?
   B. No, it isn't.
6. A. Are doctors rich?
   B. Yes, they are.
7. A. Are blue jeans popular?
   B. Yes, they are.
8. A. Are houses expensive?
   B. Yes, they are.
9. A. Are Americans friendly?
   B. Yes, they are.
10. A. Is English the official language?
    B. Yes, it is.
11. A. Are Japanese cars popular?
    B. Yes, they are.
12. A. Are fast food restaurants popular?
    B. Yes, they are.
13. A. Are movie tickets cheap?
    B. No, they aren't.
14. A. Are public schools closed on Christmas?
    B. Yes, they are.

Exercise 29

Answers will vary, but some possible answers are:

1. Are January and February warm months? No, they aren't.
2. Is Chicago a big city? Yes, it is.
3. Are Alaska and Texas big states? Yes, they are.
4. Are movie stars rich? Yes, they are.
5. Is Washington state in the East? No, it isn't.
6. Is California on the East coast? No, it isn't.
7. Is Illinois a state? Yes, it is.
8. Is education in private schools free? No, it isn't.

Exercise 30

1. Where's
2. When's

3. Who's
4. What's

5. Why are
6. Where are
7. How are
8. Where's
9. Where are
10. When's
11. Why are
12. What's

Exercise 31

1. b	4. c	7. b
2. a	5. c	8. c
3. b	6. b	9. a

Exercise 32

1. nationality is
2. time is
3. kind of, is
4. kind of, are
5. color is
6. old is your son
7. tall is your brother
8. old are you
9. much does that car cost
10. long is the movie

Exercise 33

Answers will vary, but some possible answers are:

1. A. My name is Mitsuki. What's your name?
   B. My name's Walter.
2. A. I'm from Japan. Where are you from?
   B. I'm from Brazil.
3. A. The president of my country is Keizo Obuchi. Who's the president of your country?
   B. He's Fernando Henrique Cardoso.
4. A. The president of my country is about 60 years old. How old is the president of your country?
   B. He's about 67 years old.

5. A. The flag of my country is red and white. What color is the flag of your country?
   B. It's yellow and green.
6. A. My country is in Asia. Where's your country?
   B. It's in South America.
7. A. I'm five feet, nine inches tall. How tall are you?
   B. I'm six feet tall.
8. A. My birthday is in February. When's your birthday?
   B. It's in May.
9. A. My favorite TV show is *ER*. What's your favorite TV show?
   B. It's *The X Files*.
10. A. My favorite color is blue. What's your favorite color?
    B. It's green.

Exercise 34

1. Where is Washington, D.C.? It's in the U.S.
2. What is the capital of the U.S.? It's Washington, D.C.
3. Where are Los Angeles and San Francisco? They're in California.
4. What is Philadelphia? It's a city.
5. Where is Peru? It's in South America.
6. Where are Ethiopia and Nigeria? They're in Africa.
7. Where is Columbia? It's in South America.
8. What color is the American flag? It's red, white, and blue.
9. What kind of names are James and William? They're English names.
10. What time is it in L.A.? It's 3:00 in L.A.

Exercise 35

1. are you?
2. Is it interesting?
3. is the weather?
4. Are you alone?
5. is with you? OR are you with
6. How old is she?
7. What time is it

LESSON ONE TEST / REVIEW

Part 1

1. big cities	13. You're
2. C	14. This
3. isn't	15. C
4. am not; C	16. They're
5. The students	17. the U.S.
6. big	18. a cold month
7. C; C	19. tall OR a tall man
8. C	20. big
9. C; wife is from	21. an
10. is 10 years old OR is 10.	22. he is
11. French is	23. is
12. C	

Part 2

1. This book is very long.
2. She has a very beautiful car.
3. Why are you late?
4. C

5. What nationality is your wife?
6. C
7. Why is the teacher absent?
8. C

Part 3

A. Where are you from?
B. I'm from Mexico.
A. Are you happy in the U.S.?
B. Yes, I am. The U.S. is a great country.
A. Are you from a big city?
B. Yes. I'm from Mexico City. It's a very big city. This city is big and beautiful too. But it's cold in the winter.
A. Is your roommate from Mexico too?
B. No, my roommate is from Taiwan. I'm happy in the U.S., but he's not happy here. He is homesick.
A. Why is he homesick?
B. His parents are in Taiwan. He's alone here.
A. How old is he?

B. He's very young. He's only 18 years old.
A. What's his name?
B. His name's Lu.

Part 4

1. we're
2. you're not OR you aren't
3. I'm not
4. they're
5. X
6. X
7. Mary's not OR Mary isn't
8. he's not OR he isn't
9. what's
10. X

Part 5

1. 'm
2. I
3. are you
4. m
5. 's
6. She's
7. 's your teacher?
8. He's
9. Is he
10. isn't
11. a
12. 's
13. old
14. old is your teacher?
15. is
16. tall is she
17. is
18. Is your class big?
19. are
20. are
21. are
22. is
23. from
24. isn't
25. are the students from?
26. are
27. 're all
28. Is Mr. Kane
29. an
30. Is that Mr. Kane?
31. 's
32. 'm

LESSON TWO

Exercise 1

1. lives
2. work
3. has
4. visit
5. show
6. has
7. means

Exercise 2

Answers will vary, but some possible answers are:

1. has many parks
2. have big families
3. like the restaurants
4. visit the museums
5. has a lot of bilingual
6. lives near the beach
7. live in a city
8. has a lot of fast food restaurants
9. attend a small
10. has many good teachers

Exercise 3

1. tries
2. plays
3. has
4. goes
5. worries
6. finishes
7. does
8. pushes
9. enjoys
10. thinks
11. says
12. changes
13. brushes
14. obeys
15. reaches
16. fixes
17. works
18. raises
19. charges
20. sees

Exercise 5

1. flies
2. washes
3. watches
4. obeys
5. pays
6. fixes
7. studies
8. does
9. manages
10. uses
11. teaches

Exercise 6

Answers will vary, but a possible answer is:

I'm a secretary. A secretary does a lot of things in an office. He or she answers the telephone and uses a computer. A secretary enters data into the computer, and writes letters and other documents. A secretary receives his or her salary every month or every two weeks.

Exercise 7

1. studies
2. gets
3. has
4. 's
5. live
6. 'm
7. study
8. watch
9. eat

Exercise 8

1. doesn't see
2. don't have
3. don't live
4. don't visit
5. doesn't have
6. doesn't live
7. doesn't work
8. doesn't take
9. doesn't have
10. doesn't visit

Exercise 9

Answers will vary, but some possible answers are:

1. This school has a library.
2. This school has a cafeteria.
3. This school has copy machines.
4. This school has a parking lot.
5. This school doesn't have a swimming pool.
6. This school has a gym.
7. This school has a student newspaper.
8. This school doesn't have a theatre.
9. This school doesn't have dormitories.
10. This school doesn't have classes for children.
11. This school has a computer lab.
12. This school doesn't have e-mail for students.

Exercise 10

Answers will vary, but some possible answers are:

1. The teacher doesn't talk fast.
2. The teacher speaks English well.
3. The teacher doesn't speak my language.
4. The teacher gives a lot of homework.
5. The teacher gives tests.
6. The teacher doesn't pronounce my name correctly.
7. The teacher wears glasses.
8. The teacher doesn't wear jeans to class.
9. The teacher teaches this class everyday.
10. The teacher watches the students during a test.

Exercise 11

Answers will vary, but some possible answers are:

1. Marta doesn't speak Chinese.
2. Marta doesn't live alone.
3. Marta lives near school.
4. Mara walks to school.
5. Marta speaks Spanish.
6. Marta likes summer.
7. Marta doesn't like cold weather.
8. Marta has a computer.
9. Marta doesn't use the Internet.

Exercise 12

1. doesn't live
2. doesn't serve
3. doesn't make
4. doesn't live
5. don't see
6. doesn't run
7. don't pay
8. doesn't need
9. don't live
10. don't study
11. don't need
12. don't live
13. don't go
14. doesn't have

Exercise 13

Answers will vary, but some possible answers are:

1. Margarita isn't married.
2. Margarita doesn't have children.
3. Margarita has a computer.
4. Margarita isn't an American citizen.
5. Margarita likes this city.
6. Margarita doesn't have a job.
7. Margarita is a full time student.
8. Margarita doesn't have a pet.
9. Margarita isn't an immigrant.
10. Margarita isn't unhappy in the U.S.
11. Margarita likes baseball.
12. Margarita doesn't understand American TV.

Exercise 14

Answers will vary, but some possible answers are:

4. a good adult son or daughter
A good adult son or daughter visits his or her parents often.
A good adult son or daughter is respectful to his or her parents.
A good adult son or daughter does not neglect his or her parents.

Exercise 15

1. Brazilians don't speak Spanish.
2. I don't speak my native language in class.
3. B, C, and D aren't vowels.
4. I'm not from the U.S.
5. Washington isn't a state.
6. The subway in Washington isn't dirty.
7. My brother doesn't live in Washington.
8. New York doesn't have an Air and Space Museum.
9. Sara isn't busy on the weekend.
10. Sara isn't married.
11. A bus ride isn't expensive.

Exercise 16

Answers will vary, but some possible answers are:

1. A. Do you like your job?
   B. Yes, I do.
2. A. Do you teach in the summer?
   B. Yes, I do.
3. A. Do you have another job?
   B. No, I don't.
4. A. Do you speak another language?
   B. Yes, I do.
5. A. Do you teach English to Americans?
   B. No, I don't.
6. A. Do you know my language?
   B. No, I don't.
7. A. Do you like to read students' homework?
   B. Yes, I do.
8. A. Do you live far from school?
   B. No, I don't.
9. A. Do you have a fax machine?
   B. No, I don't.
10. A. Do you have trouble with English spelling?
    B. Yes, I do.
11. A. Do you have an e-mail address?
    B. Yes, I do.
12. A. Do you like soccer?
    B. Yes, I do.

Exercise 17

1. do
2. have
3. Does she speak
4. speaks
5. talks
6. don't understand
7. gives
8. Does your teacher give
9. gives
10. wears
11. Does your teacher wear

Exercise 18

Answers will vary, but some possible answers are:

1. Does he use a map? Yes, he does.
2. Do you bring your dictionary to class. No, I don't.
3. Do we need practice with spelling? Yes, we do.
4. Does the teacher speak another language? Yes, he does.
5. Do you understand the teacher? Yes, I do.

6. Does the present tense have a lot of irregular verbs? No, it doesn't.
7. Do the students speak English fluently? No, they don't.
8. Does Washington have a zoo? Yes, it does.
9. Do people pay to enter the White House? No, they don't.
10. Do the subway trains run after midnight? No, they don't.

6. Do American people eat with chopsticks? No, they don't.
7. Does Spanish have a lot of irregular verbs? Yes, it does.
8. Are you interested in American history? Yes, I am.
9. Is the subway in Washington quiet? Yes, it is.
10. Does Sara work on the weekend? No, she doesn't.

Exercise 19

1. A. Russians take off their shoes before they enter a house. Do Spanish people take off their shoes before they enter a house?
   B. No, we don't.
2. A. Russians don't bow when they say hello. Do Spanish people bow when they say hello?
   B. No, we don't.
3. A. Russians shake hands when they say hello. Do Spanish people shake hands when they say hello?
   B. Yes, we do.
4. A. Russians bring a gift when they visit a friend's house. Do Spanish people bring a gift when they visit a friend's house?
   B. Yes, we do.
5. A. Russians don't eat with chopsticks. Do Spanish people eat with chopsticks?
   B. No, we don't.
6. A. In Russia, on the bus, younger people stand up to let an older person sit down. In Spain, on the bus, do younger people stand up to let an older person sit down?
   B. Yes, we do.
7. A. Russians women don't cover their faces with a veil. Do Spanish women cover their faces with a veil?
   B. No, we don't.
8. A. In Russia, people don't visit friends without calling first. In Spain, do people visit friends without calling first?
   B. Yes, we do.
9. A. In Russia, men usually don't open doors for women. In Spain, do men hold doors open for women?
   B. Yes, we do.
10. A. In Russia, men give flowers to women for their birthdays. In Spain, do men give flowers to women for their birthdays?
    B. Yes, we do.
11. A. In Russia, people don't celebrate children's day. In Spain, do people celebrate children's day?
    B. No, we don't.
12. A. In Russia, high school students usually don't wear a uniform. In Spain, do high school students wear a uniform?
    B. No, they usually don't.

Exercise 20

Answers will vary, but some possible answers are:

1. Do Mexicans shake hands when they meet? Yes, they do.
2. Do adults learn a language easily? No, they don't.
3. Do Australians speak English? Yes, they do.
4. Are tacos popular in the U.S.? Yes, they are.
5. Do you understand British English? No, I don't.

Exercise 21

Answers will vary, but some possible answers are:

1. A. I speak my native language at home. Do you speak English or your native language at home?
   B. I speak my native language at home too.
2. A. I prefer popular music. Do you prefer classical music or popular music?
   B. I prefer classical music.
3. A. I'm a resident of the U.S. Are you a resident of the U.S. or a visitor?
   B. I'm a visitor.
4. A. I'm single. Are you married or single?
   B. I'm single too.
5. A. I live in an apartment. Do you live in an apartment or a dormitory?
   B. I live in an apartment too.
6. A. I write with my right hand. Do you write with your right hand or your left hand?
   B. I write with my left hand.
7. A. I'm from a big city. Are you from a big city or a small town?
   B. I'm from a small town.
8. A. I prefer morning classes. Do you prefer morning classes or evening classes?
   B. I prefer morning classes too.

Exercise 22

1. does
2. many
3. Where do
4. don't
5. does; speak
6. does; work

Exercise 23

Answers will vary, but some possible answers are:

1. A. Do you speak Spanish?
   B. No, I don't.
   A. What language do you speak?
   B. I speak Farsi.
2. A. Do you need English in your country?
   B. Yes, I do.
   A. Why do you need English?
   B. Because I want to work in tourism.
3. A. Do you have American friends?
   B. Yes, I do.
   A. How many American friends do you have?
   B. I have three or four good American friends.
4. A. Do you like this city?
   B. No, I don't.
   A. Why don't you like it?
   B. It's very noisy.
5. A. Do you live near the school?
   B. No, I don't.
   A. Where do you live?
   B. I live on Spruce Street.

6. A. Do you plan to go back to your country?
   B. Yes, I do.
   A. When do you plan to go back?
   B. I plan to go back next summer.
7. A. Do you live alone?
   B. No, I don't.
   A. Who do you live with?
   B. I live with my cousin.
8. A. Do you practice English outside of class?
   B. Yes, I do.
   A. Who do you practice English with?
   B. I practice English with my American friends.
9. A. Do you bring your dictionary to class?
   B. No, I don't.
   A. Why don't you bring your dictionary to class?
   B. Because it's very heavy.
10. A. Do you have a cell phone?
    B. Yes, I do.
    A. Why do you have a cell phone?
    B. Because I'm not at home very much.

Exercises 24

Answers will vary, but some possible answers are:

1. A. Do you have an office mate?
   B. Yes, I do.
   A. What does your office mate teach?
   B. She teaches chemistry.
2. A. Do you get paid on the first of the month?
   B. No, I don't.
   A. When do you get paid?
   B. I get paid on the 5th of the month.
3. A. Do you have a computer?
   B. Yes, I do.
   A. What kind of computer do you have?
   B. I have a Macintosh.
4. A. Do you speak another language?
   B. Yes, I do.
   A. What language do you speak?
   B. I speak Spanish.
5. A. Do you teach summer school?
   B. Yes, I do.
   A. Why do you teach summer school?
   B. Because I need the money.
6. A. Do you work in another school?
   B. Yes, I do.
   A. What other school do you work in?
   B. I work in a secretarial school.
7. A. Do you correct the homework in school?
   B. No, I don't.
   A. Where do you correct the homework?
   B. I correct the homework at my kitchen table.
8. A. Do you prefer evening classes?
   B. No, I don't.
   A. Why don't you prefer evening classes?
   B. Because I'm always tired in the evening.
9. A. Do you drive to school?
   B. No, I don't.
   A. How do you get to school?
   B. I walk or take a bus.
10. A. Do you like to teach English?
    B. Yes, I do.

A. Why do you like to teach it?
B. Because it's fun.
11. A. Do you come from this city?
    B. No, I don't.
    A. What city do you come from?
    B. I come from Houston.
12. A. Do you have children?
    B. Yes, I do.
    A. How many children do you have?
    B. I have one daughter.

Exercise 25

Answers will vary, but some possible answers are:

1. A. Does your teacher give a lot of homework?
   B. Yes, she does.
   A. Why does she give a lot of homework?
   B. Because we need it.
2. A. Does your teacher write on the blackboard?
   B. Yes, she does.
   A. When does she write on the blackboard?
   B. When we learn something new.
3. A. Does your teacher use a tape recorder in class?
   B. Yes, she does.
   A. Why does she use a tape recorder?
   B. She uses it for listening practice.
4. A. Does your teacher come to class late?
   B. No, she doesn't.
   A. What time does she come to class?
   B. She comes to class five minutes before it begins.
5. A. Does your teacher call you by your first name?
   B. No, she doesn't.
   A. Why doesn't she call you by your first name?
   B. Because I prefer my last name.
6. A. Does she pronounce your name correctly?
   B. No, she doesn't.
   A. How does she pronounce it?
   B. She pronounces it like an English name.
7. A. Does your teacher use a textbook?
   B. Yes, she does.
   A. What textbook does she use?
   B. She uses *Readings for Today*.
8. A. Does your teacher wear jeans to class?
   B. Yes, she does.

Exercise 26

A. How do you spell "Gomez"?
B. G-O-M-E-Z. It's a Spanish name.
A. Are you from Spain?
B. No, I'm not.
A. What country do you come from?
B. I come from Guatemala.
A. Is your family here?
B. No. My family is still in Guatemala. I call them once a week.
A. Isn't that expensive?
B. Yes, it is.
A. How much does it cost?
B. A phone call to Guatemala costs about 25 cents a minute. But we don't talk for long. We just say hello.

A. How do you say "hello" in Spanish?
B. We say "hola." Please excuse me now. I'm late for class. Hasta luego.
A. What does "hasta luego" mean?
B. It means "see you later" in Spanish.

Exercise 27

Answers will vary, but some possible answers are:

1. A. Where does the American President live?
   B. He lives in Washington, D.C.
2. A. What language do Canadians speak?
   B. They speak English and French.
3. A. How much does this course cost?
   B. It costs a few hundred dollars.
4. A. What does "L.A." mean?
   B. It means Los Angeles.
5. A. How do you spell "enough"?
   B. E-N-O-U-G-H.
6. A. How many people does the U.S. have?
   B. It has about 270 million people.
7. A. When do Americans celebrate the New Year?
   B. They celebrate the New Year in January.
8. A. What does "large" mean?
   B. It means "big."
9. A. How do you say "book" in Spanish?
   B. We say "libro" in Spanish.
10. A. Why doesn't the teacher speak a foreign language in class?
    B. Because he's here to teach us English.

11. A. When does the U.S. have cold weather?
    B. The U.S. has cold weather in December, January, February, and March.
12. A. When do Americans celebrate Labor Day?
    B. They celebrate Labor Day in September.
13. A. What does "automobile" mean?
    B. It means "car."
14. A. When does the school year end?
    B. It ends in June.

Exercise 28

1. 's your name
2. are you from
3. 'm
4. do you speak
5. Are you
6. are you
7. 'm from
8. 's Peru
9. do you want
10. does "export" mean?
11. do you need
12. does your father speak
13. Do you like
14. is
15. How do you spell "Nowak"?
16. does your class have
17. is it on
18. does
19. begin
20. How do you say

LESSON TWO TEST / REVIEW

Part 1
1. C
2. don't have
3. Where do
4. doesn't need
5. C
6. don't need
7. C
8. Do
9. C;C;does
10. does this school have
11. How do you spell
12. C
13. don't you
14. does, C
15. does a stamp cost
16. C
17. C
18. doesn't have
19. I don't like
20. How do you say
21. goes
22. C
23. C
24. does "adjective" mean?

Part 2
1. goes
2. carries
3. mixes
4. drinks
5. plays
6. studies
7. catches
8. says

Part 3
1. uses; doesn't use
2. speak; don't speak
3. has; doesn't have
4. are; aren't
5. pronounce; don't pronounce
6. teaches; doesn't teach
7. means; doesn't mean
8. come; don't come
9. is; isn't

Part 4
1. Does Mexico have 50 states? No, it doesn't.
2. Does the bank sell stamps? No, it doesn't.
3. Is Los Angeles in California? Yes, it is.
4. Does Burger King sell hamburgers? Yes, it does.
5. Do April and June have 31 days? No, they don't.

6. Does the Vice President live in the White House? No, he doesn't.
7. Do Canadians speak English? Yes, they do.
8. Does the teacher come to class on time? Yes, she does.
9. Is the U.S. a big country? Yes, it is.

Part 5
1. What language do Canadians speak?
2. How many states does Mexico have?
3. Where does the Vice President live?
4. When is Christmas?
5. How do you spell "tomorrow"?
6. What does "occasion" mean?
7. Why doesn't the President make the laws?
8. Where do you come from?

Part 6
A. How old are you?
B. I'm 30 years old.
A. Are you married?
B. No, I'm single.
A. Do you live with your parents?
B. No, I don't live with my parents.
A. Why don't you live with your parents?
B. I don't live with my parents because they live in a different city.
A. Where do they live?
B. They live in Chicago.
A. Do you like Washington?
B. Yes, I like it very much.
A. Why do you like Washington?
B. I like it because it has so many interesting museums and galleries. But I don't have time to visit these places

very often. I work every day. When my parents visit, we go to galleries and museums.
A. When do your parents visit?
B. They visit me in the spring. They love Washington.
A. Why do they love Washington?
B. They love it because it's a beautiful, interesting city. And they love it because I'm here.
A. What kind of job do you have?
B. I have a job with the government. I work in the Department of Commerce.
A. What does "commerce" mean?
B. Commerce means business.
A. How do you spell "commerce"?
B. C-O-M-M-E-R-C-E.
A. Do you like your job?
B. Yes. I like my job very much.
A. Where do you live?
B. I live a few blocks from the White House.
A. Do you have a car?
B. No, I don't. I don't need a car.
A. How do you get to work?
B. I go to work by subway. If I'm late, I take a taxi.
A. How much does that cost?
B. A taxi ride from my house to work costs about $12.
A. Is the subway clean?
B. Oh yes. The subway is very clean.
A. Does it run all night?
B. No, it doesn't run all night. It runs until midnight.
A. In my country, we don't say "subway." We use a different word.
B. How do you say "subway" in your country?
A. We say "metro."

LESSON THREE

Exercise 1
1. dishes
2. countries
3. halves
4. books
5. boys
6. girls
7. benches
8. boxes
9. tables
10. stereos
11. knives
12. stories
13. sofas
14. keys
15. movies
16. baths
17. mosquitoes
18. lions
19. flies
20. cows
21. sharks
22. roaches
23. foxes
24. horses
25. turkeys
26. chickens
27. wolves
28. dogs
29. squirrels
30. ponies
31. ducks
32. moths

Exercise 3
1. feet
2. women
3. policemen
4. children
5. fish
6. mice
7. sheep
8. teeth

Exercise 4
Answers will vary, but some possible answers are:
1. A. How many children do you have?
   B. I don't have children.
2. A. How many brothers do you have?
   B. I have one brother.
3. A. How many sisters do you have?
   B. I have two sisters.
4. A. How many nieces do you have?
   B. I have three nieces.
5. A. How many nephews do you have?
   B. I have one nephew.
6. A. How many aunts do you have?
   B. I have six aunts.
7. A. How many telephones do you have?
   B. I have two telephones.
8. A. How many watches do you have?
   B. I have one watch.
9. A. How many televisions do you have?
   B. I have one television.
10. A. How many radios do you have?
    B. I have three radios.
11. A. How many cousins do you have?
    B. I have seven cousins.

12. A. How many computers do you have?
    B. I don't have any computers.

Exercise 5

1. An adult has a lot of responsibilities.
2. A child likes to play.
3. A single parent has a hard job.
4. A woman lives longer than a man.
5. A car is expensive.
6. A house costs a lot of money.

Exercise 6

1. Children need love.
2. Eggs have protein.
3. Bananas are yellow.
4. Dolphins are intelligent.
5. Dolphins don't live on land.
6. Mice are small.

Exercise 7

Answers will vary, but some possible answers are:

1. Americans eat a lot of hamburgers.
2. American children have a lot of toys.
3. Big cities in the U.S. all look the same.
4. Teachers at this college work very hard.
5. Students at this college have a lot of homework.
6. American doctors live well.
7. Old people in the U.S. prefer warm climates.
8. American women are very independent.

Exercise 8

Answers will vary, but some possible answers are:

1. Generally, people don't eat on the street in my country.
2. Generally, old people live with their children.
3. Generally, women in my country do all the housework.
4. Generally, men open doors for women.
5. Generally, houses are very expensive in my country.
6. Generally, poor people beg in the center of the city.
7. Generally, students don't have their own cars in my country.
8. Generally, doctors work long hours in my country.

Exercise 9

Answers will vary, but some possible answers are:

1. Lawyers
2. Homeless people
3. Teenagers
4. Aerobics instructors
5. Children
6. Parents

Exercise 10

Answers will vary, but some possible answers are:

1. I like tomatoes.
2. I like oranges.
3. I like strawberries.
4. I don't like grapes.
5. I like bananas.
6. I like peaches.
7. I don't like radishes.
8. I like pears.
9. I like potatoes.
10. I like cherries.

Exercise 11

Answers will vary, but some possible answers are:

1. A. Do you like cats?
   B. Yes, I do.
2. A. Do you like dogs?
   B. No, I don't.
3. A. Do you like American doctors?
   B. Yes, I do.
4. A. Do you like American cars?
   B. No, I don't.
5. A. Do you like American movies?
   B. Yes, I do.
6. A. Do you like fashion magazines?
   B. Yes, I do.
7. A. Do you like comic books?
   B. Yes, I do.
8. A. Do you like computers?
   B. No, I don't.
9. A. Do you like computer games?
   B. No, I don't.
10. A. Do you like strict teachers?
    B. No, I don't.
11. A. Do you like American supermarkets?
    B. Yes, I do.
12. A. Do you like American textbooks?
    B. Yes, I do.

Exercise 12

Answers will vary, but some possible answers are:

1. There isn't a closet in the living room.
2. There aren't any blinds on the windows.
3. There's a door in every room.
4. There's a window in every room.
5. There's a lease.
6. There's a porch.
7. There's a number on the door of the apartment.
8. There's an overhead light in every room.
9. There isn't a microwave oven in the kitchen.
10. There isn't a back door.
11. There's no fireplace.
12. There's a smoke detector in the living room.

Exercise 13

Answers will vary, but some possible answers are:

1. There's a closet in the room.
2. There are two beds in the room.
3. There isn't a private bath for every room.
4. There are men and women in the dorm.
5. There's a cafeteria in the dorm.
6. There are snack machines in the dorm.
7. There are noisy students in the dorm.
8. There are numbers on the doors of the rooms.
9. There are elevators in the dorms.
10. There's a laundry in the dorm.

Exercise 14

Answers will vary, but some possible answers are:

1. A. Are there any children in your building?
   B. Yes, there are.

2. A. Is there a dishwasher in the kitchen?
   B. No, there isn't.
3. A. Is there a yard in front of your building?
   B. No, there isn't.
4. A. Are there any trees in front of your building?
   B. No, there aren't.
5. A. Is there a basement in the building?
   B. Yes, there is.
6. A. Is there a laundry room in the basement?
   B. Yes, there is.
7. A. Is there a janitor in the building?
   B. Yes, there is.
8. A. Are there any noisy neighbors in the building?
   B. Yes, there are.
9. A. Are there any nosy neighbors in the building?
   B. No, there aren't.
10. A. Is there an elevator in the building?
    B. No, there isn't.
11. A. Are there any parking spaces for the tenants?
    B. No, there aren't.
12. A. Are there a lot of closets in the apartment?
    B. Yes, there are.
13. A. How many apartments are there in your building?
    B. There are sixty.
14. A. How many parking spaces are there in front of your building?
    B. There are none.

Exercise 15

Answers will vary, but some possible answers are:

1. A. Are there any married students in your dorm?
   B. Yes, there are.
2. A. Are there any private rooms in your dorm?
   B. Yes, there are.
3. A. Is there a bicycle room in your dorm?
   B. No, there isn't.
4. A. Is there a computer room in your dorm?
   B. No, there isn't.
5. A. Is there an elevator in your dorm?
   B. Yes, there is.
6. A. Is there a bulletin board in your dorm?
   B. Yes, there is.
7. A. Are there any graduate students in your dorm?
   B. Yes, there are.
8. A. Is there a quiet place to study in your dorm?
   B. No, there isn't.
9. A. Is there an air conditioner in your room?
   B. Yes, there is.
10. A. Is there a parking lot for your dorm?
    B. Yes, there is.
11. A. How many rooms are there in your dorm?
    B. There are 400.
12. A. How many floors are there in your dorm?
    B. There are six.

Exercise 16

Answers will vary, but some possible answers are:

1. A. Is there a phone in your office?
   B. Yes, there is.

2. A. Is there an answering machine in your office?
   B. Yes, there is.
3. A. Are there any photos of your family in your office?
   B. No, there aren't.
4. A. Is there a radio in you office?
   B. No, there isn't.
5. A. Is there a copy machine in your office?
   B. No, there isn't.
6. A. Are there any windows in your office?
   B. Yes, there are.
7. A. Is there a calendar in your office?
   B. Yes, there is.
8. A. Are there any bookshelves in your office?
   B. Yes, there are.
9. A. Are there any plants in your office?
   B. No, there aren't.
10. A. Is there a file cabinet in your office?
    B. Yes, there is.

Exercise 17

1. Is there
2. are there
3. There are
4. Are there
5. There are
6. many
7. are there
8. There are
9. there aren't
10. there are
11. Is there

Exercise 18

1. There are; They're
2. There's; It's
3. They're
4. They're
5. It's
6. It's
7. It's
8. there are
9. It's
10. it's

Exercise 19

Answers will vary, but some possible answers are:

1. A. Is there a library at this school?
   B. Yes, there is.
   A. Where is it?
   B. It's next to the office.
2. A. Are there any vending machines at this school?
   B. Yes, there are.
   A. Where are they?
   B. They're in the cafeteria.
3. A. Are there any public telephones at this school?
   B. Yes, there are.
   A. Where are they?
   B. They're next to the gym.
4. A. Is there a computer room at this school?
   B. Yes, there is.
   A. Where is it?
   B. It's across from the library.
5. A. Is there a cafeteria at this school?
   B. Yes, there is.
   A. Where is it?
   B. It's opposite the auditorium.
6. A. Is there a gym at this school.
   B. Yes, there is.
   A. Where is it?
   B. It's opposite the auditorium.

7. A. Is there a swimming pool at this school?
   B. Yes, there is.
   A. Where is it?
   B. It's in the basement.
8. A. Are there any tennis courts at this school?
   B. Yes, there are.
   A. Where are they?
   B. They're next to the parking lot.
9. A. Are there any dormitories at this school?
   B. No, there aren't.
10. A. Is there a parking lot at this school?
    B. Yes, there is.
    A. Where is it?
    B. It's between the tennis courts and the football field.
11. A. Is there a bookstore at this school?
    B. No, there isn't.
12. A. Are there any copy machines at this school?
    B. Yes, there are.
    A. Where are they?
    B. They're in the library.
13. A. Is there a student lounge at this school?
    B. Yes, there is.

A. Where is it?
B. It's across from the cafeteria.
14. A. Is there a fax machine at this school?
    B. Yes, there is.
    A. Where is it?
    B. It's in the office.

Exercise 20

Conversation 1

| 1. the | 3. a |
| 2. the | 4. the |

Conversation 2

1. a	5. the
2. the	6. a
3. the	7. The
4. any	

Conversation 3

1. a	4. a
2. the	5. The
3. a	

LESSON THREE TEST / REVIEW

Part 1

A. It's big enough for my family. There are four bedrooms and two bathrooms. Each bedroom has a large closet [OR There is a large closet in each bedroom]. Let me show you my kitchen too.
B. Oh. There's a new dishwasher in your kitchen.
A. It's wonderful. You know how I hate to wash dishes.
B. Is there a microwave oven?
A. No, there isn't, unfortunately.
B. Are there any washers and dryers for clothes?
A. Oh yes. They're in the basement. There are five washers and dryers in the laundry room. I never have to wait.
B. Are there a lot of people in your building?
A. There are thirty apartments in my building.
B. Is there a janitor in your building?
A. Yes. There's a very good janitor. He keeps the building very clean.
B. I suppose this apartment costs a lot.
A. Well, yes. The rent is high. But I share the apartment with my cousins.

Part 2

cards	matches	desks
feet	shelves	keys
potatoes	radios	stories
women	mice	buses
months	children	

Part 3

1. there are	8. Is there
2. Is there	9. It's
3. there	10. are there
4. is	11. There are
5. It's	12. Is there
6. Are there	13. there is
7. They're	14. it's

Part 4

1. a	6. some
2. The	7. the
3. some	8. the
4. a	9. a
5. X	

LESSON FOUR

Exercise 1

1. always	7. always
2. often	8. always
3. usually	9. never
4. usually	10. always
5. always	11. never
6. never	

Exercise 2

Answers will vary, but some possible answers are:

1. I never cook the meals in my house.
2. I usually stay home on Sundays.
3. I always buy the Sunday newspaper.
4. I usually read the newspaper in English.

5. I never use public transportation.
6. I'm never tired in class.

Exercise 3

Answers will vary.

Exercise 4

Answers will vary.

Exercise 5

1. Do you ever use public transportation?
2. Do you ever drink coffee at night?
3. Do you ever drink tea in the morning?
4. Do you ever speak English at home?
5. Do you ever watch TV at night?
6. Do you ever rent videos?
7. Are you ever late for class?
8. Do you ever ask for directions on the street?
9. Are you ever homesick?
10. Are you ever lazy on Saturdays?
11. Does it ever snow in March?

Exercise 7

1. Do Americans ever eat with chopsticks?
2. Do Americans ever carry radios?
3. Do Americans ever say "Have a nice day"?
4. Do Americans ever kiss when they meet?
5. Do Americans ever shake hands when they meet?
6. Are Americans ever impolite to you?
7. Do Americans ever pronounce your name incorrectly?
8. Do Americans ever ask you what country you're from?
9. Are Americans ever curious about your country?

Exercise 8

Answers will vary

Exercise 9

Answers will vary

Exercise 10

Answers will vary, but some possible answers are:

1. How often does she pick up her son at baseball practice?
   She picks up her son twice a week.

2. How often does she shop for groceries?
   She shops for groceries once a week.
3. How often does she take the dog for a haircut?
   She takes the dog for a haircut once a month.
4. How often does she go to the beauty salon?
   She goes to the beauty salon once a month.
5. How often does she visit Mom?
   She visits her Mom every Friday.
6. How often does she go to the gym?
   She goes to the gym three times each week.
7. How often does she prepare the kids' lunches?
   She prepares the kids' lunches every weekday.
8. How often does she change the oil in her car?
   She changes the oil in her car four times a year.

Exercise 11

Answers will vary

Exercise 12

1. usually complains
2. How often do you call
3. I call her every day.
4. 's often
5. always watches
6. Does she ever
7. rarely does
8. usually cooks
9. never changes
10. do you usually do
11. usually buy
12. usually says
13. always die
14. Is she always
15. Is she ever
16. always says

Exercise 13

Answers will vary

C	often brings
gives	C
C	C
English is	I always
C	sometimes go
C	tries
C	C
she explains	C
do the	she usually wears
has	she looks
are	a teacher never wears
say	understands
C	C
C	She comes
C	C
makes	knows

Exercise 14

Answers will vary

LESSON FOUR TEST / REVIEW

Part 1
1. I always
2. C
3. They are never
4. It seldom snows
5. C; Yes, I do
6. C; I always am
7. C; I always do
8. How often; C
9. Once in a while I
10. C

Part 2
1. is
2. Do you like
3. Does
4. doesn't
5. wears
6. How old is he
7. is
8. Does he speak
9. speaks
10. when

11. meets
12. is
13. wears
14. always
15. never speaks
16. speaks
17. gives us
18. When
19. don't
20. Does
21. teach
22. or sing to
23. does
24. do you use
25. does "Context" mean
26. do you spell it

Part 3
1. in
2. always in
3. always on
4. at
5. every
6. during
7. from; to
8. in
9. in

LESSON FIVE

Exercise 1

Answers will vary, but some possible answers are:

1. father's
2. mother's
3. husband's
4. husband's
5. father's
6. wife's
7. mother's

Exercise 2
1. The teacher always corrects the students' homework.
2. No change
3. The teacher's job is to explain the grammar.
4. What are your parents' names?
5. No change.
6. Do you use your father's last name?
7. What is your dog's name.
8. My children's names are Jason and Jessica.

Exercise 3
1. his
2. her
3. its
4. their
5. her; her
6. their
7. your
8. my
9. our
10. his OR her
11. their

Exercise 4
1. Whose office is this? This is the dean's office.
2. Whose offices are those? Those are the teachers' offices.
3. Whose dictionary is that? That's the teacher's dictionary.
4. Whose books are those? Those are the students' books.
5. Whose car is that? That's my parents' car?
6. Whose house is this? This is my cousins' house.
7. Whose papers are those? Those are Mr. Ross's [OR Mr. Ross'] papers.
8. Whose diskettes are these? These are the programmer's diskettes.

Exercise 5
1. Hers
2. Yours
3. his
4. yours
5. mine
6. Whose
7. Ours
8. Paula's

Exercise 6
1. him
2. me
3. it
4. it
5. them
6. him OR her
7. us
8. him
9. you
10. them

Exercise 7
1. it
2. it
3. it
4. you
5. them
6. you
7. me
8. you
9. us
10. him
11. you
12. him
13. you
14. you

Exercise 8
1. I'm
2. My
3. I
4. My
5. I
6. My; Mine
7. My; me

Exercise 9
1. He's
2. He
3. He's
4. His; him; his
5. He's; His
6. his
7. His

Exercise 10
1. She's
2. her
3. She's
4. She
5. Hers
6. She's; She; her
7. Her

Exercise 11
1. They're
2. They
3. They
4. Their
5. Theirs
6. They're
7. them

Exercise 12
1. It
2. It's
3. Its
4. It
5. Its
6. It's
7. it

Exercise 13
1. We
2. We're
3. Our
4. us
5. Ours
6. We're

BOOK I/ ANSWER KEY   **179**

Exercise 14

1. You
2. you
3. Yours
4. You're
5. Your
6. You

Exercise 15

Answers will vary, but some possible answers are:

1. A. Who cooks the meals in your house?
   B. My mother does.
2. A. Who makes your bed?
   B. I do.
3. A. Who pays the bills?
   B. My parents do.
4. A. Who washes the dishes?
   B. My brother and I do.
5. A. Who shops for groceries in your house?
   B. We all do.
6. A. Who washes the clothes?
   B. My brother does.
7. A. Who vacuums the carpet?
   B. I do.
8. A. Who dusts the furniture?
   B. I do.
9. A. Who sweeps the floor?
   B. My brother does.

Exercise 16

1. Who
2. Who's
3. Whose
4. Whom

Exercise 17

B. *My* teacher's name is Charles Flynn.
A. *Mine* is Marianne Petters. She's Mr. Flynn's wife.
B. Oh, really? His last name is different from *hers*.
A. Yes. She uses *her* father's last name, not her *husband's*.
B. Do they have children?
A. Yes.
B. *Whose* name do the children use?
A. *Their* children use both last names.
B. How do you know so much about *your* teacher and *her* children?
A. We talk about *our* names in class. We also talk about American customs. She explains her customs and we explain *ours*.
B. Mr. Flynn doesn't talk about *his* family in class.
A. Do you call *him* "mister"?
B. Of course. *He's* the teacher. We show respect.
A. But we call Marianne by *her* first name. *She* prefers that.
B. I prefer to call *our* teachers by *their* last names. That's the way we do it in my country.
A. And in *mine* too. But *we're* in the U.S. now. There's an expression: When in Rome, do as the Romans do.

LESSON FIVE TEST / REVIEW

Part 1

1. your
2. he's
3. it's
4. C; C; C
5. C
6. C
7. Her; C
8. C
9. the teacher's first name
10. My brothers' wives
11. You're
12. My brother's
13. Whose umbrella is this?
14. her husband's mother
15. their
16. C; C
17. C
18. Who has
19. My friend and I
20. C

Part 2

1. a
2. a
3. b
4. c
5. b
6. a
7. c
8. a
9. a
10. b
11. c
12. d
13. a
14. d
15. b
16. c
17. c

Part 3

1. my
2. your
3. I
4. it
5. your
6. you
7. '
8. her
9. s'
10. her
11. 's
12. her
13. 's
14. her
15. 's
16. Her
17. our
18. 's
19. 's
20. Their
21. '
22. ours
23. 's
24. them
25. their
26. 's
27. her
28. Her
29. 's
30. his
31. him
32. He's
33. his
34. him

LESSON SIX

Exercise 1

1. are
2. ing
3. are
4. ing
5. 'm; ing
6. major
7. wearing
8. throw

Exercise 2

Answers will vary, but some possible answers are:

1. It's improving because he's practicing a lot.
2. He's learning to play the guitar.
3. He's taking five courses.

4. He's unhappy because the food in the dorm is fattening.
5. They're thinking about getting an apartment next semester.
6. He's wearing a sweater and jeans.
7. I'm majoring in economics.
8. I'm taking twelve credit hours.

Exercise 3

1. planning
2. opening
3. sitting
4. beginning
5. hurrying
6. happening
7. staying
8. growing
9. marrying
10. grabbing
11. writing
12. fixing
13. wiping
14. carrying
15. drinking
16. driving
17. waiting
18. serving
19. visiting
20. preferring

Exercise 4

1. is living
2. are gaining
3. is not majoring
4. are making; throwing
5. is writing
6. am filling
7. is making
8. are using
9. are not studying
10. are finishing

Exercise 5

Answers will vary, but some possible answers are:

1. I'm sitting in the back of the room.
2. I'm not speaking my native language.
3. I'm paying attention.
4. I'm asking questions.
5. I'm learning the present continuous tense.
6. I'm not looking out the window.
7. I'm looking at the blackboard.
8. I'm not writing a composition.
9. I'm using my textbook.
10. I'm not wearing jeans.

Exercise 6

Answers will vary, but some possible answers are:

1. I'm looking for a new apartment.
2. I'm learning a lot of English.
3. I'm not gaining weight.
4. I'm losing weight.
5. I'm not spending a lot of money.
6. I'm saving my money.
7. I'm writing a term paper.
8. I'm trying to understand American customs.
9. I'm meeting Americans.
10. I'm not learning how to drive.
11. I'm not living in a dorm.
12. I'm planning to return to my hometown.

Exercise 7

Answers will vary, but some possible answers are:

1. A. Is the teacher wearing a sweater?
   B. No, he isn't.
2. A. Is the teacher writing on the blackboard?
   B. Yes, he is.
3. A. Is the teacher erasing the blackboard?
   B. No, he isn't.
4. A. Is the teacher sitting at the desk?
   B. No, he isn't.
5. A. Is the teacher taking attendance?
   B. No, he isn't.
6. A. Is the teacher explaining the grammar?
   B. Yes, he is.
7. A. Is the teacher helping the students?
   B. Yes, he is.
8. A. Are we practicing the present continuous tense?
   B. Yes, we are.
9. A. Are we practicing the past tense?
   B. No, we aren't.
10. A. Are we reviewing Lesson 6?
    B. No, we aren't.
11. A. Are we making mistakes?
    B. No, we aren't.
12. A. What is the teacher wearing?
    B. He's wearing a jacket and tie.
13. A. Where is the teacher standing?
    B. He's standing in front of the blackboard.
14. A. What exercise are we doing?
    B. We're doing exercise 7.
15. A. What are you thinking about?
    B. I'm thinking about lunch.

Exercise 8

Answers will vary, but some possible answers are:

1. A. Are you planning to buy a car?
   B. No, I'm not.
2. A. Are you studying biology this semester?
   B. No, I'm not.
3. A. Are you taking other courses this semester?
   B. Yes, I am.
4. A. Are you looking for a new apartment?
   B. Yes, I am.
5. A. Are you looking for a job?
   B. No, I'm not.
6. A. Is your English improving?
   B. Yes, it is.
7. A. Is your vocabulary growing?
   B. Yes, it is.
8. A. Is the teacher helping you?
   B. Yes, she is.
9. A. Are the students making progress?
   B. Yes, they are.
10. A. Are you learning about other students' countries?
    B. Yes, I am.

Exercise 9

1. A. Is Dan living in an apartment?
   B. No, he isn't. He's living in a dormitory.
2. A. Is he majoring in art?
   B. No he isn't. He's majoring in music.
3. A. Is he studying the guitar?
   B. Yes, he is. He's learning to play the guitar.
4. A. Is his roommate majoring in chemistry?
   B. Yes, he is.

5. A. Is Dan wearing a new sweater?
   B. Yes, he is.
6. A. Is he taking 10 credit hours?
   B. No, he isn't. He's taking 18 credit hours.
7. A. What is Dan majoring in?
   B. He's majoring in music.
8. A. How many courses is Dan taking?
   B. He's taking five courses.

Exercise 10

Answers will vary, but some possible answers are:

1. A. What tense are we practicing?
   B. We're practicing the present continuous tense.
2. A. What kind of book are we using?
   B. We're using a grammar book.
3. A. Why are you listening to the teacher?
   B. Because she's explaining something.
4. A. Why is the teacher helping the students?
   B. Because they're having trouble with the exercise.
5. A. Which question am I answering?
   B. You're answering question number 5.
6. A. What kind of questions are we practicing?
   B. We're practicing present continuous questions.
7. A. Why is your English ability improving?
   B. Because I'm working hard.
8. A. How is your life changing?
   B. I'm living in a different culture. OR I'm learning a new language.
9. A. How many courses are you taking?
   B. I'm taking four courses.

Exercise 11

1. A. What instrument is he learning?
   B. He's learning the guitar.
2. A. Why is he gaining weight?
   B. Because the dormitory food is greasy.
3. A. Who is he studying with? OR With whom is he studying?
   B. He's studying with some friends.
4. A. What's he wearing?
   B. He's wearing a new sweater.
5. A. Why is his English improving?
   B. Because he's living with an American.
6. A. How many courses is he taking?
   B. He's taking five courses.
7. A. What kind of students is he meeting.
   B. He's meeting students from all over the world.

Exercise 12

Answers will vary, but some possible answers are:

1. A. I'm wearing jeans. Are you wearing jeans?
   B. Yes, I am.
2. A. I'm not holding a pencil. Are you holding a pencil?
   B. Yes, I am.
3. A. I'm not chewing gum. Are you chewing gum?
   B. No, I'm not.
4. A. I'm thinking about the weekend. Are you thinking about the weekend?
   B. Yes, I am.

5. A. I'm living in a dorm. Are you living in a dorm?
   B. No, I'm not.
6. A. I'm not planning to take a vacation. Are you planning to take a vacation?
   B. No, I'm not.
7. A. I'm looking for a new job. Are you looking for a new job?
   B. No, I'm not.
8. A. I'm planning to buy a computer. Are you planning to buy a computer?
   B. Yes, I am.
9. A. I'm taking a computer class this semester. Are you taking a computer class this semester?
   B. No, I'm not.
10. A. I'm getting tired. Are you getting tired?
    B. Yes, I am.
11. A. I'm not gaining weight. Are you gaining weight?
    B. No, I'm not.
12. A. I'm learning about the history of the U.S. Are you learning about the history of the U.S.?
    B. Yes, I am.
13. A. I'm not learning how to drive. Are you learning how to drive?
    B. No, I'm not.

Exercise 13

Answers will vary, but some possible answers are:

A. Hello?
B. Hi. It's Betty.
A. Oh, hi, Betty. This connection is so noisy. Where are you calling from?
B. I'm calling from the car. I'm on the cell phone.
A. Are you driving home now?
B. No, I'm not. I'm going to the airport.
A. Why are you going to the airport?
B. I'm going to pick up a client of mine.
A. I can't hear you. There's so much noise.
B. Airplanes are flying overhead. They're very low.
A. I can't hear you. Talk louder please.
B. I am talking as loud as I can. I am going to the airport to pick up a client of mine. I'm late. Her plane is landing now and I'm stuck in traffic. I'm getting nervous. Cars aren't moving.
A. Why aren't they moving?
B. There's an accident on the highway.
A. I worry about you. Are you wearing your seatbelt?
B. Of course, I'm wearing my seat belt.
A. That's good.
B. What are you doing now?
A. I'm using the computer. I'm looking for information about cars on the Internet.
B. What are the kids doing?
A. The kids? I can't hear you.
B. Yes, the kids.
A. Meg is watching TV. Pam is doing her homework.
B. Why isn't Meg doing her homework?
A. She doesn't have any homework today.
B. Are you preparing dinner for the kids?
A. No, I'm not preparing dinner. I'm waiting for you to come home and prepare the dinner.
B. Please don't wait for me. Oh. Traffic is finally moving. Talk to you later.

Exercise 14

1. am eating
2. eat
3. am also observing
4. is wearing
5. wear
6. is wearing
7. is wearing
8. use
9. is using
10. write
11. belong
12. sits
13. stands
14. stand up
15. enters
16. study
17. is taking
18. are you taking
19. take
20. is waiting

Exercise 15

1. am studying
2. are using
3. need
4. are comparing
5. don't remember
6. see
7. am not looking; am looking
8. don't need
9. are not writing
10. don't hear
11. are learning
12. know

Exercise 16

1. is smelling
2. smell
3. are thinking
4. think
5. am having
6. have
7. do not have
8. has; am having
9. is looking
10. looks

Exercise 17

1. is writing
2. is sitting
3. sees
4. goes

5. writes
6. thinks; wants
7. is looking; are kissing
8. looks
9. is thinking
10. are wearing
11. wear
12. seem

Exercise 18

1. The mother isn't feeding the baby.
2. Dan isn't sitting in class.
3. He doesn't understand American customs.
4. Arab men and women don't kiss in public.
5. They don't use their hands to eat spaghetti.
6. He isn't wearing earrings in both ears.
7. Arabs don't seem strange to him.
8. Dan doesn't like to take care of a baby.
9. Moslem women never wear shorts.

Exercise 19

1. Is Dan writing his homework? No, he isn't.
2. Is he watching American people? Yes, he is.
3. Does he understand American customs? No, he doesn't.
4. Do American women wear shorts in the summer? Yes, they do.
5. Is he eating a hot dog? Yes, he is.

Exercise 20

1. To whom is he writing a letter? OR Who is he writing a letter to?
2. Why does he want to know about American customs?
3. Where are they putting on makeup?
4. Why do American men and women touch and kiss in public?
5. How often does he write to his family?
6. Why isn't he using a fork?
7. Why don't women wear shorts in some countries?
8. Why do Americans wear blue jeans?
9. What does "behavior" mean?

LESSON SIX TEST / REVIEW

Part 1

1. Why aren't you listening to me?
2. I usually go home after class. OR Usually I go home after class.
3. C
4. C
5. Does she need help with her homework?
6. C
7. Why is he studying now?
8. Does he have any children?
9. C
10. My teacher speaks English well.
11. I speak my native language at home.
12. The baby's sleeping now.
13. When does summer begin?
14. Where does your family live?

Part 2

1. am looking
2. am returning
3. Do you want
4. am waiting
5. are working
6. need
7. Do you like
8. like
9. wears
10. has
11. seems
12. think
13. does Bob teach
14. usually work
15. helps
16. Does he give
17. doesn't believe
18. doesn't he believe
19. thinks
20. says
21. are working
22. sounds
23. are you asking
24. am thinking
25. fill
26. see
27. is walking

Part 3

1. doesn't want
2. isn't looking
3. aren't talking
4. don't have
5. don't work
6. doesn't give
7. isn't waiting
8. doesn't seem
9. isn't returning

Part 4

1. Does he like tests? No, he doesn't.
2. Does Teresa have time? No, she doesn't.
3. Are they talking about their teachers? Yes, they are.
4. Does Bob ever wear a suit to class? No, he doesn't.

5. Does Alicia want to go for coffee? No, she doesn't.
6. Do American teachers seem strange to Teresa? No, they don't.
7. Is Alicia working on a geography project? No, she isn't.

Part 5

1. Why does he sound interesting?
2. Why doesn't he like tests?
3. What kind of projects are they working on?
4. How often does she study in the library?
5. What kind of book is she looking for?
6. Why is Teresa waiting for her friend?
7. Why aren't her classmates writing a term paper?

LESSON SEVEN

Exercise 1

Answers will vary, but some possible answers are:

1. will be
2. will give
3. will buy
4. will read
5. will open

Exercise 2

Answers will vary, but some possible answers are:

1. are going to send
2. are going to open
3. am going to bring
4. are going to go
5. are going to be

Exercise 3

Answers will vary, but some possible answers are:

1. I'm going to get something to eat after class.
2. I'm not going to watch TV tonight.
3. I'm going to eat dinner at home tonight.
4. I'm not going (to go) to the library this week.
5. I'm going (to go) shopping for groceries this week
6. I'm going to stay home this weekend.
7. I'm not going to take a vacation this year.
8. I'm not going to move to another apartment this year.
9. I'm going to buy a car this year.

Exercise 4

Answers will vary, but some possible answers are:

1. The teacher is going to give a test soon.
2. The test isn't going to be hard.
3. Most students are going to pass the test.
4. I am going to pass the test.
5. The teacher isn't going to give everyone an "A."
6. My English is going to improve.
7. We are going to finish this book by the end of the semester.
8. The next test is going to cover the future tense.
9. We are going to have a party at the end of the semester.

Exercise 5

Answers will vary, but some possible answers are:

1. am going to open
2. am going to go to
3. is going to eat
4. am going to call her
5. am going to buy
6. is going to go to
7. am going to quit
8. am going to move
9. are going to fly here

Exercise 6

Answers will vary, but some possible answers are:

1. There won't be another world war.
2. The economy of the U.S. will get worse.
3. People in the U.S. will have fewer children.
4. Americans will live longer.
5. Health care will improve.
6. Cars will use solar energy.
7. Divorce will increase.
8. Crime will not get worse.
9. People won't get tired of computers.
10. Technology will continue to grow.

Exercise 7

Answers will vary, but some possible answers are:

1. I'll take him fishing.
2. I'll take her to a restaurant.
3. I'll buy him a new radio.
4. I'll buy him some CDs.
5. I'll buy her a new swimsuit.
6. I'll take him to a movie.

Exercise 8

1. will always
2. will do
3. will work
4. will have; will be
5. will grow
6. will be
7. will not look

Exercise 9

Answers will vary, but some possible answers are:

1. I'll open it for you.
2. I'll pick up stamps for you.

3. I'll cook.
4. I'll type up your composition on my computer.
5. I'll drive.
6. I'll pay for dinner.
7. I'll lend you the money.
8. I'll get the phone.

Exercise 10

Answers will vary, but some possible answers are:

1. A. Are you going to watch TV tonight?
   B. Yes, I am.
   A. What show are you going to watch?
   B. The news.
2. A. Are you going to listen to the radio?
   B. Yes, I am.
   A. When are you going to listen to the radio?
   B. On the way home from class.
3. A. Are you going to read the newspaper?
   B. Yes, I am.
   A. What newspaper are you going to read?
   B. *The Daily News.*
4. A. Are you going to eat dinner tonight?
   B. Yes, I am.
   A. Who are you going to eat dinner with?
   B. With my roommate.
5. A. Are you going to take a shower?
   B. Yes, I am.
   A. When are you going to take a shower?
   B. Before dinner.
6. A. Are you going to go shopping?
   B. Yes, I am.
   A. Why are you going to go shopping?
   B. Because I need shoes.
7. A. Are you going to call someone?
   B. Yes, I am.
   A. Whom are you going to call?
   B. My mother.
8. A. Are you going to use a computer?
   B. Yes, I am.
   A. Why are you going to use a computer?
   B. Because I need to do research on the Internet.
9. A. Are you going to do your homework?
   B. Yes, I am.
   A. When are you going to do your homework?
   B. Tonight.

Exercise 11

Answers will vary, but some possible answers are:

1. A. Are you going to go back to your country?
   B. Yes, I am.
   A. Why are you going to go back to your country?
   B. Because I want to see my family.
2. A. Are you going to study something new?
   B. Yes, I am.
   A. What are you going to study?
   B. I'm going to study economics.
3. A. Are you going to look for a job?
   B. Yes, I am.
   A. When are you going to look for a job?
   B. After graduation.

4. A. Are you going to get an "A" in this course?
   B. No, I'm not.
   A. What grade are you going to get?
   B. I'm going to get a "B."
5. A. Are you going to transfer to another school?
   B. Yes, I am.
   A. Why are you going to transfer to another school?
   B. Because this school doesn't have the program I want.
6. A. Are you going to visit other American cities?
   B. Yes, I am.
   A. Which cities are you going to visit?
   B. I'm going to visit San Diego and San Francisco.
7. A. Are you going to buy a computer?
   B. Yes, I am.
   A. Why are you going to buy a computer?
   B. Because it will help me with my school work.

Exercise 12

1. I have	5. will I do
2. will I have	6. Will; be; will; be
3. Will I be	7. will I live?
4. will pay for	8. Will there be

Exercise 13

1. hatch; will have	4. will go; have
2. will sell; are	5. will notice; wear
3. sell; will have	6. see; will want

Exercise 14

Answers will vary, but some possible answers are:

1. I'll feel much happier.
2. I'm going to go to a movie.
3. I'll give you a call.
4. I'll have to start looking for a job.
5. I'll miss the U.S. a lot.
6. I'm going to live on a beach.
7. I'll be able to get a better job.

Exercise 15

Answers will vary, but some possible answers are:

1. my English will get better.
2. I won't pass the course.
3. I'll lose this apartment.
4. I'll take you out to dinner.
5. I'm going to have to study this weekend.
6. we're going to go to the movies.
7. I'll be able to buy a car.

Exercise 16

Answers will vary, but some possible answers are:

1. will write OR are going to write
2. will give OR am going to give
3. will we have OR are we going to have
4. do not take
5. will get
6. Will you tell OR Are you going to tell
7. will you give OR are you going to give
8. Will it be OR Is it going to be
9. study

10. are we going to study OR will we study
11. Will we finish OR Are we going to finish
12. When will the semester be
13. will give OR am going to give

Exercise 17

Answers will vary, but some possible answers are:

Will we be able to use dictionaries on the exams?
Are you going to give us daily quizzes?

Exercise 18

1. Are you going to buy OR Will you buy
2. leave
3. will you be in OR are you going to be in
4. are you going to live OR will you live
5. get
6. will decide
7. Are you going to work OR Will you work
8. are you going to study OR will you study
9. will you return OR are you going to return
10. will return OR am going to return
11. graduate
12. will you graduate OR are you going to graduate
13. Will you miss me OR Are you going to miss me
14. Will you write to me
15. I'll write
16. find

Exercise 19

1. are going to invite OR will invite
2. will it be OR is it going to be
3. are going to have OR will have
4. Are you going to buy OR Will you buy
5. am going to use OR will use
6. am going to wear OR will wear
7. are you going to live OR will you live
8. are going to live OR will live
9. finishes
10. gets
11. will get OR are going to get

12. won't be OR isn't going to be
13. are not going to have OR won't have
14. Are your parents going to come OR Will your parents come
15. are going to take OR will take
16. When are you going to get
17. will send OR are going to send
18. will be

Exercise 20

1. will have; graduates
2. often studies
3. rarely go
4. are thinking
5. are saving

Exercise 21

1. don't have
2. don't want
3. isn't working
4. don't depend
5. won't graduate

Exercise 22

1. Is Katie a student? Yes, she is./No, she isn't.
2. Are they thinking about having children? Yes, they are./No, they aren't.
3. Will Jason have a good job? Yes, he will./No, he won't.
4. Is Katie attending college now? Yes, she is./No, she isn't.
5. Are they going to have five children? Yes, they are./No, they aren't.

Exercise 23

1. Why are they saving their money?
2. Why don't they want to depend on their parents?
3. When will Jason make good money?
4. Why does Jason want to be a lawyer?
5. Why isn't Katie going to work when her children are small?
6. When will Jason pay back his student loans?
7. Why don't they go out very much?
8. What college is Jason attending?
9. When is he going to graduate?
10. Who is earning money now?
11. Who wants to help them?
12. How are they learning about responsibilities?

LESSON SEVEN TEST / REVIEW

Part 1

1. will you
2. will buy
3. Are you going to eat
4. he; C
5. I am going
6. C
7. They're going to graduate
8. I will be happy; know
9. am going to leave
10. C; C
11. will be
12. C

Part 2

1. are going to
2. is going to
3. will
4. will
5. will OR am going to
6. will OR is going to
7. will OR are going to
8. will
9. will OR is going to

Part 3

1. isn't going to invite
2. won't wear
3. am not going to buy
4. won't help
5. aren't going to meet

Part 4

1. Will they send money. No, they won't.
2. Are you going to invite your relatives? Yes, I am.
3. Are they going to open the gifts? Yes, they are.
4. Will they need things for their bathroom? Yes, they will.
5. Will there be food at the party? Yes, there will.

Part 5

1. How will they use the money?
2. What kind of gift are you going to send?
3. When will they thank us?
4. Where are they going to get married?
5. Why aren't they going to open the gifts?
6. How many people will there be at the wedding?
7. Who will give money?

TEST ON COMPARISON OF TENSES

Part 1

1. is working
2. is sleeping
3. have
4. am
5. go
6. is
7. walk
8. drive
9. watches
10. am studying
11. am going to take
12. think
13. will help
14. is
15. are going (to go) OR will go
16. are going to visit OR will visit
17. lives
18. are going to spend OR will spend
19. get
20. will send

Part 2

1. isn't writing
2. doesn't take
3. aren't going to visit
4. doesn't go
5. don't go
6. won't go

Part 3

1. Is her husband sleeping? No, he isn't.
2. Does she ever walk to school? Yes, she does.
3. Is she going to take a math class? Yes, she is.
4. Will she go to Montreal? Yes, she will.
5. Is she going to send Judy a letter? No, she isn't.
6. Is she writing a letter now? Yes, she is.
7. Does her sister-in-law live in Toronto? No, she doesn't.

Part 4

1. A. What is her husband doing?
   B. He's working on his car.
2. A. What course is she taking?
   B. She's taking English and math.
3. A. Who watches her baby?
   B. Her mother does.
4. A. What course is she going to take?
   B. She's going to take a computer course.
5. A. Where will they go for Christmas?
   B. They'll go to Montreal.
6. A. Where does she live?
   B. She lives in Montreal.
7. A. Why doesn't she usually drive to school?
   B. Because the school is only a few blocks from her house.

LESSON EIGHT

Exercise 1

1. played
2. studied
3. decided
4. wanted
5. liked
6. showed
7. looked
8. stopped
9. happened
10. carried
11. enjoyed
12. dragged
13. dropped
14. started
15. followed
16. preferred
17. liked
18. mixed
19. admitted
20. developed

Exercise 3

1. dreamed
2. studied
3. started
4. used
5. tried
6. stayed
7. offered
8. decided
9. died
10. lived
11. changed

Exercise 4

1. were
2. was
3. were
4. were
5. was
6. was
7. Were
8. was
9. were

Exercise 5

1. The airplane wasn't common transportation in the early 1900s.
2. Lindbergh wasn't from Kansas.
3. Earhart's last flight wasn't successful.
4. The Wright Brothers' first plane wasn't in the air for many hours.
5. Earhart wasn't an inventor.
6. There weren't a lot of planes 100 years ago.
7. The Wright Brothers weren't born in the twentieth century.

Exercise 6

1. Was the telephone an important invention? Yes, it was.
2. Were the Wright Brothers inventors? Yes, they were.
3. Was Lindbergh American? Yes, he was.
4. Was travel by plane common 75 years ago. No, it wasn't.
5. Were there airplanes 100 years ago? No, there weren't.
6. Were you in class yesterday. Yes, I was. OR No, I wasn't.
7. Were you interested in the story about the aviators? Yes I was. OR No, I wasn't.
8. Were you born in the U.S.? Yes, I was. OR No, I wasn't.

Exercise 7

Answers will vary, but some possible answers are:

1. I was born in Nepal.
2. I was sad when I left my country.
3. No one was with me on my trip to the U.S.
4. I was happy when I arrived in the U.S.
5. Everybody moved very quickly.
6. Yes, I was.
7. My cousins were at the airport to meet me.
8. It was cold.

Exercise 8

1. A. Why was Lindbergh a hero?
   B. Because he was the first person to fly from New York to Paris nonstop.
2. A. What nationality was Earhart?
   B. She was American.
3. A. How old was Lindbergh when he crossed the Atlantic?
   B. He was twenty-five.
4. A. Why wasn't her last flight successful?
   B. Because she disappeared somewhere over the Pacific Ocean.
5. A. Who were the Wright Brothers?
   B. They were American inventors.
6. A. When was Earhart born?
   B. She was born in 1897.
7. A. Why were the Wright Brothers famous?
   B. Because they invented the first powered airplane.

Exercise 9

1. was
2. thought
3. put, drove
4. flew, fell
5. saw
6. wrote

Exercise 10

1. had
2. became
3. read
4. sold
5. built
6. had
7. made
8. flew
9. saw
10. heard
11. brought

Exercise 11

1. didn't fly
2. didn't want
3. didn't write
4. didn't stay
5. didn't think
6. didn't see
7. didn't go
8. didn't put
9. didn't walk
10. didn't dream

11. didn't sell
12. didn't have
13. didn't build
14. didn't want

Exercise 12

Answers will vary, but some possible answers are:

1. changed
2. got
3. applied
4. studied
5. sold
6. said
7. didn't buy
8. didn't have
9. wasn't
10. didn't go
11. didn't understand
12. didn't know

Exercise 13

Answers will vary, but some possible answers are:

1. I found a job in a restaurant three days after I arrived.
2. I registered for English classes the first week I was in the U.S.
3. My husband and I didn't rent an apartment right away. We lived with friends.
4. We bought a car after one year.
5. I got a Social Security card two months ago.
6. I got a driver's license a week before we bought our car.
7. We visited the Art Museum last week.
8. We saw relatives the day we arrived in the U.S.
9. We didn't buy clothes when we arrived in the U.S. We bought all our clothes before we left our country.
10. We went to the bank the day after we arrived in the U.S.

Exercise 14

Answers will vary, but some possible answers are:

1. I didn't receive a letter last week.
2. I wrote three letters on Sunday.
3. I went to the library on Tuedsay and Thursday.
4. I did my laundry on Sunday morning.
5. I didn't buy groceries this week. I had plenty of food in the house.
6. I made a long-distance call to my parents.
7. I bought a magazine to read about my favorite movie star last week.
8. I worked hard all week.
9. I didn't look for a job because I had to study for exams.
10. I didn't rent any videos this week.
11. I sent an email to my friend in Italy last week.
12. I didn't read a newspaper last week because I was too busy.

Exercise 15

Answers will vary, but some possible answers are:

1. Yes, I did.
2. Yes, I did.
3. Yes, I did.
4. No, I didn't, but I thought I did.
5. No, I wasn't.
6. Yes, I finished high school just before I left my country.
7. No, I didn't own a car.
8. Yes, I had a part-time job.

9. Yes, I thought about my future a lot.
10. Yes, I was happy in my country, but I'm happy here too.

Exercise 16
1. Did his brother die in 1912? No, he didn't.
2. Did Goddard build an airplane? No, he didn't.
3. Did Lindbergh love to fly? Yes, he did.
4. Did Earhart cross the Ocean? Yes, she did.
5. Did Earhart work for the U.S. Postal System? No, she didn't.
6. Did Earhart become famous? Yes, she did.
7. Did Lindbergh disappear? No, he didn't.
8. Was Earhart born in the twentieth century? No, she wasn't.
9. Did the Wright Brothers win money for their first flight? No, they didn't.
10. Did people believe Goddard at first? No, they didn't.
11. Did Goddard dream about flight? Yes, he did.
12. Did the Americans send a rocket into space in 1957? No, they didn't.
13. Did the Americans put a man in space in 1961? Yes, they did.
14. Did Goddard see the first moon landing? No, he didn't.

Exercise 17
1. did the Wright brothers build their plane
2. did the first plane crash
3. was the plane
4. didn't newspapers report
5. did Lindbergh work
6. did he cross the ocean
7. did he win
8. was he
9. did his plane land
10. did Lindbergh die
11. didn't Earhart return
12. was Earhart born
13. did she disappear
14. was Earhart with
15. did the first man walk on the moon
16. didn't Goddard see

Exercise 18
1. When was Lindbergh born? He was born in 1902.
2. What kind of toy did the Wright Brothers' father give them? He gave them a flying toy.
3. What kind of shop did they have? They had a bicycle shop.
4. Where did they design airplanes? They designed airplanes in their bicycle shop.
5. When did they fly their first plane? They flew their first plane in 1903.
6. How many seconds did the first plane stay in the air? It stayed in the air for 12 seconds.
7. Why didn't the U.S. government want to see the airplane at first? They didn't want to see the plane because they didn't believe it.
8. What did Goddard invent? Goddard invented the rocket.
9. Why did Goddard take his rocket to his aunt's farm? He took it to his aunt's farm to see if it would fly.

10. Why did people laugh at Goddard? They laughed at Goddard because they didn't believe him.

Exercise 19
Answers will vary, but some possible answers are:

1. A. I graduated from high school.
   B. When did you graduate from high school?
   A. I graduated from high school five years ago.
2. A. I studied biology.
   B. When did you study biology?
   A. I studied biology last year.
3. A. I bought an English dictionary.
   B. Where did you buy an English dictionary?
   A. I bought it in a store near my house.
4. A. I left my country.
   B. When did you leave your country?
   A. I left my country three months ago.
5. A. I came to the U.S.
   B. Why did you come to the U.S.?
   A. I came to the U.S. to join my family.
6. A. I brought my clothes to the U.S.
   B. What else did you bring to the U.S.?
   A. I brought a few books and some family photographs.
7. A. I rented an apartment.
   B. Where did you rent an apartment?
   A. I rented an apartment near my work.
8. A. I started to study English.
   B. When did you start to study English?
   A. I started to study English 15 years ago.
9. A. I chose this college.
   B. Why did you choose this college?
   A. I chose this college because it's in a big city.
10. A. I found my apartment.
    B. When did you find your apartment?
    A. I found an apartment my first week in the U.S.
11. A. I started to study English.
    B. When did you start to study English?
    A. I started to study English five years ago.
12. A. I got married.
    B. When did you get married?
    A. I got married ten years ago.

Exercise 20
Answers will vary, but some possible answers are:

1. A. I participated in a sport.
   B. What sport did you participate in?
   A. I participated in swimming.
2. A. I enjoyed school.
   B. What subject did you enjoy most?
   A. I enjoyed mathematics the most.
3. A. I got good grades in school.
   B. How did you get good grades?
   A. I studied hard.
4. A. I didn't take music lessons.
   B. Why didn't you take music lessons?
   A. I have never been interested in playing an instrument.
5. A. I didn't live with my grandparents.
   B. Why didn't you live with your grandparents?
   A. My grandparents lived in a different city.

6. A. I got an allowance.
   B. What did you do with your allowance?
   A. I went to see movies.
7. A. I had a pet.
   B. What kind of pet did you have?
   A. I had a cat.
8. A. I didn't live on a farm.
   B. Why didn't you live on a farm?
   A. Because my family preferred living in a city.
9. A. I didn't play soccer.
   B. Why didn't you play soccer?
   A. I'm not very athletic.
10. A. I studied English.
    B. How long did you study English?
    A. I studied English for five years.
11. A. I had a bike.
    B. How often did you ride the bike?
    A. I rode my bike every day.
12. A. I thought about my future.
    B. How often did you think about your future?
    A. I thought about my future all of the time!

Exercise 21

1. Neil Armstrong
2. Charles Lindbergh
3. Goddard
4. Earhart
5. Lindbergh
6. T. Roosevelt
7. *The New York Times*

Exercise 22

Answers will vary, but some possible answers are:

1. A. Who brought a dictionary to class today?
   B. I did.
   A. What kind of dictionary did you bring?
   B. I brought a Spanish-English dictionary.
2. A. Who drank coffee this morning?
   B. I did.
   A. How much coffee did you drink?
   B. I drank 2 cups of coffee.

3. A. Who wrote a composition last night?
   B. I did.
   A. For what class did you write a composition?
   B. I wrote the composition for my American history class.
4. A. Who watched TV this morning?
   B. I did.
   A. What did you watch?
   B. I watched the morning news.
5. A. Who came to the U.S. alone?
   B. I did.
   A. Why did you come to the U.S. alone?
   B. I came alone because my family was already here.
6. A. Who made a long distance call last night?
   B. I did.
   A. Who did you call?
   B. I called my mother in Argentina.
7. A. Who studied English before coming to the U.S.?
   B. I did.
   A. How long did you study English?
   B. I studied English for one year.
8. A. Who bought a newspaper today?
   B. I did.
   A. Which newspaper did you buy?
   B. I bought *The New York Times*.

Exercise 23

1. came
2. were you
3. moved
4. was
5. did you move
6. were
7. were you
8. was
9. did you stay
10. came
11. Did they come
12. didn't
13. found
14. saved
15. brought
16. didn't come
17. started
18. arrived
18. supported
20. did
21 didn't go
22. had
23. got
24. started
25. did you chose

LESSON EIGHT TEST / REVIEW

Part 1

1. decided to fly
2. stayed
3. did Lindbergh cross
4. was born
5. C
6. did Goddard invent
7. did Goddard die
8. C
9. C
10. saw
11. was
12. walked
13. C
14. didn't return
15. C
16. didn't believe
17. C
18. did men land
19. C
20. C

Part 2

1. ate
2. saw
3. got
4. sat
5. hit
6. made
7. took
8. found
9. said
10. read
11. drank
12. built
13. stopped
14. left
15. bought
16. thought
17. ran
18. carried
19. sold
20. stood

Part 3

1. weren't
2. didn't fly
3. wasn't
4. didn't invent
5. didn't die
6. didn't go
7. didn't come
8. wasn't born
9. didn't build
10. didn't become

Part 4

1. Did Orville Wright become famous? Yes, he did.
2. Was Goddard an aviator? No, he wasn't.

3. Did Earhart fly across the Atlantic ocean? Yes, she did.
4. Was Goddard born in the U.S.? Yes, he was.
5. Did the Wright Brothers write about rockets? No, they didn't.
6. Did the Americans send a man into space? Yes, they did.
7. Did Wilbur Wright die in 1945? No, he didn't.
8. Did Russia put men on the moon in 1969? No, it didn't.
9. Did people laugh at Goddard's ideas in 1969? No, they didn't.
10. Did Goddard think about computers? No, he didn't.

Part 5

1. When did Lindbergh become famous?
2. What did the Wright Brothers invent?
3. Who invented the airplane?
4. When did Earhart cross the ocean?
5. How much money did he get for his flight?
6. Why did she want to fly around the world?
7. How many people saw Lindbergh in Paris?
8. Why didn't Goddard's colleagues believe his ideas?
9. When did Orville Wright die?
10. Which president examined Goddard's ideas?

LESSON NINE

Exercise 1

Answers will vary, but some possible answers are:

1. Fill
2. Don't use
3. Write
4. include
5. Don't write
6. fill
7. include
8. Put
9. Bring

Exercise 2

Answers will vary, but some possible answers are:

1. Don't talk
2. Come home
3. Wash your hands
4. Look both ways
5. Don't fight with
6. Don't play
7. Write to
8. Finish your homework

Exercise 3

Answers will vary, but a possible answer is:

10. how to use a washing machine
    Put the clothes in the machine and add some detergent. Close the lid of the machine. Choose the water temperature. Put coins in the slot of the washing machine. Push them in. The washer will start working.

Exercise 4

Answers will vary, but some possible answers are:

1. Don't forget to do your homework.
2. Pass your papers to the front of the classroom.
3. Keep your eyes on your own paper.

Exercise 5

Answers will vary, but some possible answers are:

A. I need to cash a check.
B. We need to get some groceries. Let's go to the supermarket.
A. Do you want to drive there?
B. The supermarket is not so far. Let's walk.
A. It looks like rain.
B. No problem. Let's take an umbrella.
A. Let's hurry. It's late and the store will close soon.
B. Don't worry. This store is open 24 hours a day.

A. We're almost out of dog food. Let's buy a 20-pound bag.
B. Let's not walk then. I don't want to carry a 20-pound bag home. Let's drive instead.

Exercise 6

Answers will vary, but some possible answers are:

1. Let's have class outside.
2. Let's not have a test on Monday.
3. Let's invite a famous person to class.

Exercise 7

Answers will vary, but some possible answers are:

1. I love to go to the beach.
2. I like to play tennis.
3. I need to have my hair cut.
4. I expected to get a letter yesterday.
5. I want to go to the movies this weekend.
6. I'm planning to buy a TV soon.
7. I need to understand Americans better.
8. I don't need to have a car.
9. I tried to learn to play the piano, but I gave it up.

Exercise 8

Answers will vary, but some possible answers are:

1. A. Do you expect to pass this course?
   B. Yes, I do.
2. A. Do you plan to graduate soon?
   B. No, I don't.
3. A. Do you plan to transfer to another college?
   B. No, I don't.
4. A. Do you like to read?
   B. Yes, I do.
5. A. Do you like to study grammar?
   B. No, I don't.
6. A. Do you try to understand Americans?
   B. Yes, I do.
7. A. Do you try to learn idioms?
   B. Yes, I do.
8. A. Do you expect to return to your country?
   B. No, I don't.

Exercise 9

Answers will vary, but some possible answers are:

1. A. Do you want to take a computer course next semester?
   B. Yes, I do.
   A. Why do you want to take one?
   B. Because I want to be able to get a job.
2. A. Do you want to move?
   B. Yes, I do.
   A. Why do you want to move?
   B. Because I live really far from school.
3. A. Do you want to return to your country?
   B. Yes, I do.
   A. When do you want to return to your country?
   B. Next year.
4. A. Do you want to get a job?
   B. Yes, I do.
   A. What kind of job do you want to get?
   B. I want to get a job in a hotel.
5. A. Do you want to become an American citizen?
   B. Yes, I do.
   A. Why do you want to become an American citizen?
   B. Because I want my children to grow up here.
6. A. Do you want to transfer to a different school?
   B. Yes, I do.
   A. Why do you want to transfer to a different school?
   B. Because this school doesn't have the kind of program I want.
7. A. Do you want to take another English course next semester?
   B. Yes, I do.
   A. Which course do you want to take?
   B. I want to take "Introduction to American Literature."
8. A. Do you want to learn another language?
   B. Yes, I do.
   A. What language do you want to learn?
   B. I want to learn Arabic.
9. A. Do you want to review the last lesson?
   B. No, I don't.
   A. Why don't you want to review the last lesson?
   B. Because I know the material by heart.

Exercise 10

Answers will vary, but some possible answers are:

1. another language.
2. the word "desks."
3. a large box of books.
4. a sense of humor.
5. the past tense.
6. irregular verbs.
7. every word in the dictionary.

Exercise 11

Answers will vary, but some possible answers are:

1. to speak another language.
2. to hear with all this noise.
3. to get to New York by train.
4. to be on time for a job interview.
5. to talk on the phone when you're driving.
6. to get a good job.

7. to skip meals.
8. to buy a movie ticket in advance.

Exercise 12

Answers will vary, but some possible answers are:

1. to have so much freedom.
2. to be from my country.
3. to have no classes on weekends.
4. to go out at night.
5. to speak to strangers.
6. to take the test?
7. to hand out the homework?

Exercise 13

Answers will vary, but some possible answers are:

1. Yes, I am happy to be in this country.
2. Yes, it is important to know English in my country.
3. No, I am not afraid to make a mistake when I speak English.
4. Yes, it is possible to find a job without knowing any English.
5. No it isn't easy to learn English grammar.
6. Yes, it is important to wear a seatbelt when you are a passenger in a car.
7. No, it isn't necessary to have a computer.
8. Yes, I was sad to leave my country.
9. Yes, I am prepared to have a test on this lesson.

Exercise 14

Answers will vary, but some possible answers are:

1. look up unfamiliar words.
2. show their appreciation.
3. complain.
4. earn some extra money.
5. look through the classified section to find a job.
6. be allowed into a bar.
7. take a nail out of a wall.
8. loose weight.
9. move the cursor around the screen.
10. prove that you bought the item in that store.

Exercise 15

Answers will vary, but some possible answers are:

1. can
2. can't
3. can
4. can't
5. can
6. can
7. can't
8. can't

Exercise 16

Answers will vary, but some possible answers are:

1. Can you write with your left hand? No, I can't.
2. Can you type sixty words per minute? Yes, I can.
3. Can you use a computer? Yes, I can.
4. Can you play chess? No, I can't.
5. Can you ski? Yes, I can.
6. Can you play the piano? Yes, I can.
7. Can you speak Arabic. No, I can't.
8. Can you bake a cake? No, I can't.

9. Can you play the guitar? Yes, I can.
10. Can you sew? Yes, I can.

Exercise 17

Answers will vary, but a possible answer is:

I can cook well. Sophia can cook well, too.

Exercise 18

Answers will vary.

Exercise 19

Answers will vary, but some possible answers are:

1. He should drink some soda.
2. She should put a bandage on it.
3. He should run water on it.
4. She should take vitamin C.
5. He should get a lot of sleep.
6. She should go to a dentist.
7. He should drink less coffee.
8. She should take a hot bath.

Exercise 20

Answers will vary, but some possible answers are:

1. You should go out and get fresh air.
2. You should get a job and be more independent.
3. You should start studying earlier.
4. You should get a haircut.
5. You should buy some new clothes.
6. You should spend less time on the phone.
7. You should straighten up your room.
8. You should listen to your mother.
9. You should take on more responsibility before you start driving.

Exercise 21

Answers will vary.

Exercise 22

Answers will vary, but some possible answers are:

1. A. Why should they study the lessons?
   B. It helps them improve their English.
2. A. When should the teacher take attendance?
   B. At the beginning of the lesson.
3. A. What else should they bring to class?
   B. A notebook and a pen or pencil.
4. A. Why should I study modals.
   B. Because you can't speak English well without them.
5. A. Why should we register for classes early?
   B. Because popular classes fill up quickly.
6. A. Why should the teacher speak clearly?
   B. So the students can understand his or her instructions.
7. A. Why shouldn't the students talk during a test?
   B. Because everyone is trying to concentrate.
8. A. Where should we do the homework?
   B. You should do the homework at home or in the library.

9. A. Why should the teacher announce a test ahead of time?
   B. So the students can prepare for it.

Exercise 23

1. must
2. must
3. must not OR mustn't
4. must
5. must not OR mustn't
6. must

Exercise 24

Answers will vary, but some possible answers are:

1. You must have a passport.
2. You must not carry a gun onto an airplane.
3. You must not smoke in the classroom.
4. You must not talk during a test.
5. You must not store gasoline in your apartment.
6. You must fill out an application.

Exercise 25

Answers will vary, but some possible answers are:

1. I don't have to wear a suit to school.
2. I have to come to class on time.
3. I don't have to stand up to ask a question in class.
4. I have to do homework.
5. I don't have to notify the teacher if I'm going to be absent.
6. I don't have to call the teacher "professor."
7. I don't have to raise my hand to answer a question.
8. I have to take a final exam.
9. I don't have to wear a uniform.
10. I have to buy my own textbooks.

Exercise 26

Answers will vary, but some possible answers are:

1. A. Do you have to take attendance?
   B. Yes, I do.
2. A. Do you have to give the students a grade?
   B. Yes, I do.
3. A. Do you have to call the students by their last names?
   B. No, I don't.
4. A. Do you have to wear a suit?
   B. No, I don't.
5. A. Do you have to work in the summer?
   B. No, I don't.
6. A. Do you have to have a master's degree?
   B. Yes, I do.
7. A. Do you have to work on Saturdays?
   B. No, I don't.
8. A. Do you have to come to this school every day?
   B. Yes, I do.

Exercise 27

Answers will vary, but some possible answers are:

1. In my country, a teacher has to wear a suit.
2. Teachers have to work on Saturdays.
3. Students have to call the teacher "professor."
4. Students have to stand up to ask a question.

Exercise 28

Answers will vary, but some possible answers are:

1. buy two boxes of cereal
2. buy
3. go to
4. put back
5. send
6. show her driver's license

Exercise 29

Answers will vary, but some possible answers are:

1. be
2. get
3. get a shipment of
4. go down
5. spoil
6. buy a different brand

Exercise 30

Answers will vary, but some possible answers are:

1. you may get a ticket.
2. you may lose your license.
3. they will die.
4. you may not pass the course.
5. you might be robbed.
6. you will get fat.
7. you may be able to buy a car.
8. I may go to the beach.

Exercise 31

W: What would you like to order?
C: I'd like the roast chicken dinner.
W: Anything else?
C: Yes. Would/Could you bring me a salad, please?
W: What kid of dressing would you like?
C: I'd like garlic dressing, please.

. . .

W: Here you are miss.
C: You know, it's a little cold at this table. May/Can I sit at another table?
W: Of course. There's a nice table in the corner. Would you like to sit over there?
C: Thanks, and could/would you bring me another glass of water, please?
W: Of course.

LESSON NINE TEST / REVIEW

Part 1

1. need to cash
2. can I
3. I am afraid
4. C
5. to go
6. It is necessary
7. go
8. can speak English
9. walk
10. must I
11. C
12. want to learn
13. can speak
14. It's impossible to learn
15. C
16. not
17. to meet
18. C
19. to talk
20. should look
21. Do not
22. to check

Part 2

1. to; don't need to learn
2. X; mustn't stop
3. to; doesn't expect to pass
4. to; don't want to study
5. to; doesn't have to give
6. X; might not have
7. to; isn't important to practice
8. to; isn't easy to learn
9. X; Let's not speak
10. X; Don't be

Part 3

Answers will vary, but some possible answers are:

1. Why should I wear a seat belt?
2. Why do you want to buy some grapes?
3. When must he fill out the application?
4. When does she need to drive to New York?
5. Why can't I park at a bus stop?
6. Why is it necessary to eat vegetables?
7. Why does she have to buy a car?
8. When would they like to see me?

Part 4

1. Could
2. can
3. Can
4. may
5. should
6. Do I have to
7. don't have to
8. should
9. may
10. will
11. would
12. Can
13. should

LESSON TEN

Exercise 1

Answers will vary, but some possible answers are:

1. water
2. milk
3. cholesterol
4. sugar
5. nutrition
6. cream
7. calcium

Exercise 2

Answers will vary, but some possible answers are:

1. a piece of
2. a pound of
3. a loaf of
4. a slice of
5. a pound of
6. a bowl of
7. five pounds of
8. a spoon of

9. ten gallons of
10. a can of
11. three pieces of

12. six rolls of
13. a bowl of
14. an ear of

Exercise 3

1. a lot of
2. a lot of
3. A lot of OR Many
4. a lot of OR much
5. a lot of OR many

6. a lot of
7. many
8. much
9. much
10. a lot of

Exercise 4

1. a little
2. a few
3. a little
4. a few
5. A few

6. a little
7. a few
8. a little
9. a little
10. a few

Exercise 5

1. some
2. any
3. any
4. any
5. some

6. an
7. any
8. a
9. any

Exercise 6

Answers will vary, but some possible answers are:

1. There's one Polish student in this class.
2. There are three Spanish-speaking students in this class.
3. There are two Americans in this class.
4. There aren't any children in this class.
5. There are seven women in this class.
6. There are five men in this class.
7. There's one teacher in this class.
8. There are two American citizens in this class.
9. There aren't any senior citizens in this class.
10. There are three teenagers in this class.

Exercise 7

1. a lot of
2. no
3. any
4. a little
5. a lot of

6. a little
7. much
8. a little
9. some
10. any; no

Exercise 8

Answers will vary, but some possible answers are:

1. A. Do you eat much rice?
   C. Yes, I eat a lot of rice.
2. A. Do you eat much fish?
   B. No, I don't eat much fish.
3. A. Do you eat much chicken?
   B. Yes, I eat a lot of chicken.
4. A. Do you eat much pork?
   C. No, I don't eat any pork.
5. A. Do you eat much bread?
   B. Yes, I eat a lot of bread.

6. A. Do you eat much cheese?
   B. Yes, I eat a lot of cheese.
7. A. Do you drink much apple juice?
   B. No, I don't drink much apple juice.
8. A. Do you drink much lemonade?
   B. I drink a little lemonade.
9. A. Do you drink much milk?
   B. No, I don't drink a lot of milk.
10. A. Do you drink much tea?
    B. Yes, I drink a lot of tea.
11. A. Do you drink much coffee?
    B. No, I drink very little coffee.
12. A. Do you drink much soda?
    B. No, I don't drink soda at all.

Exercise 9

Answers will vary, but some possible answers are:

1. A. Do you have any money with you now?
   B. No, I don't have any money with me now.
2. A. Do you have any credit cards?
   B. Yes, I have some credit cards.
3. A. Do you have any bread at home?
   B. Yes, I have some bread at home.
4. A. Do you have any bananas at home?
   B. No, I don't have any bananas at home.
5. A. Do you have any orange juice in your refrigerator?
   B. Yes, I have some orange juice in my refrigerator.
6. A. Do you have any plants in your apartment?
   B. No, I don't have any plants.
7. A. Do you have any family pictures in your wallet?
   B. Yes, I have some family pictures in my wallet.
8. A. Do you have time to relax?
   B. Yes, I have a little time to relax.

Exercise 10

1. a few
2. a lot of
3. any
4. much
5. a lot of
6. many

7. a lot of
8. a lot of
9. much
10. much
11. a lot of
12. a lot

Exercise 11

Answers will vary, but some possible answers are:

W. Would you like any coffee, sir?
D. Yes, and please bring me some cream too. I don't need any sugar. And I'd like a glass of orange juice too.
A few minutes later:
W. Are you ready to order, sir?
D. Yes, I'd like the scrambled eggs with 3 strips of bacon. And some pancakes too.
W. Do you want some syrup with your pancakes?
C. Yes. What kind do you have?
W. We have a few different kinds: strawberry, cherry, blueberry, maple. . .
C. I'll have the strawberry syrup. And bring me some butter too.

After the customer is finished eating:
W. Would you like some dessert?
C. Yes, I'd like a slice of cherry pie. And put a scoop of ice cream on the pie. And I'd like a little more coffee, please.

After the customer eats dessert:
W. Would you like anything else?
D. Just the check. I don't have any cash with me. Can I pay by credit card?
W. Of course.

Exercise 12

Answers will vary, but some possible answers are:

1. much; I won't be able to finish it.
2. many; I won't make good grades.
3. much; I'll ruin my teeth.
4. many; I'll get behind my studies.
5. much; is bad for your heart.

Exercise 13

Situation A	Situation B
1. too	1. too
2. too many	2. too many
3. too	3. too
4. too	4. too much
5. too much	5. too many

Exercise 14

Answers will vary, but some possible answers are:

My dormitory is too big. There are too many students in it. Some of them drink too much on the weekends and make too much noise.

Exercise 15

1. a lot of/many
2. too

3. too
4. a lot of
5. too much/a lot of
6. a lot of
7. a lot of
8. too many/a lot of; too much/a lot of
9. a lot of
10. too much/a lot of

Exercise 16

Answers will vary, but some possible answers are:

D. I'm looking at your lab results and I see that your cholesterol level is very high. Also your blood pressure is too high. Do you use a lot of salt on your food?
P. Yes, doctor. I love salt. I eat a lot of potato chips and popcorn.
D. That's not good. You're overweight too. You need to lose 50 lbs. What do you usually eat?
P. For breakfast I usually grab a cup of coffee and a doughnut. I don't have much time for lunch, so I eat a bag of potato chips and drink a can of soda while I'm working. I'm so busy that I have no time to cook at all. So for dinner, I usually stop at a fast-food place and get a burger and fries.
D. That's a terrible diet! How much exercise do you do?
P. I never exercise. I don't have much time at all. I own my own business and I have a lot of work. Sometimes I work 80 hours a week.
D. I'm going to give you an important piece of advice. You're going to have to change your lifestyle.
P. I'm too old to change my habits.
D. You're only 45 years old. You're too young to die. And if you don't change your habits, you're going to have a heart attack. I'm going to give you a booklet about staying healthy. It has some information that will teach you about diet and exercise. Please read it and come back in six months.

LESSON TEN TEST / REVIEW

Part 1

Answers will vary, but some possible answers are:

1. any
2. many
3. many
4. C
5. too
6. C
7. any
8. a
9. a lot of
10. C
11. C
12. C
13. C
14. four glasses of milk
15. pounds of sugar
16. How many
17. C
18. C
19. a lot of
20. some good advice
21. too
22. a lot of cassettes
23. C
24. many
25. C

Part 2

Answers will vary, but some possible answers are:

1. glass
2. cup
3. carton
4. piece
5. piece
6. piece
7. slice
8. sheet
9. pound
10. bowl

Part 3

1. much
2. A few
3. some
4. an
5. some
6. any
7. a few
8. a
9. much
10. much

LESSON ELEVEN

Exercise 1
1. frustrated
2. 7
3. hard
4. graduated
5. equally

Exercise 2
Answers will vary, but some possible answers are:

1. large
2. difficult
3. young
4. interesting
5. beautiful
6. inspiring
7. rich
8. fast

Exercise 3
Answers will vary, but some possible answers are:

1. A. Do you prefer a big city or a small one?
   B. I prefer a small one.
2. A. Do you prefer an old house or a new one?
   B. I prefer a new one.
3. A. Do you prefer a cold climate or a warm one?
   B. I prefer a cold one.
4. A. Do you prefer a small car or a big one?
   B. I prefer a big one.
5. A. Do you prefer a soft mattress or a hard one?
   B. I prefer a hard one.
6. A. Do you prefer green grapes or red ones?
   B. I prefer green ones.
7. A. Do you prefer red apples or yellow ones?
   B. I prefer yellow ones.
8. A. Do you prefer strict teachers or easy ones?
   B. I prefer strict ones.
5. A. Do you prefer noisy children or quiet ones?
   B. I prefer quiet ones.
10. A. Do you prefer used textbooks or new ones?
    B. I prefer new ones.

Exercise 4
1. letter carrier
2. phone call
3. cell phone
4. paint brush
5. driver's license
6. earrings
7. wedding ring
8. garbage can
9. winter holiday
10. TV program
11. math course
12. flower shop
13. tooth brush

Exercise 5
1. False
2. True
3. True
4. False
5. False
6. False

Exercise 6
1. closely
2. well
3. frequently
4. slowly
5. unnecessarily
6. fast
7. immediately

Exercise 7
1. beautifully
2. responsibly
3. neatly
4. well
5. cheerfully
6. fluently
7. politely
8. hard
9. sadly
10. patiently
11. correctly

Exercise 8
Answers will vary, but some possible answers are:

1. I speak English slowly.
2. I speak my native language fluently.
3. I dance badly.
4. I walk fast.
5. I study hard.
6. I do my homework carefully.
7. I drive carefully.
8. I sing well.
9. I type slowly.
10. I work hard.
11. I dress for class quickly.
12. I dress for a party carefully.

Exercise 9
Answers will vary, but some possible answers are:

1. I cook well.
   I dance well.
2. I don't swim well.
   I don't sew well.
3. I speak quickly.
   I eat quickly.
4. I do my homework slowly.
   I walk slowly.
5. I learned to drive easily.
   I learned to cook easily.

Exercise 10
A. I heard you moved last month.
B. Yes, we did. The move was difficult. We had terrible movers. They didn't behave responsibly. They arrived late and worked slowly. So the move was very expensive. And they didn't do a good job.
A. What happened?
B. They were so careless with the furniture. They broke a few of my favorite dishes.
A. You seem very upset about this.
B. Of course I'm upset.
A. Well, the move's over now. Are you happy with your new apartment?
B. We like the apartment. It's very big and comfortable. All of our furniture fits easily. But we're not happy with our rude neighbors. They have loud fights. I can hear them clearly right through the walls. I think both of them are crazy. And they have a dog. The dog barks constantly. I can't sleep peacefully with all the noise.
A. Are you going to talk to them about it?

B. I already did. I tried talking to them politely. They said that would try to be more quiet but nothing changed. I'm so angry.

A. When you were polite, nothing changed. You need to speak to them more directly and honestly. Tell them to be quiet or you're going to call the police.

Exercise 11

1. too
2. very
3. very
4. too

5. very
6. too
7. very
8. too
9. too
10. very
11. very
12. very
13. too

Exercise 12

1. too hard
2. old enough
3. too sick
4. enough money
5. enough experience
6. strong enough
7. too heavy
8. enough exercise

LESSON ELEVEN TEST / REVIEW

Part I

1. old; shoe
2. too
3. very
4. C
5. C
6. C; very
7. too
8. well
9. worried
10. C
11. C
12. married
13. is located
14. C; a large one
15. Happy
16. very much

3. He ate breakfast early.
4. She opened the door slowly.
5. C
6. C

Part 3

1. neat; sloppily
2. carefully; fast
3. fluently; hard
4. easily; difficult
5. accurately; carefully
6. soft; loudly
7. beautifully; sick
8. responsible; childishly
9. carefully; foolishly
10. regularly; lazy

Part 2

1. I got my driver's license last year.
2. My brother is only 15 years old. He's not old enough to drive.

LESSON TWELVE

Exercise I

1. isn't
2. California
3. Isn't
4. Alaska
5. Hispanic

Exercise 2

1. more interesting; the most interesting
2. younger, the youngest
3. more beautiful; the most beautiful
4. better; the best
5. more common OR commoner;
6. the most common OR the commonest
7. thinner; the thinnest
8. more carefully; the most carefully
9. prettier; the prettiest
10. worse; the worst
11. more famous; the most famous
12. luckier; the luckiest
13. simpler OR more simple;
14. the simplest OR the most simple
15. higher; the highest
16. more delicious; the most delicious
17. farther; the farthest
18. more foolishly; the most foolishly

Exercise 3

1. The biggest
2. The longest
3. The highest
4. the most important
5. the commonest OR the most common
6. the most popular
7. the most expensive
8. the most beautiful
9. the best
10. the tallest
11. the worst
12. the oldest

Exercise 4

Answers will vary, but some possible answers are:

1. My brother is the most intelligent person in my family.
2. My mother is the kindest person in my family.
3. My cousin Martha is the most beautiful person in my family.
4. I'm the most stubborn person in my family.
5. My cousin Don is the laziest person in my family.
6. My uncle David is the tallest person in my family.

7. My aunt Katherine is the most serious person in my family.
8. My sister Louise is the most nervous person in my family.
9. The strongest person in my family is my cousin Peter.
10. The funniest person in my family is my cousin Dick.
11. The most responsible person in my family is my father.
12. I am the neatest person in my family.

Exercise 5

Answers will vary, but some possible answers are:

1. The most exciting sport is soccer.
2. One of the worst wars of this century was the Second World War.
3. One of the worst tragedies in recent U.S. history was the bombing in Oklahoma City.
4. One of the most important inventions of the last hundred of years is the telephone.
5. New York is the most interesting city in the world.
6. Crime is the biggest problem in the U.S. today.
7. The worst job is cleaning up after other people.
8. The best job is supervising other people.
9. Dave Bell is the hardest teacher at this school.
10. Julia Roberts is one of the most popular movie stars.

Exercise 6

Answers will vary, but some possible answers are:

1. My father talks the most in my family.
2. My aunt Carolyn drives the best in my family.
3. My brother walks the fastest in my family.
4. My sister speaks English the best in my family.
5. My brother stays up the latest in my family.
6. My father gets up the earliest in my family.
7. My grandmother speaks the most softly in my family.
8. My brother eats the most in my family.

Exercise 7

Answers will vary, but some possible answers are:

1. My sister spends the most money.
2. I get the most mail.
3. My aunt drinks the most coffee.
4. My sister spends the most time in the bathroom.
5. My sister and I spend a lot of time on the telephone.
6. My little brother has the worst temper.
7. My sister wears the most makeup.

Exercise 8

1. smaller
2. more
3. less expensive
4. slower
5. more dangerous

Exercise 9

Answers will vary, but some possible answers are:

1. My father is taller than my mother.
2. My mother is more educated than my father.
3. My mother is friendlier than my father.
4. My father is lazier than my mother.
5. My father is thinner than my mother.

6. My father is quieter than my mother.
7. My mother is more stubborn than my father.
8. My father is more patient than my mother.
9. My father is more successful than I am.
10. My mother is stronger than I am.
11. My mother is more nervous than my father.
12. My father is more polite than my mother.

Exercise 10

Answers will vary, but some possible answers are:

1. In general, women are more polite than men.
2. In general, men are stronger than women.
3. In general, men are taller than women.
4. Some men are more intelligent than some women, and some women are more intelligent than some men.
5. In general, women are kinder than men.
6. In general, women are friendlier than men.
7. In general, women are more talkative than men.
8. In general, women are more patient than men.
9. In general, women are more romantic than men.
10. In general, women are more sensitive than men.
11. In general, men are more logical than men.
12. Some women are more responsible than men, and some men are more responsible than women.

Exercise 11

Answers will vary, but some possible answers are:

1. Madrid is more crowded than Dallas.
2. Dallas is more modern than Madrid.
3. Dallas is bigger than Madrid.
4. Madrid is noisier than Dallas.
5. Madrid is more beautiful than Dallas.
6. Madrid is more interesting than Dallas.
7. Madrid is colder in winter than Dallas.
8. Dallas is safer than Madrid.
9. Madrid is dirtier than Dallas.
10. Madrid is sunnier than Dallas.

Exercise 12

Answers will vary, but some possible answers are:

1. In my opinion, men run faster than women.
2. In my opinion, men gossip more than women.
3. In my opinion, women take care of children better than men.
4. In my opinion, women worry more than men.
5. In my opinion, women work harder than men.
6. In my opinion, men drive more foolishly than women.
7. In my opinion, men drive faster than women.
8. In my opinion, women spend more on clothes than men.
9. In my opinion, men think faster than women.
10. Women live longer than men.
11. In my opinion, men get old faster than women.
12. In my opinion, men make decisions faster than women.

Exercise 13

Answers will vary, but some possible answers are:

1. Athens has more traffic than Baltimore.
2. Athens has a better climate than Baltimore.
3. Baltimore has more rain than Athens.

4. Baltimore has more crime than Athens.
5. Athens has more pollution than Baltimore.
6. Baltimore has more job opportunities than Athens.
7. Baltimore has more factories than Athens.
8. Baltimore has more tall buildings than Athens.
9. Athens has more people than Baltimore.
10. Athens has more sunshine than Baltimore.
11. Baltimore has more homeless people than Athens.

Exercise 14

Answers will vary, but some possible answers are:

1. Women have an easier life than men. Men have more to worry about.
2. Women live longer than men. They take better care of themselves.
3. American women have an easier life than women in my country. They have a lot more freedom and more money to spend.
4. American couples have fewer children than couples in my country. Both parents usually work, so it's difficult to take care of more than one or two children.
5. Married men are more responsible than single men. They have to think of their wives and children.
6. American teenagers have more freedom than teenagers in my country. Their parents give them more independence.
7. American teenagers have less responsibility than teenagers in my country. They don't have as many duties inside and outside the house.
8. American children have more toys than children in my country. Parents spend more money on toys in this country.
9. American children don't have as good an education as children in my country. My country has a very good educational system.
10. American teachers have higher salaries than teachers in my country. Salaries are higher in America.
11. American teachers get less respect than teachers in my country. Students are more respectful in my country.

Exercise 15

1. bigger than	6. the most crowded
2. the biggest	7. more crowded
3. more intelligent than	8. the most beautiful
4. the most intelligent	9. The shortest
5. more crowded than	10. shorter than

Exercise 16

Answers will vary, but some possible answers are:

A. I'm planning to visit Chicago.
B. You're going to love it. It's a beautiful city. In fact, it's one of the most beautiful cities in the U.S.
A. It's the second largest city, isn't it?
B. Not any more. Los Angeles is now bigger than Chicago.
A. What should I see while I'm there?
B. You can visit the Sears Tower. It's the biggest building in the U.S. It has 110 stories. On a clear day, you can see many miles.
A. Did you go to the top when you were there?
B. When I was there, the weather was bad. It was raining. I hope you have better weather than I had. When are you going?
A. In August.
B. Ugh! August in the worst month of the year. It's often 90 degrees or more. If you get hot, you can always go to the beach and cool off.
A. Is Chicago near an ocean?
B. Of course not. It's near Lake Michigan.
A. Is it big like Lake Washington?
B. It's much bigger than Lake Washington. In fact, it's one of the largest lakes in the U.S.
A. Is it very rainy?
B. Not in the summer. It's sunny. In fact, it's much dryer than Seattle.
A. What do you suggest that I see?
B. You should see the famous architecture downtown. The most famous architects in the U.S. built buildings in Chicago.
A. Do I need to take taxis everywhere or does Chicago have a good public transportation system?
B. Taxis are so expensive! They're much more expensive than the buses and trains. You should use the public transportation. But remember there's a lot of crime in Chicago, so it's not safe to travel alone at night. It's better in the daytime.
A. Does Chicago have higher crime than Seattle?
B. Yes. But if you're careful, you'll be OK. I'm sure you'll enjoy it. It's an interesting place because it has people from all over the world. In fact, I think it's one of the most interesting cities in the U.S.

LESSON TWELVE TEST / REVIEW

Part 1

1. the youngest students	7. oldest
2. older than	8. C
3. the tallest	9. C
4. more educated than	10. bigger
5. C	11. better than
6. the biggest	12. easier

Part 2

1. I have more problems than you.
2. I woke up earlier than you.
3. Paris is the most beautiful city in the world.
4. C
5. You type faster than I do.
6. C

7. Your car is more expensive than my car.
8. C
9. C
10. C

Part 3

1. the highest
2. worse than
3. the most common
4. more populated than

5. the longest
6. better than
7. the largest
8. more quickly than
9. better than
10. friendlier than
11. more carefully than
12. the best
13. more fluently than
14. more intelligent

LESSON THIRTEEN

Exercise 1

1. is too.
2. does too.
3. did too.
4. will too.
5. can too.

Exercise 2

1. doesn't either.
2. can't either.
3. won't either.
4. isn't either.
5. didn't either.

Exercise 3

1. doesn't.
2. does.
3. can.
4. didn't.
5. will.

Exercise 4

Answers will vary, but some possible answers are:

1. but Paraguay doesn't.
2. but Paraguay isn't.
3. and Paraguay does too.
4. and Paraguay doesn't either.
5. but Paraguay didn't.
6. but Paraguay wasn't.
7. but Paraguayans don't.
8. but Paraguayans do.
9. and Paraguayan schools are too.
10. and Paraguay does too.

Exercise 5

Answers will vary, but some possible answers are:

1. I speak Spanish, and Carlos does too.
2. I'm not interested in football, and Carlos isn't either.
3. I'm interested in soccer, and Carlos is too.
4. I don't have a car, but Carlos does.
5. I use the Internet, but Carlos doesn't.
6. I can't drive, but Carlos can.
7. I plan to go back to my country, and Carols does too.
8. I'm going to buy a computer this year, and Carlos is too.
9. I wouldn't like to live in a small American town, but Carlos would.
10. I don't exercise everyday, and Carlos doesn't either.
11. I'm not studying math this semester, and Carlos isn't either.
12. I studied English when I was in my country, and Carlos did too.

13. I came to the U.S. directly from my country, and Carlos did too.
14. I haven't finished college in my country, but Carlos did.
15. I'm not a vegetarian, and Carlos isn't either.
16. I have a cell phone, and Carlos does too.

Exercise 6

1. does
2. doesn't either
3. does too
4. would too
5. either
6. don't either

Exercise 7

1. aren't you?
2. can't you?
3. won't we?
4. shouldn't we?
5. isn't there?
6. wouldn't you?
7. isn't it?
8. aren't I?

Exercise 8

1. are you?
2. can he?
3. should we?
4. were you?
5. are there?
6. is it?

Exercise 9

1. doesn't it?
2. don't you?
3. didn't you?
4. doesn't it?
5. didn't they?
6. didn't we?

Exercise 10

1. does she?
2. did he?
3. did you?
4. do we?
5. do I?
6. does she?

Exercise 11

1. weren't we?
2. didn't we?
3. didn't she?
4. isn't it?
5. didn't you?
6. didn't you?
7. didn't she?

Exercise 12

1. can't you?
2. aren't there?
3. do you?
4. won't they?

Exercise 13

A. You don't have a car do you?
B. Yes, I do. (Person B has a car.)
A. You aren't American, are you?
B. No, I'm not. (Person B isn't American.)

A. You don't like this city, do you?
B. No, I don't. (Person B doesn't like this city.)
A. The U.S. is the best country in the world, isn't it?
B. No, it isn't. (Person B doesn't agree with the statement.)
A. You don't speak Russian, do you?
B. No, I don't. (Person B doesn't speak Russian.)
A. You can drive, can't you?
B. No, I can't. (Person B can't drive.)
A. You don't have a watch, do you?
B. Yes, I do. (Person B has a watch.)
A. You work on Saturday, don't you?
B. Yes, I do. (Person B works on Saturday.)

Exercise 14

Answers will vary, but some possible answers are:

1. You're married, aren't you? Yes, I am.
2. You have children, don't you? Yes, I do.
3. You didn't study English in your country, did you? Yes, I did.
4. You have a car, don't you? No, I don't.
5. You don't live alone, do you? No, I don't.

6. You'll take another English course next semester, won't you? Yes, I will.
7. You won't return to your country, will you? No, I won't.
8. You took the last test, didn't you? Yes, I did.
9. You have to work on Saturdays, don't you? Yes, I do.
10. The teacher doesn't speak your language, does he? No, he doesn't.
11. You can type, can't you? Yes, I can.
12. This class isn't too hard for you, is it? No, it isn't.
13. There was a test last Friday, wasn't there? Yes, there was.
14. You don't speak German, do you? No, I don't.
15. I'm asking you a lot of personal questions, aren't I? Yes, you are.

Exercise 15

1. Yes, I do.
2. don't they?
3. No, they don't.
4. is it?
5. No, it isn't.
6. don't you?
7. Yes, I do.
8. are they?
9. Yes, they are.
10. didn't you?
11. No, I didn't.
12. are you?
13. No, I'm not.

LESSON THIRTEEN TEST / REVIEW

Part 1

1. but
2. C
3. No
4. does too
5. either
6. are
7. did
8. C
9. C
10. isn't it?

Part 2

1. do too
2. don't
3. does
4. don't
5. does too
6. doesn't either
7. don't either
8. did too

Part 3

1. isn't she?
2. does she?
3. won't we?
4. don't we?
5. can we?
6. aren't you?
7. is it?
8. shouldn't I?
9. do you?

LESSON FOURTEEN

Exercise 1

1. was
2. stayed
3. is
4. has
5. plays
6. sleep
7. go
8. love
9. go
10. eat
11. had
12. was
13. will try OR are going to try
14. am sitting
15. am getting
16. are playing
17. is reading
18. likes
19. prefer
20. are going (to visit)
21. are going to leave OR will leave
22. will be OR are going to be
23. have
24. will write
25. will return OR are going to return
26. will call
27. get
28. will tell

Exercise 2

1. didn't go
2. aren't staying
3. doesn't have
4. aren't
5. doesn't play
6. won't be
7. doesn't like
8. aren't going
9. aren't going to spend

Exercise 3

1. Does her husband like to swim? Yes, he does.
2. Is her husband getting a suntan now? No, he isn't.
3. Does her husband prefer the sun? No, he doesn't.
4. Does Jane get up early every day? No, she doesn't.
5. Did they eat dinner in a French restaurant? No, they didn't.
6. Does the hotel have tennis courts? Yes, it does.
7. Was the flight comfortable? Yes, it was.
8. Will they visit Saint John? No they won't.
9. Are there a lot of children at the beach? Yes, there are.

Exercise 4

1. A. How did they get to Puerto Rico?
   B. They went by plane. OR They flew there.
2. A. Why isn't Ed sitting in the sun?
   B. Because he prefers the shade.
3. A. Where did they eat dinner last night?
   B. They ate in a Puerto Rican restaurant.
4. A. When will Jane call Rosemary?
   B. She'll call her when she gets home.
5. A. Where are the children playing now?
   B. They're playing in the water.
6. A. What time are they going to leave on Friday?
   B. They're going to leave at 7 o'clock on Friday morning.
7. A. Who plays tennis every morning?
   B. Ed plays tennis every morning. OR Ed does.
8. A. Why doesn't Jane go shopping in the morning?
   B. Because she usually sleeps late.
9. A. How many swimming pools are there at the hotel?
   B. There are two swimming pools at the hotel.

Exercise 5

I come from India. I decided to move to the U.S. ten months ago. It was difficult to leave my friends and family, but I wanted to come to the U.S. and have more opportunities.

When I lived in India, I was a draftsman. When I cam to the U.S. in July, I didn't find a job at first because my English wasn't good enough. Last September I found a job in a laundromat. I don't like my job at all. I want to find a better job soon. I know I will get a better job when I speak English better. I am saving my money now. When I have enough money, I will begin to take engineering courses at the university. My parents will be proud of me when I graduate.

Right now, I am taking ESL courses at a college near my house. I studied English in India, but it was different from American English. When I listen to Americans at my job or on TV, I can't understand a lot of things they say. Sometimes when I speak with Americans at my job, they don't understand me. They sometimes laugh at my pronunciation. They aren't bad people, but they don't understand that it is hard to learn another language and live in another country. I usually stay by myself at work. I know I should practice more, but I'm very shy.

When I was in India, I lived in a big house with my parents, sisters and brothers, and grandparents. No I have a small apartment and live alone. Sometimes I am lonely. I would like to get married someday, but first I want to earn some money and save for my future.

Exercise 6

1. didn't study
2. doesn't want to work
3. isn't going to study
4. isn't taking
5. isn't saving
6. don't know
7. shouldn't
8. can't understand

Exercise 7

1. Will he study accounting? No, he won't.
2. Do Indians understand him? Yes, they do.
3. Is he studying American history now? No, he isn't.
4. Does he live with his family? No, he doesn't.
5. Can he understand American English? No, he can't.
6. Is it hard to live in another country? Yes, it is.
7. Does he want to get married next year? No, he doesn't.
8. Did he live with his grandparents in India? Yes, he did.

Exercise 8

1. Why is he saving his money?
2. When is he going to get married?
3. Who laughs at him?
4. Why is he lonely?
5. Why aren't his parents in the U.S.?
6. Why didn't he find a job at first?
7. When will he graduate from the university?
8. Why did he come to the U.S. alone?
9. Why don't his coworkers understand his accent?
10. When did he live in a big house?

Exercise 9

Answers will vary, but some possible answers are:

1. How often do we have a test?
   We have a test once a month.
2. Why are we reviewing tenses now?
   Because it will help our English.
3. Why do we need more practice with verbs?
   Because we still make a lot of mistakes.
4. When will we have a final exam?
   We'll have a final exam at the end of this month.
5. Why doesn't the teacher speak fast in class?
   Because she wants to make sure we understand her.
6. What time does the teacher usually come to class?
   She usually comes about five minutes before class begins.
7. When did we study the present tense?
   We studied the present tense last month.
8. Why should we study every day?
   Because it will help us learn English faster.
9. When are we going to finish this lesson?
   We're going to finish this lesson this week.
10. Why is the school closed on January 1st?
    The school is closed January 1st because it's New Year's day.
11. How is the teacher helping the students?
    She is helping them with their pronunciation.
12. What kind of exercise are we doing?
    We're doing a question and answer exercise.
13. When did we read a story about Hellen Keller?
    We read a story about Hellen Keller in chapter eleven.
14. When is vacation going to start?
    It will start in a few weeks.

15. How many students does this class have?
    It has twenty-five students.
16. How does the teacher explain the grammar?
    She explains it very clearly and slowly.
17. Why doesn't the classroom have a computer?
    Because all of the computers are in the computer lab.
18. When did we have a test on modals?
    We had a test on modals a few weeks ago.
19. Why should I register for classes early?
    It will help ensure you get the classes you want.
20. Why is it important to learn English?
    Because you'll have more opportunities.
21. How many questions are there in this exercise?
    There are twenty-seven questions in this exercise.
22. Why shouldn't the teacher speak our language in class?
    Because we are in class to learn English.
23. Who will get an A?
    Students who study very hard will get an A.
24. Who went back to his country?
    Eduardo went back to his country.
25. Who sits near the door?
    Yumiko sits near the door.
26. How many students come from Mexico?
    Twelve students come from Mexico.
27. Who will be our teacher next semester?
    I don't know who our teacher will be next semester.

BOOK 2 / ANSWER KEY

LESSON ONE

Exercise 1
1. 're
2. 's
3. 's
4. are; 're; 're
5. 's
6. are; are
7. 's
8. are
9. 're
10. are

Exercise 2
1. are; 're not
2. 's; isn't
3. 'm; isn't
4. 's. isn't
5. 's; isn't
6. are; aren't
7. 's; isn't
8. is; isn't

Exercise 3
1. son's not; 's; old
2. isn't; 's
3. are
4. are
5. 'is
6. is; 's; old
7. It's
8. 's
9. This
10. window
11. 'm; 's
12. is

Exercise 4
1. Yes, I am. OR No, I'm not.
2. Yes, I am. OR No, I'm not.
3. Yes, she is. OR No, she's not. OR No, she isn't.
4. Yes, they are. OR No, they're not. OR No, they aren't.
5. Yes, they are. OR No, they're not. OR No, they aren't.
6. Yes, it is. OR No, it's not. OR No it isn't.
7. Yes, I am. OR No, I'm not.
8. Yes, it is. OR No, it's not. OR No, it isn't.
9. Yes, there is. OR No, there's not. OR No, there isn't.
10. Yes, it is. OR No, it's not. OR No, it isn't.

Exercise 5
Answers will vary.

1. I'm from Osaka.
2. It's red and white.
3. It's 8 o'clock in Osaka now.
4. Baseball, sumo, and volleyball are popular sports in Japan.
5. Dogs and cats are popular pets in Japan.
6. Toyotas, Hondas, and Mitsubishis are popular cars in Japan.
7. Tokyo is Japan's capital.
8. Keizo Obuchi is the Prime Minister of Japan.
9. November 23 is Labor Day in Japan.
10. Shogatsu is a popular holiday in Japan.

Exercise 6
B. Hello?
A. Hi. This is Alice.
B. Hi, Alice. How are you?
A. I'm fine. This is a long distance call. I'm not at home now.
B. Where are you?
A. I'm at Disneyland.
B. What's Disneyland? Is it a city?
A. No, it's not. It's a park in California.
B. What kind of park is it?
A. It's a place for children to have fun. There are a lot of things to do here.
B. Who's with you?
A. My daughter's with me. We're here for her birthday.
B. How old is she?
A. She's 10 years old. She's very excited about the trip.
B. Why isn't your husband with you?
A. My husband isn't here because he's too busy. Anyway, he's not interested in Disneyland.
B. How is the weather in California?
A. It's sunny and warm. Is it warm in New York?
B. No. The weather here is terrible. It's only 50° and rainy. You're lucky to be in California.
A. Yes, I am. My daughter and I are tired now. And we are hungry. I'll talk to you when I get home.
B. Thanks for calling. Bye.

Exercise 7
1. gives
2. get
3. needs
4. costs
5. talk
6. wants
7. barks
8. travel
9. have
10. has
11. protect
12. loves
13. knows
14. thinks

Exercise 8
1. don't eat
2. don't like
3. doesn't sleep
4. don't buy
5. doesn't allow
6. don't need
7. don't go
8. don't like
9. don't have
10. doesn't like

Exercise 9
Answers will vary.

Exercise 10
A. Do you like animals?
B. Yes, I do. In fact, I love animals very much. I especially like dogs.

A. Do you have a dog?
B. No, I don't.
A. If you love dogs, why don't you have a dog?
B. Because my landlord won't permit dogs.
A. Will he permit cats?
B. Yes, he will.
A. Do you have a cat?
B. Yes, I do, but I need to find a new home for my cat. Do you know anyone who wants a cat?
A. Why don't you want your cat?
B. I'm getting married in three months and my girlfriend doesn't want to live with cats.
A. Why doesn't she want to live with cats? Doesn't she like them?
B. She likes them, but she's allergic to them. When she comes over, she sneezes and coughs. She doesn't want to come over any more.
A. That's a big problem.
B. Yes, it is. I need to find a good home for my cat. Do you want my cat?
A. Sorry. My landlord doesn't allow dogs or cats. Maybe you need a new girlfriend.
B. I don't think so. I love her and she loves me.
A. Well, I hope you find a good home for your cat soon.

Exercise 11

Answers will vary.

1. Do you live alone?
   Who do you live with? OR With whom do you live?
2. Do you go to bed early?
   What time do you go to bed?
3. Does the teacher come to class on time?
   What time does she come to class?
4. Does the teacher come from this city?
   Where does she come from?
5. Do you practice English outside of class?
   Who do you practice English with. OR With whom do you practice English?
6. Do you think about your future?
   What else do you think about?
7. Do you complain about English grammar?
   What else do you complain about?
8. Do you listen to the radio?
   What station do you listen to?
9. Does the teacher talk about spelling?
   What else does she talk about?
10. Are you interested in animals?
    What animals are you interested in?
11. Do you come from Mexico?
    Where in Mexico do you come from?
12. Do you go to sleep at midnight?
    What time do you go to sleep?

Exercise 12

1. much
2. do
3. does; cost
4. does it cost
5. much does it cost
6. mean
7. it mean
8. does it mean
9. you say
10. do you say
11. do you say school
12. spell
13. do you
14. do you spell

Exercise 13

A. How is your cousin Bill? I never see him.
B. He's fine. But he doesn't live here anymore.
A. Where does he live now?
B. He lives in L.A. now.
A. What does L.A. mean?
B. L.A. means Los Angeles. We say L.A. for short.
A. Where is L.A.?
B. L.A. is on the west coast. It's in California. I plan to visit him next month.
A. How much does an airplane ticket to Lost Angeles cost?
B. An airplane ticket to Los Angeles costs about $200.
A. Why does he live in L.A.?
B. He lives in L.A. because he goes to school there now.
A. What college does he go to?
B. He goes to Los Angeles City College.
A. Does he like California?
B. Oh, he likes it very much.
A. Do you have his address? I want to write to him.
B. Yes, I have his address. He lives at 734 Sierra Avenue.
A. How do you spell "Sierra"?
B. S-I-E-R-R-A.
A. Sierra sounds like a Spanish word. What does it mean?
B. It means "mountain." Many places in California have Spanish names. In fact, Los Angeles means "the angels."

Exercise 14

1. thinks
2. carries
3. eat
4. asks
5. shares
6. arrives; divide
7. ask
8. don't wait

Exercise 15

Answers will vary.

1. sometimes
2. often
3. always
4. never
5. often
6. usually
7. always
8. frequently
9. never
10. rarely

Exercise 16

Answers will vary.

1. often
2. never
3. rarely
4. usually
5. never
6. always
7. always
8. sometimes
9. often
10. frequently
11. always
12. rarely

Exercise 17

Answers will vary.

1. I rarely talk to my neighbors.
2. I always pay my rent on time.
3. I'm usually busy on Saturdays.
4. I sometimes receive letters from my friends.
5. I often call my family in my country.
6. I occasionally travel in the summer.
7. I sometimes speak English at home with my family.
8. I usually eat meat for dinner.

9. I often go downtown.
10. I hardly ever study in the library.
11. I sometimes eat cereal for breakfast.
12. I always bring my dictionary to class.

Exercise 18

Answers will vary.

1. I rarely cook dinner on Sunday.
2. I usually go to the movies on the weekend.
3. I hardly ever go to bed early.
4. I sometimes go to a club at night.
5. People from my country often visit each other without calling first.

6. People from my country seldom work on weekends.
7. Americans sometimes eat while walking on the street.
8. Americans rarely have more than three or four children.
9. Women from my country hardly ever wear shorts.
10. Men from my country hardly ever help with the housework.

Exercise 19

Answers will vary.

Exercise 20

Answers will vary.

LESSON ONE TEST / REVIEW

Part 1

1. do
2. C
3. don't you
4. does your brother speak
5. doesn't
6. live
7. C
8. doesn't like pizza
9. How do you spell
10. does "occasion" mean
11. does the textbook cost
12. am never
13. C
14. C
15. never
16. C
17. How often
18. Every other day she
19. Needs
20. lives
21. he is
22. France is
23. C
24. It is
25. is located
26. C
27. isn't the teacher
28. is 10 years old
29. am not interested
30. doesn't have
31. am not
32. have
33. She comes

Part 2

1. knows; doesn't know
2. has; doesn't have
3. lives; doesn't live
4. is; isn't
5. understand; don't understand

6. are; are not
7. wait; don't wait
8. asks; doesn't ask

Part 3

1. Does Elena have a dog? No, she doesn't.
2. Does Sofia live in the U.S.? No, she doesn't.
3. Does Sofia have an American friend? No, she doesn't.
4. Do Americans ever ask "How's it going?" Yes, sometimes they do.
5. Do you live in New York? No, I don't. OR Yes, I do.
6. Are American customs strange for Marianne? No, they aren't.

Part 4

1. How do you spell "custom"?
2. Where does Sofia live?
3. What does "kitten" mean?
4. How do you say "How are you?" in Russian?
5. Why isn't "How are you?" a serious question in the U.S.?
6. Why doesn't Marianne wait for an answer?
7. Does Sofia write to Elena once a week?
8. Why do they divide the check in a restaurant?
9. Why doesn't Elena have a dog?
10. Why do you pay for your friends in a restaurant?

LESSON TWO

Exercise 1

1. is sitting
2. isn't sitting
3. is watching
4. is writing
5. are wearing
6. isn't wearing
7. is talking
8. is working
9. is pushing
10. are listening
11. are playing
12. is jogging
13. is playing
14. isn't playing
15. is running
16. are reading
17. am filling
18. aren't studying

Exercise 2

Answers will vary.

1. is shining
2. isn't raining
3. am writing
4. am using
5. aren't doing
6. is helping
7. is wearing
8. am not using
9. aren't practicing
10. am wearing
11. is standing
12. am not sitting

Exercise 3

Answers will vary.

1. I'm learning English.
2. I'm studying psychology and math, too.
3. I'm taking three courses.

Exercise 4

Answers will vary.

1. I'm thinking about taking a vacation. Are you thinking about taking a vacation?
2. I'm starting art lessons soon. Are you starting art lessons soon?
3. I'm going on a diet. Are you going on a diet?

Exercise 5

1. Is Sarah learning
2. Is she wearing
3. Is she sitting
4. Is the man playing
5. Is Sarah writing
6. Are the elderly men playing
7. Are most people wearing
8. Is Sarah trying

Exercise 6

1. Why is she watching Americans?
2. Why isn't she wearing a bathing suit?
3. What are they playing with?
4. Why aren't they relaxing?
5. How is she learning about American customs?
6. Why are they sitting alone?
7. Why is the dog running?
8. Why isn't she sitting in the sun?
9. Who is she writing to?
10. Who is she looking at?
11. What is she writing about?
12. What are they playing?
13. What are they reading?
14. What is she doing?

Exercise 7

Answers will vary.

1. I'm wearing blue jeans now.
2. Pierre is wearing an earring now.
3. I'm not standing in class to answer the teacher's questions.
4. I'm not making a mistake with English grammar now.
5. My teacher is wearing running shoes now.
6. I'm studying a foreign language now.
7. My teacher isn't sitting behind the desk now.
8. I'm writing in my textbook now.

Exercise 8

Answers will vary.

1. Is the teacher giving a test now? No, he isn't.
2. Are the students asking questions now? Yes, they are.
3. Are you using your dictionary now? No, I'm not.
4. Is the teacher explaining the grammar now? Yes, he is.
5. Are you listening to the teacher now? Yes, I am.
6. Is the teacher using the blackboard now? Yes, he is.
7. Are you writing the answers in your book now? Yes, I am.
8. Are the students making mistakes now? No, they aren't.
9. Is the teacher standing in class now? Yes, he is.
10. Are you using a pencil now? No, I'm not.

Exercise 9

1. knows
2. wants
3. seem
4. is talking
5. isn't relaxing
6. sees
7. are playing
8. aren't wearing
9. want; don't care
10. is describing
11. is taking
12. needs

Exercise 10

1. is sitting
2. sits; doesn't like; thinks
3. doesn't know
4. are reading; aren't talking
5. reads; is writing
6. are listening; hears; doesn't like; don't care
7. wants
8. doesn't live
9. doesn't like
10. are looking
11. look
12. is taking
13. doesn't look
14. thinks; don't care
15. loves; wants
16. don't need

Exercise 11

1. When does she like to sit in the park?
2. Why doesn't she like to sit in the sun?
3. Why is she surprised by American customs?
4. Who is he playing Frisbee with? OR With whom is he playing Frisbee?
5. Why do the people in the park seem strange to her?
6. What is Sarah wearing?
7. Why is it bad for the skin?
8. Where is he jogging?
9. Who is she speaking to? OR With whom is she speaking?
10. Where are they playing tennis?
11. Why do they need exercise?
12. Why is she pushing her wheelchair?

Exercise 12

1. Do you want
2. am cooking
3. have
4. am waiting
5. are you doing
6. am studying
7. want
8. need
9. talk
10. have
11. is visiting
12. am preparing
13. sounds
14. is happening
15. are planning
16. don't like
17. doesn't matter
18. matters
19. are thinking
20. don't think
21. don't know
22. hear

Exercise 13

Answers will vary.

1. will increase
2. will be
3. will; live
4. Will; take
5. Will; be

Exercise 14

Answers will vary.

M. I'm worried about you. You will be alone for the first time in your life.
S. Don't worry, Mom. I won't be alone. There will be a lot of people on campus.
M. Who will wash your clothes for you?
S. I'll wash them myself.
M. What will you eat?
S. I'll eat the food in the dorm.
M. Make sure you eat a lot of fruits and vegetables.
S. Don't worry. I will.
M. When will your classes begin?
S. My classes will begin next week.
M. What will you do this week?
S. This week I will meet my new roommate. He's from Germany.
M. When will he arrive
S. He'll probably arrive tomorrow. This week I will unpack my suitcases and set up my computer. Also I will buy my books at the bookstore. I will use a map of the campus and learn how to get around.
M. Will you have enough money?
S. Yes, I'll have enough money. Remember, I have your credit card. But I will only use it for necessary things.
M. Will you call me once a week?
S. Yes, I will call you. And I will send you email too.
M. Will you come home for the holidays?
S. Yes, I will. I'll come home for Thanksgiving and Christmas. But I won't come home for Labor Day.
M. Why won't you come home for Labor Day?
S. Because I won't have enough time.
M. Drive carefully.
S. I will.
M. I will miss you.
S. I'll miss you too, Mom.

Exercise 15

Answers will vary.

1. is going to increase
2. are going to pay
3. is; going to be
4. are; going to take
5. are going to be

Exercise 16

Answers will vary.

1. 's going to rain
2. 'm going to bring
3. 'm going to have
4. 'm going to meet
5. 's going to give us a test soon.
6. 's going to increase
7. 're going to move
8. 's going to retire
9. 'm going to clean
10. 's going to send

Exercise 17

Answers will vary.

1. Are you going to continue to teach English as a Second Language?
2. Are we going to have a final examination?
3. How many classes are you going to teach next semester?

Exercise 18

Answers will vary.

1. A. Where are you going?
   B. I'm going to the park this afternoon. I am going to meet my friend and play tennis with her. I have to return some videos to the video store, but I don't have time.
   A. Give them to me. I'm going to pass that way. I'll return them for you.
2. A. I have to go to the airport. My sister's plane is going to arrive at 4 o'clock this afternoon.
   B. I'll go with you. I'll stay in the car while you go into the airport. That way, you won't have to pay for parking.
3. A. My sister's birthday is next week.
   B. Are you going to give her a birthday present?
   A. Of course, I will.
   B. What are you going to give her?
   A. She loves the theater. I'm going to buy her tickets to a play.
   A. How old will she be?
   B. She'll be 21 years old.
4. Teacher: Next week we are going to have our midterm test.
   Student: Will it be hard?
   Teacher: Yes, but I'll help you prepare for it.
5. Wife: I won't have time to pick up the children this afternoon. I have to work late.
   Husband: Don't worry. I'll pick them up.
   Wife: I won't have time to cook either.
   Husband: Just relax. I'll prepare dinner tonight.
6. Man: I want to marry you.
   Woman: But we're only 19. We're too young.
   Man: I'll be 20 in April.
   Woman: But you don't even have a job.
   Man: I'll find a job.
   Woman: Let's wait a few years.
   Man: I'll wait for you forever. I will always love you.
7. A. Do you want to watch the football game with me on Saturday?
   B. I can't. My brother is going to move. I am going to help him.
   A. Do you need any help?
   B. We need boxes. Do you have any?
   A. No, but I'll look for boxes. I'm going to go to the supermarket this afternoon. I'll get boxes there. I'll bring them to your house.
   B. Thanks.

8. A. I'm so excited. I'm going to get a puppy.
   B. That's a big responsibility. You're never home. How will you take care of it?
   A. My cousin lives with me now. She doesn't have a job. She'll help me take care of the dog.
   B. What about your landlord? Is it OK with him?
   A. I'm not going to tell him.
   B. You have to tell him. He'll know if you have a dog. You have to take the dog out three times a day. And the dog is going to bark.

Exercise 19

1. When I retire, I'm going to live with my children.
   OR I will live with my children when I retire.
2. When I am old, I will take care of myself.
   OR I will take care of myself when I am old.
3. If my parents need help, I'll take care of them.
   OR I'll take care of my parents if they need help.
4. If I am not healthy, I'll live with my children.
   OR I'll live with my children if I am not healthy.
5. If I don't have money, I will get help from the government.
   OR I will get help from the government if I don't have money.
6. After my parents die, I'll move to another city.
   OR I'll move to another city after my parents die.
7. If I get a pension, I won't need to depend on my children.
   OR I won't need to depend on my children if I get a pension.
8. Before I retire, I'm going to save my money.
   OR I'm going to save my money before I retire.

Exercise 20

Answers will vary.

1. When I graduate, I'm going to get a good job.
2. When I graduate, I'm going to find a new apartment.
3. When I graduate, I'll have better English.

Exercise 21

1. 's going (to go)

2. 'll be OR 's going to be
3. 's going to get
4. is he doing OR is he going to do
5. will you do OR are you going to do
6. 'll be OR 's going to be
7. 'll outlive OR 's going to outlive
8. 'll probably need OR 's probably going to need
9. 'll cross
10. are
11. 'll live OR 're going to live
12. 'm
13. 'll take OR 'm going to take
14. 'll change
15. are
16. 'll see
17. 'll drive

Exercise 22

1. are you going to do OR will you do
2. retire
3. sell
4. will move OR am going to move
5. are you going to do OR will you do
6. am going to buy OR will buy
7. am
8. am going to start OR will start
9. will get OR am going to get
10. sell
11. are you going to do OR will you do
12. retire
13. retire
14. save
15. will have OR are going to have
16. don't think
17. comes
18. will not have
19. will worry
20. comes
21. wait
22. are
23. will be OR are going to be
24. are
25. will introduce
26. talk
27. will change

LESSON TWO TEST / REVIEW

Part 1

1. He is sitting
2. C
3. C
4. He's listening to
5. She's going to leave
6. I'm going to watch
7. I'm going to watch
8. are you going to do
9. C
10. There will be
11. I will know
12. will be hungry
13. C
14. I will get
15. C
16. C
17. isn't she
18. C

Part 2

1. are moving OR are going to move
2. have
3. am having OR am going to have
4. 'll need OR are going to need
5. arrives
6. has
7. always likes
8. brings
9. needs

10. are staying
11. is helping
12. 'll come
13. are going to use
14. want
15. will be OR are going to be
16. hear
17. 's calling
18. wants
19. 'll call
20. 'll see

Part 3
1. isn't talking
2. isn't going to move
3. doesn't need
4. won't go
5. won't move
6. doesn't have

Part 4
1. Is her mother helping her pack? Yes, she is.
2. Does her husband work at home? Yes, he does.
3. Does her present apartment have an extra room for the baby? No, it doesn't.
4. Will her friends move the furniture? No, they won't.
5. Is her husband staying home this week? Yes, he is.
6. Is Sue going to have a baby? No, she isn't.

Part 5
1. Why are they going to move to a bigger apartment?
2. Why does her husband need an extra bedroom?
3. Why doesn't she want her friends to help her move?
4. When is she going to have a baby?
5. Why is Bill calling Mary now?
6. When will they use professional movers?

LESSON THREE

Exercise 1
1. was
2. was not
3. were
4. was
5. were not
6. was
7. Was there; was
8. Was she
9. was she
10. weren't they allowed
11. was he; was
12. was he
13. Were his children

Exercise 2
1. ended; continued
2. wanted
3. worked
4. separated
5. attended
6. disliked
7. ordered; refused
8. called
9. arrested
10. organized
11. changed
12. occurred; killed

Exercise 3
1. was
2. became
3. got
4. found
5. had
6. sat
7. got
8. told
9. came
10. heard
11. gave
12. went
13. won
14. shot

Exercise 4
1. didn't live
2. didn't want
3. didn't think
4. didn't believe
5. didn't become
6. wasn't
7. didn't have
8. didn't ride
9. didn't go
10. didn't die

Exercise 5
S. Do you remember Martin Luther King?
T. Of course I do. I saw him on TV many times when I was young.
S. Did you see him on TV when he was in Washington, DC?
T. Yes, I did. I remember his famous speech in Washington in 1963.
S. What did he speak about?
T. He spoke about equality for everyone.
S. Did a lot of people go to Washington?
T. Oh, yes. 250,000 went to Washington.
S. Do you remember when he died?
T. I was in high school when he died. The principal came to our class and told us the news.
S. What did you do when you heard the news?
T. At first we didn't believe it. Then we all started to cry. We went home from school and watched the news on TV.
S. Where was he when he died?
T. He was on the balcony of a hotel in Memphis when a man came and shot him. It was terrible. But we should remember King for his life, not his death. We celebrate Martin Luther King's birthday.
S. Really? I didn't know that. When is it?
T. He was born on January 15th. We don't have school on that date.
S. Did this date become a holiday right after he died?
T. No. It became a holiday in 1985.
S. How do you remember so much about King?
T. I wrote a paper on him when I was in college.

Exercise 6
1. lived
2. started
3. invaded
4. went
5. had
6. went
7. ended
8. returned
9. came
10. got
11. were
12. led
13. thought
14. suffered
15. wanted
16. was
17. didn't want
18. was
19. moved
20. missed
21. died
22. realized
23. had
24. was
25. left
26. went
27. got
28. didn't receive

29. came
30. saw
31. started
32. was
33. was
34. didn't understand
35. learned

36. found
37. began
38. didn't study
39. studied
40. was
41. made

Exercise 7

1. wasn't born
2. didn't go
3. didn't get
4. weren't
5. didn't move
6. didn't die

7. wasn't
8. didn't leave
9. didn't receive
10. didn't learn
11. didn't study

Exercise 8

1. Was Irina born in Moscow? No, she wasn't.
2. Did she live in a small town after the war? No, she didn't.
3. Did their German army invade Ukraine? Yes, it did.
4. Did her family return to their hometown? No, they didn't.
5. Did her daughter live in Lvov until 1989? No, she didn't.
6. Was it hard for Irina to leave her job? Yes, it was.
7. Did she go to Rome? Yes, she did.
8. Did all her friends get permission to come to America? No, they didn't.
9. Did Irina learn English quickly? No, she didn't.

Exercise 9

1. Why did she leave her town in 1941?
2. When did the war end?
3. When did the German army invade her country?
4. Where did her family go after the war?
5. Why did she want to leave her country in the 1980s?
6. How many reasons did she have for leaving her country?
7. When did her father die?
8. Why was her future uncertain in the U.S.?
9. When did her daughter come to the U.S.?
10. Whom did she see in the Chicago airport?
11. Whey didn't she understand English at first?

Exercise 10

Answers will vary. See example.

Exercise 11

Answers will vary.

1. I used to enjoy school.
2. I used to obey my parents.
3. I didn't use to attend religious school.
4. I didn't use to play with dolls.
5. I didn't use to play soccer.
6. I used to draw pictures.
7. I didn't use to have a pet.
8. I didn't use to tell lies.
9. I used to read mystery stories.

Exercise 12

Answers will vary.

1. I used to play the piano.
2. I used to enjoy mysteries.
3. I used to believe in the tooth fairy.
4. I used to believe in Santa Claus.
5. I used to like to eat candy.
6. My parents used to tell me I was a smart child.
7. I used to roller skate.

Exercise 13

Answers will vary.

1. spend my money
2. be a lazy student
3. live with my parents
4. watch TV
5. relax when I came home
6. have long hair
7. walk
8. be heavy
9. do what my parents told me to do
10. use cash for most of my purchases

Exercise 14

Answers will vary.

1. I used to go to private school. Now I go to public school.
2. I didn't used to work. Now I work part time.
3. I used to play soccer. Now I am too busy to play soccer.
4. I used to live in a house. Now I live in an apartment.
5. I used to live with my family. Now I live with my friend.

LESSON THREE TEST / REVIEW

Part 1

1. ate
2. put
3. gave
4. wrote
5. sent
6. listened
7. read
8. took
9. brought

10. talked
11. knew
12. found
13. stood
14. left
15. sat
16. went
17. made
18. heard

19. felt
20. fell

21. got

Part 2

1. was born
2. didn't you eat
3. Did you study
4. did your uncle arrive
5. There were
6. were you

7. Were you afraid
8. C
9. C
10. died
11. decided to drive
12. I was excited

13. C

14. wasn't he

15. did you buy

16. used to live

Part 3

1. wasn't
2. didn't go
3. didn't tell
4. didn't stand
5. didn't come
6. didn't take
7. didn't organize
8. didn't end
9. didn't believe
10. didn't speak

Part 4

1. Why did King become a minister?
2. When was he born?
3. Why didn't he like segregation?
4. Why did black children go to separate schools?

5. Why didn't some restaurants permit black people to eat there?
6. How many times was King in jail?
7. When did he win the Nobel Prize?
8. Where did Parks work?
9. Why was she tired?
10. How many times did she go home by bus?
11. Where did she live?
12. Why didn't she want to obey the law?
13. Why did the police take her to jail?

Part 5

Answers will vary.

1. I used to live with my family. Now I live alone.
2. I used to work full time. Now I'm a full time student.

LESSON FOUR

Exercise 1

1. her; him
2. it
3. it; her
4. it
5. them
6. him
7. them

Exercise 2

1. told
2. say
3. tell
4. tell
5. tell
6. say
7. tell
8. say
9. say
10. say
11. said
12. told

Exercise 3

1. 's
2. 's
3. '
4. '
5. 's
6. '
7. '
8. 's

Exercise 4

1. bride's grandmother
2. teachers' offices
3. windows of the rooms
4. children's toys
5. name of this school
6. women's names
7. Mr. Harris' class
8. parents' house

Exercise 5

1. My
2. her
3. his
4. Their
5. Their
6. our
7. your
8. its

Exercise 6

A. What are you going to wear to your sister's wedding?
B. I'm going to wear my new blue dress.
A. Did your sister buy a new dress for her wedding?
B. No, she's going to borrow her best friend's dress.
A. Will the wedding be at your house?
B. Oh, no. We live in an apartment. Our apartment is too small. We're going to invite over 200 guests. The wedding is going to be at a church. Afterwards, we're going to have a dinner in a restaurant. The restaurant has its own reception hall.
A. Are the newlyweds going on a honeymoon after the wedding?
B. Yes. They have friends who have a cottage. They're going to stay at their friends' cottage in the country for a week.
A. Is the groom's mother a nice woman?
B. I don't know his mother. I'll meet her at the wedding for the first time.

Exercise 7

1. Whose car is that?
2. Whose toys are those?
3. Whose music do you listen to?
4. Whose bike are you using?
5. Whose cooking do you like?
6. Whose dress did the bride borrow?

Exercise 8

1. Mine
2. her
3. Theirs
4. Our
5. My
6. Yours
7. Your

Exercise 9

1. I'm
2. I
3. My
4. My; me
5. Mine

Exercise 10

1. Our
2. We
3. We're
4. us
5. ours

Exercise 11

1. You're
2. You
3. Yours
4. Your
5. you

Exercise 12

1. His
2. He's
3. He
4. His
5. him

Exercise 13

1. Her
2. her
3. She
4. She's; Her
5. Hers

Exercise 14

1. It's
2. It
3. Its
4. it
5. It's

Exercise 15

1. their
2. theirs
3. They're
4. They
5. them

Exercise 16

Answers will vary.

1. Who explains the grammar?
2. How many students speak Spanish?
3. Who usually sits near the door?
4. What usually happens after class?
5. Who wants to repeat this course?
6. Who needs help with this lesson?
7. Who has a computer?
8. How many students live in a dorm?
9. Who has a cell phone?
10. Who lives alone?

Exercise 17

Answers will vary.

1. Who moved last year?
2. Who found a job?
3. Who took a trip recently?
4. Who brought a dictionary to class today?
5. Who passed the last test?
6. Which students came late today?
7. Which student arrived first today?
8. How many students did today's homework?
9. How many students studied English in their countries?
10. How many students brought a cell phone to class?

Exercise 18

1. Who dances the first dance?
2. Who holds the rings?
3. How many people say, "Congratulations"?
4. Which woman wears a white dress?
5. Who pays for the bridesmaids' dresses?

Exercise 19

1. When does the bride throw the bouquet?
2. Which women try to catch the bouquet?
3. On which hand does the groom put the ring?
4. What kind of music does the band play?

5. Who dances with the bride?
6. What kind of presents do the guests give?
7. Who cries at the wedding?
8. What happens after the dinner?

Exercise 20

1. cooks in your house
2. cleans in your house
3. children do you have
4. children go to school
5. one goes to private school
6. do you use
7. does she work for

Exercise 21

1. Who's
2. Who(m)
3. Who
4. Whose
5. Whose

Exercise 22

1. myself
2. yourselves
3. themselves
4. himself
5. herself
6. ourselves
7. yourself
8. yourself
9. themselves
10. itself
11. ourselves
12. yourself; myself
13. yourself
14. yourself

Exercise 23

Answers will vary.

1. I like to walk by myself.
2. I don't like to exercise by myself.

Exercise 24

Answers will vary.

Exercise 25

Frank and Sylvia used to do a lot of things together. They went to movies, went out to restaurants, and took vacations together. But now they are always too busy for each other. They have two children and spend most of their time taking care of them.

Frank and Sylvia bought a house recently and spend their free time taking care of it. It's an old house and needs a lot of work.

When Frank and Sylvia have problems, they try to solve them by themselves. But sometimes Sylvia goes to her mother for advice. Frank never goes to his mother. He doesn't want to bother her with his problems. Frank often complains that Sylvia cares more about the kids and the house than about him.

Sylvia wants to go to a marriage counselor, but Frank doesn't want to go with her. He always says to Sylvia, "We don't need a marriage counselor. We can solve our problems by ourselves. You just need to pay more attention to me. If you want to see a counselor, you can go by yourself. I'm not going." Sylvia feels very frustrated. She thinks that the marriage isn't going to get better by itself.

LESSON FOUR TEST / REVIEW

Part 1
1. the bridesmaids'
2. bride's
3. her
4. his
5. their friends'
6. Their
7. The groom's friends; C
8. C
9. Her best friend's
10. C
11. my husband's mother
12. women's
13. My sister's wedding
14. C
15. her
16. He is
17. C; my wife and I; C
18. My wife and I
19. Got
20. C; the bride's mother
21. C
22. Who threw
23. Their; C
24. Your
25. happened

Part 2
1. b
2. a
3. a
4. b
5. b
6. c
7. c
8. c
9. b
10. a
11. d
12. d
13. d
14. a
15. c

Part 3
1. said
2. told
3. told
4. said
5. said
6. told
7. told
8. told

Part 4
1. does she throw the bouquet
2. try to catch the bouquet
3. does the groom put the ring
4. does the groom kiss
5. ring has a diamond
6. last name does the bride use
7. took pictures at your wedding
8. dress did the bride borrow
9. wedding was bigger
10. came to the wedding
11. cut the cake

Part 5
1. myself
2. herself
3. themselves
4. ourselves
5. himself
6. yourselves
7. yourself

LESSON FIVE

Exercise 1
1. Americans
2. families
3. leaves
4. children
5. Deer
6. cities
7. languages
8. clouds
9. potatoes
10. valleys
11. butterflies
12. men
13. fish
14. wolves
15. donkeys
16. foxes
17. countries
18. months
19. geese
20. women

Exercise 2
1. children
2. daughters
3. million people
4. news is
5. pants are
6. C
7. Every student wants
8. C; subjects
9. Everyone wants
10. C
11. C
12. C

Exercise 3
1. people
2. Men; women; children
3. lives
4. Millions
5. skills
6. months
7. fish
8. families
9. deer; turkeys
10. days

Exercise 4

Answers will vary.

1. have a lot of toys.
2. are very competitive.
3. are slow.
4. are very active.
5. are interesting.
6. make a lot of money.
7. have good careers.
8. help with the housework.

Exercise 5
1. has a challenging job.
2. has an important job.
3. has a rewarding job.
4. has a physically active job.
5. has a well paying job.
6. has a creative job.
7. has a peaceful job.
8. has a glamorous job.
9. has a detail-oriented job.
10. has an exciting job.

Exercise 6

friends = C	medicine = C/NC
meal = C	fish = NC
things = C	skills = C
lives = C	feast = C
men = C	fortune = NC
women = C	families = C
children = C	chief = C
freedom = NC	deer = NC
Indians = C	beans = C
people = C	squash = NC
food = C/NC	bread = C/NC
health = NC	berries = C
months = C	turkeys = C/NC
meat = C/NC	peace = NC
skins = C	friendship = NC
corn = NC	sweet potatoes = C
vegetables = C	cranberries = C
plants = C	

Exercise 7

1. nature; flowers; trees; birds; fish
2. peace; friendship
3. food
4. advice; corn; vegetables; knowledge
5. experience
6. meat; beans; bread; berries
7. fortune
8. plants; medicine
9. jewelry; rings; necklaces
10. information; holidays

Exercise 8

Answers will vary.

1. rolls of
2. pounds of
3. A gallon of
4. cups of
5. a loaf of
6. a piece of
7. bottle of
8. pieces of
9. a piece of
10. gallons of gas

Exercise 9

1. are
2. were; are
3. was
4. were
5. Was there
6. were there
7. will be
8. will there be

Exercise 10

Answers will vary.

1. from 2 o'clock to 3 o'clock.
2. in the Middle East.
3. in New England.
4. in the mall.
5. in big cities.
6. in the Southwest.
7. four years ago.
8. in my new school.
9. a decade ago.
10. the West.

Exercise 11

1. ten million
2. food
3. died
4. Indians
5. skills
6. food
7. Indians
8. Unemployment

Exercise 12

1. There's no university in my hometown.
2. There's a subway in my hometown. It's very efficient.
3. There's no English language newspaper in my hometown.
4. There's no airport in my hometown.
5. There's a soccer team in my hometown. It's a very successful team.
6. There's a river in my hometown. Many people go there to fish.
7. There's no jail in my hometown.
8. There's an art museum in my hometown. It has many beautiful works of art.
9. There's an English language institute in my hometown. I took classes there.
10. There's a cemetery in my hometown. Many of my ancestors are buried there.

Exercise 13

1. any
2. a
3. any
4. some
5. no
6. any
7. an
8. some
9. no
10. any
11. no
12. a

Exercise 14

1. much OR a lot of
2. a lot of OR much
3. Many OR A lot of
4. a lot of
5. much
6. many
7. much
8. much
9. a lot of OR many
10. many

Exercise 15

My name is Colleen Finn. I'm a Ho-chunk Indian. My tribal land is in Wisconsin. But I live in Chicago because there is too much (OR a lot of) unemployment on my reservation and I can't find a good job there. There are a lot of opportunities in Chicago, and I found a job as a secretary in the English Department at Truman College. I like my job very much. I have a lot of responsibilities and I love the challenge.

I like Chicago, but I miss my land, where I still have a lot of relatives and friends. I often go back to visit them whenever I get tired of life in Chicago. My friends and I have a lot of fun together, talking, cooking our native food, walking in nature, and attending Indian ceremonies, such as Pow-Wows. I need to get away from Chicago once in a while to feel closer to nature. Even though there are a lot of nice things about Chicago, there are too many (OR a lot of) cars and trucks in the big city and a lot of (OR too much) pollution. A weekend on the reservation gives me time to relax and smell fresh air.

Exercise 16

Answers will vary.

1. If I try to memorize too many words, I won't remember them all.
2. If I make too many mistakes on my homework, I won't be able to go to a good college.
3. If I spend too much money on clothes, I won't be able to afford a car.
4. If I drink too much coffee, I won't be able to sleep tonight.
5. If I spend too much time with my friends, I will be late for work.
6. If I stay up too late, I will be tired in the morning.

Exercise 17

1. a little
2. a few
3. A little
4. Several OR A few
5. A little
6. A few
7. A little
8. several OR a few
9. a few OR several
10. a little

Exercise 18

1. a little
2. very little
3. very little
4. a little
5. a little
6. very little
7. very little
8. a little
9. Very few
10. a few
11. a few
12. very few
13. a few
14. Very few
15. a few
16. very few
17. a few
18. Very few

Exercise 19

Answers will vary.

Exercise 20

Answers will vary.

Exercise 21

Answers will vary.

Exercise 22

Answers will vary.

Exercise 23

Answers will vary.

1. There's a lot of opportunity to make money in my country.
2. There aren't a lot of divorced people in my country.
3. There are a lot of foreigners in my country.
4. There's a lot of freedom in my country.
5. There aren't many American cars in my country.
6. There are many political problems in my country.
7. There isn't a lot of unemployment in my country.
8. There is a lot of crime in my hometown.

LESSON FIVE TEST / REVIEW

Part 1

1. a
2. friends
3. C
4. women
5. a lot
6. A lot of Americans
7. C
8. a lot of
9. worker
10. C
11. advice
12. luck OR a lot of luck
13. The White House is
14. a lot of
15. There are
16. teachers
17. (any) new furniture
18. men
19. C
20. C
21. some
22. C
23. a
24. C
25. C
26. C
27. very little
28. pounds of meat
29. many
30. cups of coffee
31. There are
32. some OR a piece of

Part 2

1. wars; people
2. reservations; unemployment; poverty; jobs
3. advice; jobs; cities
4. sculptures; paintings; artists; art
5. music; CDs ; tapes

Part 3

Answers will vary.

1. cup
2. glass
3. teaspoon
4. gallon
5. piece
6. assignment
7. piece
8. rolls
9. piece
10. bar

Part 4

1. a
2. very little
3. a lot of
4. some
5. a
6. many
7. no
8. a lot of
9. a few
10. A few
11. A few
12. a lot of
13. a lot of

LESSON SIX

Exercise 1
Answers will vary.

1. greasy
2. sick
3. one
4. concerned
5. tired
6. was

Exercise 2

1. tired
2. wonderful; C
3. large
4. C
5. get married
6. C
7. is located
8. C

Exercise 3

1. shopping cart.
2. teaspoon
3. frying pan.
4. taxi driver
5. spring break.
6. very long vacation.
7. factory worker; hard job.
8. automobile factories
9. College students; textbooks; book store.
10. pretty long meeting
11. health food
12. swimming pool

Exercise 4
Answers will vary.

1. I answer every question honestly. I never lie.
2. I don't drive fast. I am a careful driver.
3. I cook well. I often try new recipes.
4. I don't talk constantly. I am a good listener.
5. I work hard. I focus on what I need to do until it's done.
6. I study hard. I study at least three hours a night.
7. I don't speak Spanish fluently. I only speak a little Spanish.
8. I type fast. I type 60 words per. minute.
9. I don't type accurately. I make a lot of mistakes.
10. I choose my food carefully. I don't eat a lot of fatty foods.
11. I don't live dangerously. I don't take risks.
12. I love passionately. I really care about the people in my life.
13. I meditate quietly. I find a quiet, private place to meditate.
14. I sleep soundly. I don't wake up at all during the night.
15. I didn't learn a second language easily. It took a lot of time and effort.
16. I lived comfortably in my country. My family had a large house and a good lifestyle.

Exercise 5

1. good
2. carefully
3. professional
4. perfect

5. hard
6. carefully
7. neat
8. conservative
9. early
10. usual
11. well
12. extremely nervous
13. difficult
14. friendly
15. clearly
16. hardly
17. good
18. well

Exercise 6
Answers will vary.

1. too much food
2. calories
3. exercise
4. time
5. many
6. Cooking
7. A car
8. late
9. heavy
10. start healthy habits

Exercise 7

1. big enough
2. enough money
3. too expensive
4. old enough
5. enough time
6. too seriously

Exercise 8
Answers will vary.

1. to learn something new.
2. to retire.
3. to reach the high shelves in my kitchen.
4. to buy a house.
5. to do everything I want to do.
6. to get a better job.

Exercise 9
Answers will vary.

1. Are you too busy to go to the movies?
2. Do you work too hard?
3. Do you have enough time to do your homework?
4. Are you strong enough to lift 100 pounds?
5. Do you have enough experience to apply for a good job?

Exercise 10

1. too
2. too
3. too many
4. too much
5. too much
6. too much
7. too
8. too
9. too many
10. too

Exercise 11

1. very
2. too
3. too
4. very
5. too
6. very
7. very
8. too
9. very
10. too

LESSON SIX TEST / REVIEW

Part I

1. shoe
2. C
3. English language
4. tired; C
5. wrong
6. too
7. yellow
8. C
9. my name carefully
10. a very expensive car
11. very
12. C
13. C; married
14. C
15. C
16. C
17. C
18. C; nervous
19. C
20. like
21. C
22. many

Part 2

1. well; bad
2. fast; safely
3. slowly
4. easily
5. hard; easy
6. usual
7. softly; well
8. quickly
9. regularly; lazy
10. tired
11. busy
12. hard; happy
13. lovely; friendly
14. angry; loudly
15. extremely; perfect; absolutely; clear

LESSON SEVEN

Exercise 1

1. When
2. When
3. When; while
4. until
5. When
6. until
7. While
8. until
9. until

Exercise 2

Answers will vary.

1. I learned many interesting things.
2. I went to college.
3. I traveled around the U.S.
4. I didn't know English well.
5. I got a job.
6. I didn't know any Americans.

Exercise 3

Answers will vary.

1. my best friend moved.
2. I looked for three weeks.
3. I got a job.
4. I came to school.
5. I bought a car when I had enough money.

Exercise 4

Answers will vary.

1. I never went to a baseball game until I came to the U.S.
2. I never heard of the Super Bowl until I came to the U.S.
3. I never saw a skyscraper before I came to the U.S.
4. I never thought about taking English classes before I came to the U.S.
5. I never had a computer before I came to the U.S.
6. I never ate a hot fudge sundae before I came to the U.S.
7. I never knew Americans work so hard before I came to the U.S.

Exercise 5

Answers will vary.

1. I call my best friend.
2. I take a walk.
3. I ask my mother.
4. I feel happy.
5. I feel homesick.
6. I eat soup.
7. I go to the movies.
8. I understand it better.

Exercise 6

Answers will vary.

1. after I exercise
2. when the mail comes late.
3. when my friends are away.
4. when it's noisy.
5. after I see my family.
6. whenever it rains.
7. while I'm in class.
8. when I'm busy.

Exercise 7

1. When
2. For
3. During
4. Before
5. When
6. While
7. while
8. in OR during
9. when
10. for
11. during
12. before OR until
13. ago
14. Whenever
15. in
16. by
17. before
18. in
19. in
20. when
21. until
22. until

Exercise 8

1. was; ing
2. wasn't planning
3. was working
4. visiting
5. was; ing
6. Was; was
7. were; living
8. Were; ing; wasn't
9. weren't you
10. was watching

Exercise 9

Answers will vary.

1. I was working in January, 1999.
2. I wasn't going to school.
3. I wasn't studying English.
4. I was living in the U.S.
5. I wasn't living with my parents.

Exercise 10

Answers will vary.

1. A. What were you doing at 10 o'clock last night?
   B. I was watching TV.
2. A. What were you doing at 4 o'clock this morning?
   B. I was sleeping.
3. A. What were you doing at 5 o'clock yesterday afternoon?
   B. I was cooking dinner.
4. A. What were you doing at this time last yesterday?
   B. I was working.
5. A. What were you doing at this time last year?
   B. I was looking for a job.

Exercise 11

1. While; was writing; dropped
2. fell; broke; while; was climbing
3. was shopping; when; lost
4. was doing; when; came
5. met; while; was attending
6. While; was driving; ran
7. When; arrived; were waiting
8. were eating; when; knocked
9. While; was taking; broke
10. interrupted; while; was talking
11. broke; while; was eating
12. met; while; was walking
13. was cooking; when; went
14. was shoveling; when; lost
15. blew; while; was ironing
16. was sleeping; when; started
17. broke; while; was washing

Exercise 12

Conversation 1

1. was putting
2. found
3. were putting
4. fell

Conversation 2

1. was watching
2. heard
3. was trying
4. dropped
5. were watching
6. didn't want

Conversation 3

1. was looking
2. found
3. did you meet
4. was walking
5. stopped
6. started
7. asked
8. were dating
9. got
10. was serving
11. wrote
12. got
13. came
14. was studying
15. got

Exercise 13

Answers will vary.

1. it started to rain.
2. I fell asleep.
3. we didn't have enough money.
4. their daughter got sick.
5. she changed her mind.
6. their car broke down.
7. I decided to go to a restaurant with my friends.

Exercise 14

1. was working
2. was having
3. sang OR was singing
4. enjoyed OR enjoying
5. came
6. had
7. went
8. was preparing
9. heard
10. opened
11. said
12. were . . . doing
13. was working
14. replied
15. was singing
16. told

Exercise 15

1. Einstein passed an exam before entering the university.
2. He left high school before receiving his diploma.
3. After developing his theory of relativity, Einstein became famous.
4. He became interested in physics after receiving books on science.
5. After coming to the U.S., he got a job at Princeton.
6. Before beginning a test, you should read the instructions carefully.
7. You shouldn't talk to another student while taking a test.
8. After finishing kindergarten, children go to first grade.

LESSON SEVEN TEST / REVIEW

Part 1

1. C
2. C
3. the teacher arrived
4. when
5. C
6. When
7. C
8. C
9. C
10. when
11. C
12. For
13. C
14. ago
15. C
16. C
17. C
18. C

Part 2

1. were you doing
2. was living; started
3. found; was looking
4. bought
5. met; he was working
6. came; found
7. arrived; was waiting
8. was using; crashed
9. was cooking; started
10. was driving; listening; heard

Part 3

1. Whenever
2. when
3. While
4. After OR When
5. before
6. until
7. When
8. before
9. TK
10. after
11. TK
12. TK
13. When
14. While
15. when
16. for

LESSON EIGHT

Exercise 1

Answers will vary.

1. can't
2. look at
3. should I look at the lease
4. must we
5. have
6. put
7. use
8. I pay
9. Can I
10. can't I
11. refuse
12. He can't

Exercise 2

1. must
2. have to
3. have to
4. must
5. have to
6. have to
7. must
8. must
9. have to
10. have to

Exercise 3

Answers will vary.

1. finish my homework
2. prepare dinner for my family
3. go to the doctor
4. look them up in the dictionary
5. go on a diet
6. study hard for the test
7. become fluent speakers of English
8. eat less junk food

Exercise 4

Answers will vary.

1. I have to go grocery shopping every week.
2. I have to go to water my plants every other day.
3. I have to cook every night.

Exercise 5

Answers will vary.

1. I had to study for a test.
2. I had to write a composition.
3. I had to clean my apartment.

Exercise 6

1. You're supposed to carry your driver's license with you when you drive.
2. The teacher is supposed to give a final grade at the end of the semester.
3. Your landlord is supposed to give you notice if he wants you to leave.
4. You're supposed to stop at a red light.
5. We are supposed to put money in the parking meter during business hours.
6. The landlord is supposed to give me a smoke detector.
7. We are supposed to write five compositions in this course.
8. We are supposed to bring our books to class.

Exercise 7

Answers will vary.

1. are not supposed to have
2. am not supposed to have
3. is supposed to give
4. are supposed to clean the apartment
5. is supposed to put
6. am supposed to pay
7. is supposed to fix
8. is supposed to refund

Exercise 8

Answers will vary.

1. We're supposed to read this entire text.
2. We're supposed to give an oral presentation.
3. We're supposed to do homework every night.

Exercise 9

Answers will vary.

1. can't
2. aren't permitted to
3. may
4. may not
5. aren't allowed to
6. can
7. can't
8. aren't permitted to

Exercise 10

Answers will vary.

1. change
2. park
3. cheat
4. take pictures

5. leave
6. use a cell phone

7. leave
8. eat

Exercise 11

Answers will vary.

1. We aren't allowed to speak any language but English in class.
2. We aren't permitted to smoke in the school.
3. We aren't allowed to be late to class.

Exercise 12

Answers will vary.

1. In my country, I couldn't wear jeans to class, but I can do it here.
2. In my country, I couldn't chew gum in the school, but I can do it here.
3. In my country, I couldn't speak in class without raising my hand, but I can do it here.

Exercise 13

Answers will vary.

1. I couldn't practice my religion in my country, but I can do it now.
2. I couldn't serve on a jury in my country, but I can do it now.
3. I couldn't vote for the president in my country, but I can do it now.

Exercise 14

Answers will vary.

1. study them
2. visit her
3. get gas
4. go to bed

5. get more exercise
6. bring a coat
7. take as many classes
8. tell the truth

Exercise 15

Answers will vary.

1. You should tell the landlord.
2. You should complain to the city.
3. You should talk to a lawyer.
4. You should pay to fix it.
5. You should clean your apartment.
6. You should go to bed early.
7. You should tell the librarian.
8. You should limit the time he is allowed to use the Internet.

Exercise 16

Answers will vary.

1. clean it
2. stop coming to work late
3. study harder
4. it will be returned.

5. we'll be late.
6. have to
7. must not talk
8. must get it

Exercise 17

Answers will vary.

1. You must not smoke.
2. You must not cheat.
3. You must not speak loudly.
4. You must not chew gum.
5. You must now carry a weapon.

Exercise 18

Answers will vary.

1. I have to speak English every day.
2. I don't have to use a dictionary to read the newspaper.
3. I've got to pay rent on the first of the month.
4. I don't have to type my homework.
5. I have to work on Saturdays.
6. I don't have to come to school everyday.

Exercise 19

Answers will vary.

1. In my country, a citizen doesn't have to vote.
2. In my country, men have to serve in the military.
3. In my country, schoolchildren sometimes have to wear a uniform.
4. In my country, divorced men have to support their children.
5. In my country, people don't have to get permission to travel.
6. In my country, students have to pass an exam to get their high school diploma.
7. In my country, students don't have to pay for their own books.
8. In my country, citizens have to pay taxes.
9. In my country, people don't have to make an appointment to see a doctor.
10. In my country, young people have to show an ID to enter nightclubs.

Exercise 20

Answers will vary.

1. must not
2. must not
3. don't have to
4. don't have to
5. must not

6. don't have to
7. don't have to
8. must not
9. don't have to
10. must not

Exercise 21

Answers will vary.

1. must not
2. can't
3. can't
4. shouldn't
5. don't have to

6. may
7. shouldn't
8. must not
9. don't have to

Exercise 22

Answers will vary.

1. Lisa must not be married.
2. Lisa must be a nurse.

3. Lisa must like coffee.
4. Lisa must like classical music.
5. Lisa must sew.
6. Lisa must cook a lot.
7. Lisa must play the piano.
8. Lisa must like modern art.
9. Lisa must be very busy.
10. Lisa must like cats.

Exercise 23
Answers will vary.

1. The owner must teach English.
2. The owner must love cars.
3. The owner must be a grandmother.
4. The owner must love music.
5. The owner must love dogs.
6. The owner must love tennis.
7. The owner must be a skier.
8. The owner must be a carpenter.
9. The owner must be a busy mother.
10. The owner must be a shy man.
11. The owner must be a father of two children.
12. The owner must be a romantic woman.
13. The owner must not have a lot of time.
14. The owner must be a woman who lives in the city.
15. The owner must be a female doctor.
16. The owner must love golf.
17. The owner must be a Mexican man.
18. The owner must be a good cook.
19. The owner must often be late.
20. The owners must dance.

Exercise 24
1. My sister may (OR might) come to live with me.
2. She may (OR might) find a job in this city.
3. My landlord may (OR might) raise my rent.
4. I may (OR might) get a dog.
5. My landlord may (OR might) not allow me to have a dog.
6. I may (OR might) move next year.
7. I may (OR might) buy a house soon.
8. I may (OR might) not stay in this city.
9. I may (OR might) not come to class tomorrow.
10. The teacher may (OR might) review modals if we need more help.

Exercise 25
Answers will vary.

1. I might move.
2. I may not get my full deposit back.
3. he or she may have trouble finding a job.
4. I may fail.
5. we may not get the classes we want.
6. I might have to take it over again.

Exercise 26
Answers will vary.

1. be Thomas; be Theodore
2. not be a woman

3. have one
4. know
5. have enough change
6. be from Spain; be from South America
7. be hiding there; be outside
8. have anymore

Exercise 27
Answers will vary.

1. Can I help you?
2. Could I close the door?
3. May I leave the room?
4. Can I write you a check?

Exercise 28
Answers will vary.

1. Can you repeat the sentence, please?
2. Would you give me your paper?
3. Will you spell your name?
4. Could you tell me your phone number?

Exercise 29
1. I would like to ask you a question.
2. The teacher would like to speak with you.
3. Would you like to try out the oven?
4. Yes, I would like to see if it works.

Exercise 30
1. Why don't you take a sweater?
2. Why don't we turn off the light?
3. Why don't you turn left here?
4. Why don't we leave early?

Exercise 31
Answers will vary.

1. I'd rather live in the U.S. than in my country.
2. I'd rather live in a suburb than in the city.
3. I'd rather sleep late than get up early.
4. I'd rather take a relaxing vacation than an active vacation.
5. I'd rather live in a house than a condo.
6. I'd rather read a story than write a composition.

Exercise 32
Answers will vary.

1. A. Would you rather read fact or fiction?
   B. I'd rather read fiction.
2. A. Would you rather watch funny movies or serious movies?
   B. I'd rather watch serious movies.
3. A. Would you rather listen to classical music or popular music?
   B. I'd rather listen to popular music.

4. A. Would you rather visit Europe or Africa?
   B. I'd rather visit Africa.
5. A. Would you rather own a large luxury car or a small sports car?
   B. I'd rather own a small sports car.
6. A. Would you rather watch a soccer game or take part in a soccer game?
   B. I'd rather take part in a soccer game.
7. A. Would you rather write a letter or receive a letter?
   B. I'd rather receive a letter.
8. A. Would you rather cook or eat in a restaurant?
   B. I'd rather cook.

Exercise 33

Answers will vary.

B. Would (OR Could OR Can) you show it to me?
S. Can (OR Could OR Would) you wait a minute, please?
B. Why don't (OR Would) you plug it in?
S. would rather sell
B. Could (OR Would) you give them both to me for $15?
S. 'd rather
B. Could (OR Can OR Would) you show me some identification?
S. Will (OR Would OR Could) you spell your name for me?

LESSON EIGHT TEST / REVIEW

Part 1

1. 're not permitted to use
2. couldn't travel
3. can she
4. C
5. has to take
6. should I do
7. are not supposed to
8. C
9. C
10. C
11. I would rather
12. C
13. have to
14. might OR may
15. C
16. C
17. C; couldn't speak

Part 2

A. I'm moving on Saturday. Could you help me?
B. I would like to help you, but I have a bad back. I went to my doctor last week, and she told me that I shouldn't lift anything heavy for a while. Can I help you any other way besides moving?
A. Yes. I don't have enough boxes. Could you help me find some?
B. Sure. I have to go shopping this afternoon. I'll pick up some boxes while I'm at the supermarket.
A. Boxes can be heavy. You had better not lift them yourself.
B. Don't worry. I'll have someone put them in my car for me.
A. Thanks. I don't have a free minute. I couldn't go to class all last week. There's so much to do.
B. I know what you mean. You must be tired.
A. I am. I have another favor to ask. Can I borrow your van on Saturday?
B. I have to work on Saturday. How about Sunday? I don't have to work on Sunday.
A. That's impossible. I've got to move out on Saturday. The new tenants are moving in Sunday morning.
B. Let me ask my brother. He has a van too. He might be able to let you use his van. He's supposed to work Saturday too, but only for half a day.
A. Thanks. I'd appreciate it if you could ask him.
B. Why are you moving? You have a great apartment.
A. We decided to move to the suburbs. It's quieter there. And I want to have a dog. I'm not supposed to have a dog in my present apartment. But my new landlord says I may have a dog.
B. I would rather have a cat. They're easier to take care of.

LESSON NINE

Exercise 1

1. gone
2. seen
3. looked
4. studied
5. brought
6. taken
7. said
8. been
9. found
10. left
11. lived
12. known
13. liked
14. fallen
15. felt
16. come
17. broken
18. worn
19. chosen
20. driven
21. written
22. put
23. begun
24. wanted
25. gotten
26. flown
27. sat
28. drunk
29. grown
30. given

Exercise 2

A. Have you been in the U.S. for long?
B. No. I haven't.
A. How long have you been in the U.S.?
B. I've been here for only 6 months. I come from Guatemala.
A. I come from Mexico. I've just started to become interested in my family's history. I've read several magazine articles about genealogy. It's fascinating. Are you interested in your family's history?
B. Of course I am. I've been interested in it for a long time.

A. Have you found out anything interesting?
B. Oh, yes. I've found that some of my ancestors were Mayans and some were from Spain and France. In fact, my great-great grandfather was a Spanish prince.
A. How did you find out so much? Have you ever been to Spain or France to look at records there?
B. Not yet. I've spent many hours on the Internet. I've also gone (OR been) to libraries to get more information.
A. How many ancestors have you found so far?
B. I've found about 50, but I'm still looking. It's been very time-consuming but a lot of fun. My brother in Guatemala is also very interested in genealogy. He has helped me a lot too. He's started to make a family tree.
A. Has he learned anything interesting?
B. Oh, yes. He's found out that he's related to me!!

Exercise 3
A. Have you been in the U.S. for long?
B. No. I haven't.
A. How long have you been in the U.S.?
B. I've been here for about a year.
A. How do you like living here?
B. I like it very much.
A. There are so many nice museums here. Have you gone to any of them?
B. No, I haven't. I've been very busy. So I haven't had time to enjoy myself.
A. The last time we talked you were looking for an apartment. Have you found an apartment yet?
B. Yes, I have. It's a nice apartment. My wife and I have been very happy with it. Now that I have a job and an apartment, maybe I'll have more time.
A. I'm going to the Art Museum on Saturday. Do you want to go with me?
B. I have always wanted to see the Art Museum. I'd love to go with you. My wife has never seen the Art Museum either. Can she come along too?
A. Of course.

Exercise 4
1. since
2. has
3. long
4. began
5. been
6. for
7. have; met
8. s; since
9. How; had
10. ve; been
11. I've
12. had

Exercise 5
Answers will vary.

1. You've been reading that book for weeks.
2. I've never been to Paris.
3. I've wanted to be a nurse since I was a little girl.
4. She has known her teacher since last year.

Exercise 6
Answers will vary.

1. I've always enjoyed classical music.
2. I've always liked my mother's uncle.

3. I've always wanted to learn the piano.
4. I've always wanted to have a sailboat.
5. I've always needed to lose ten pounds.
6. I've always been interested in American history.
7. I've always thought about living on a farm.

Exercise 7
Answers will vary.

1. I've never seen *Gone with the Wind.*
2. I've never liked caviar.
3. I've never studied statistics.
4. I've never visited Seattle.
5. I've never played football.
6. I've never tasted Indian food.

Exercise 8
Answers will vary.

1. I've always been good at math.
2. I've always liked chocolate.
3. I've always worn comfortable clothes.
4. I've always hated to iron.

Exercise 9
Answers will vary.

1. I've never visited Italy, but I'd like to.
2. I've never taken singing lessons, but I'd like to.
3. I've never climbed a mountain, but I'd like to.
4. I've never seen thee Taj Mahal, but I'd like to.

Exercise 10
Answers will vary.

1. S. Have you always taught English?
   T. Yes, I have.
2. S. Have you always taught at this college?
   T. No. I have taught at a few different colleges.
3. S. Have you always thought about grammar?
   T. No, I haven't. When I was younger, I know very little about grammar.
4. S. Has English always been easy for you?
   T. Yes, it has. The language people grow up speaking is always easy for them.
5. S. Has your last name always been _____?
   T. No. I changed it after I got married.
6. S. Have you always been interested in foreigners?
   T. Yes. I love learning about different cultures.
7. S. Have you always lived in this city?
   T. No. I moved here five years ago.
8. S. Have you always been a teacher?
   T. Yes. I started teaching when I graduated from college.

Exercise 11
Answers will vary.

Exercise 12

Answers will vary.

1. I've been studying English for three years.
2. I've been working for four years.
3. She's been living here since January.
4. We've been using this book since the beginning of the semester.
5. My sister has been studying at the college for two years.

Exercise 13

Answers will vary.

1. I've lived in the U.S.
   I've been living in the U.S. since 1996.
2. I work as a computer programmer.
   I've been working as a computer programmer for four years.
3. I attend Long Island University.
   I've been attending Long Island University for one year.
4. The teacher is explaining the present perfect tense.
   The teacher has been explaining the present perfect tense for three days.
5. The students are practicing the present perfect continuous.
   The students have been practicing the present perfect continuous for a few days.

Exercise 14

Answers will vary.

1. A. Do you drive?
   B. Yes, I do.
   A. How long have you been driving?
   B. I've been driving since I was 18 years old.
2. A. Do you work?
   B. Yes, I do.
   A. How long have you been working?
   B. I've been working for four years.
3. A. Do you use the Internet?
   B. Yes, I do.
   A. How long have you been using the Internet?
   B. I've been using the Internet for two years.
4. A. Do you wear glasses?
   B. Yes, I do.
   A. How long have you been wearing glasses?
   B. I've been wearing glasses since I was a child.
5. A. Do you play a musical instrument?
   B. Yes, I do.
   A. How long have you been playing a musical instrument?
   B. I've been playing a musical instrument for ten years.

Exercise 15

Answers will vary.

1. S. How long have you been teaching English?
   T. I've been teaching English for five years.
2. S. How long have you been working at this college?
   T. I've been working at this college since September.
3. S. How long have you been living in this city?
   T. I've been living in this city for ten years.
4. S. How long have you been using this book?
   T. I've been using this book for a few years.
5. S. How long have you been living at your present address?
   T. I've been living at my present address for ten years.

Exercise 16

Answers will vary.

1. A. Do you work in a restaurant?
   B. Yes, I do.
   A. How long have you worked in a restaurant?
   B. I have worked in a restaurant since 1998.
2. A. Does your father live in the U.S.?
   B. Yes, he does.
   A. How long has he been living in the U.S.?
   B. He has been living in the U.S. since he was 25 years old.
3. A. Are you studying for the test now?
   B. Yes, I am.
   A. How long have you been studying for the test?
   B. For a week.
4. A. Is your teacher teaching you the present perfect lesson?
   B. Yes, he is.
   A. How long has he been teaching you this lesson?
   B. Since last week.
5. A. Are they using the computers now?
   B. Yes, they are.
   A. How long have they been using them?
   B. They have been using them since they started to write their compositions.
6. A. Are you studying your family history?
   B. Yes, we are.
   A. How long have you been studying your family history?
   B. Since we moved to the U.S.
7. A. Do your grandparents live in the U.S?
   B. Yes, they do.
   A. How long have they lived in the U.S?
   B. Since they were born.
8. A. Are you using the Internet?
   B. Yes, I am.
   A. How long have you been using the Internet?
   B. I've been using the Internet for two hours.

Exercise 17

S: Why am I failing this course?

T: We have had 6 tests so far, but you have taken only 4 of them. And you have failed 2 out of those 4. Also, you have been absent 5 times. You have not given me any compositions at all this semester.

S: But I have been very busy with my job this month. And my mother has been sick this month. I have taken her to the doctor twice this month.

T: I'm sorry you're having so many problems. But when you're absent, you need to call me and find out about your assignments and tests.

S: I have tried to call you several times this week, but you never answer.

T: Most of the time I'm in class. Please call the English office and leave a message with the secretary.

S: I will.

Exercise 18

Answers will vary.

1. A. Have we had any tests so far?
   B. Yes, we have. We've had two tests.
2. A. Has this lesson been difficult up to now?
   B. No, it hasn't.
3. A. Has the teacher given a lot of homework so far?
   B. No, she hasn't.
4. A. Have you understood all the explanations up to now?
   B. Yes, I have.
5. A. Have you had any questions about this lesson so far?
   C. Yes, I have.

Exercise 19

Answers will vary.

1. A. How many letters have you written this month?
   B. I haven't written letters this month.
2. A. How many times have you eaten in a restaurant this month?
   B. I've eaten in a restaurant once this month.
3. A. How many times have you gotten paid this month?
   B. I've gotten paid three times this month.
4. A. How many long distance calls have you made this month?
   B. I've made about five long distance calls this month.
5. A. How many books have you bought this month?
   B. I've haven't bought books this month.
6. A. How many times have you gone to the movies this month?
   B. I've gone to the movies twice this month.
7. A. How many movies have you rented this month?
   B. I've rented four movies this month.
8. A. How many times have you cooked this month?
   B. I've cooked many times this month.

Exercise 20

Answers will vary.

1. How many books have you read this year?
2. How many counties have you visited?
3. How much money have you earned this month?
4. How many cups of coffee have you drunk this week?

Exercise 21

Answers will vary.

1. A. How many apartments did you live in in your country?
   B. I lived in a few apartments.
2. A. How many apartments have you lived in in the U.S.?
   B. I've lived in one apartment in the U.S.
3. A. How many schools did you attend in your country?
   B. I attended three schools in my country.
4. A. How many schools have you attended in the U.S.?
   B. I've only attended one school in the U.S.
5. A. How much coffee did you drink yesterday?
   B. I drank two cups of coffee yesterday.

6. A. How much coffee have you drunk today?
   B. I've drunk one cup of coffee today.
7. A. How many jobs have you had in the U.S.?
   B. I've had two jobs in the U.S.
8. A. How many jobs did you have in your country?
   B. I had three jobs in my country.
9. A. How many compositions did you write last semester?
   B. I wrote five compositions last semester.
10. A. How many compositions have you written this semester?
    B. I've written four compositions this semester.

Exercise 22

1. gone
2. haven't
3. Have you ever lived
4. have
5. Has; been
6. has
7. have never been
8. Have your children ever attended
9. Have you ever worked

Exercise 23

1. have; eaten
2. hasn't had
3. 've already told you
4. 've just made
5. haven't made

Exercise 24

Answers to these questions will vary. See example.

1. Have you ever worked in a factory?
2. Have you ever lost a glove?
3. Have you ever run out of gas?
4. Have you ever fallen out of bed?
5. Have you ever made a mistake in English?
6. Have you ever told a lie?
7. Have you ever eaten raw fish?
8. Have you ever studied calculus?
9. Have you ever met a famous person?
10. Have you ever met a famous person?
11. Have you ever gone to an art museum?
12. Have you ever broken a window?
13. Have you ever gotten locked out of your house or car?
14. Have you ever seen a French movie?
15. Have you ever gone to Las Vegas?
16. Have you ever traveled by ship?
17. Have you ever been in love?
18. Have you ever written a poem?

Exercise 25

Answers will vary.

1. Have you ever studied another language?
2. Have you ever visited my country?
3. Have you ever lived in another country?
4. Have you ever gone camping?
5. Have you ever lost your keys?

Exercise 26

Answers will vary.

1. A. Has your country ever had a civil war?
   B. Yes. There was a civil war in my country over 100 years ago.
2. A. Has your country's leader ever visited the U.S.?
   B. Yes. He visited the U.S. last year.
3. A. Has the American president ever visited your country?
   B. Yes. I think he has visited my country a few times.
4. A. Has your country ever had a woman president?
   B. No. My country has never had a woman president.
5. A. Have you ever gone back to visit your country?
   B. No. I haven't gone back to visit my country yet.
6. A. Has there ever been an earthquake in your hometown?
   B. No. There has never been an earthquake in my hometown.

Exercise 27

Answers will vary.

1. A. Have you found a job yet?
   B. Yes, I have.
2. A. Have you made any American friends yet?
   B. Yes, I have.
3. A. Have you opened a bank account yet?
   B. Yes, I have.
4. A. Have you saved any money yet?
   B. No, I haven't.
5. A. Have you bought a car yet?
   B. No, I haven't.
6. A. Have you written to your family yet?
   B. Yes, I have.

LESSON NINE TEST / REVIEW

Part 1

1. I came
2. eaten
3. have you
4. ever gone
5. I've known
6. for
7. I've never gone
8. How long
9. C
10. He's been working
11. studied
12. C
13. already
14. C

Part 2

Conversation 1
1. studied
2. have been working OR have worked
3. Have; though
4. was
5. 've always wanted
6. was
7. graduated
8. haven't had

Conversation 2
1. have you been
2. Has; changed
3. came
4. came

5. lived
6. have lived OR have been living
7. Have you always lived
8. 've moved
9. haven't found

Part 3

Paragraph 1

    I use the Internet every day. I've used it for three years. I started to use it when I became interested in genealogy. I've worked on my family tree for three years. Last month, I found information about my father's ancestors. My grandfather lives with us and likes to tell us about his past. He was born in Italy, but he came here when he was very young, so he's lived here most of his life. He doesn't remember much about Italy. I haven't found any information about my mother's ancestors yet.

Paragraph 2

    I came to the U.S. when a war broke out in my country. I lived in the U.S. for five years. At first, everything was very hard for me. I didn't know any English when I arrived. But I've studied English for the past five years, and now I speak it pretty well. I haven't started my college education yet, but I plan to next semester.

LESSON TEN

Exercise 1

Answers will vary.

1. Teaching
2. Looking in the classified section of the newspaper
3. Eating
4. Speaking on the telephone
5. Learning English
6. Spitting
7. Exercising
8. Taking tests
9. Taking the subway at night
10. Stealing

Exercise 2

Answers will vary.

Exercising can improve a person's health.
Drinking eight glasses of water a day can improve a person's health.
Laughing can improve a person's health.

Eating a lot of sugar is bad for a person's health.
Smoking is bad for a person's health.
Feeling stress is bad for a person's health.

Exercise 3

Answers will vary.

1. going to the beach
2. cooking.
3. studying; taking tests
4. getting presents
5. playing the piano
6. doing my laundry.
7. working hard
8. smoking

Exercise 4

Answers will vary.

1. I miss eating the traditional foods of my country.
2. I miss the friendliness of the people in my hometown.
3. I miss shopping in my country.

Exercise 5

Answers will vary.

I recommend going to the museums.
I recommend visiting the countryside.
I recommend trying the local food.

You should avoid walking in the cities alone at night.
You should avoid taking your wallet out on the street.
You should avoid buying items in the tourist shops.

Exercise 6

Answers will vary.

1. I don't like to go fishing because I don't like to eat fish.
2. I like to go camping because I like being outdoors.
3. I like to go jogging because I like exercising.
4. I like going swimming because I like the water.
5. I don't like going hunting because I don't believe in killing animals.
6. I like going shopping because I like buying new things.

Exercise 7

Answers will vary.

1. I'm afraid of speaking in front of people.
2. I'm not afraid of meeting new people.
3. I'm interested in learning about art history.
4. I'm not interested in going to discos.
5. I want to succeed in creating a good life in this country.
6. I'm not very good at singing or dancing.
7. I'm accustomed to driving on the left side of the road.
8. I'm not accustomed to living alone.
9. I plan on visiting my country as soon as possible.
10. I don't care about earning a lot of money.

Exercise 8

Answers will vary.

1. In the U.S., I'm interested in making friends.
   In my country, I was interested in spending time with my friends.

2. In the U.S., I'm afraid of not understanding the culture.
   In my country, I was afraid of having limited opportunities.
3. In the U.S., I worry about getting a good job.
   In my country, I worried about passing my exams.
4. In the U.S., I dream about falling in love and getting married.
   In my country, I dreamed about coming to the U.S.
5. In the U.S., I look forward to speaking fluent English.
   In my country, I looked forward to going to university in the U.S.
6. In the U.S., I often think about how to improve my English.
   In my country, I often thought about what career to choose.
7. In the U.S., people often complain about politicians.
   In my country, people often complain about politicians.
8. In the U.S., families often talk about what they want to buy.
   In my country, families often talk about what activities they want to do.
9. In the U.S., teenagers are usually interested in going to the mall.
   In my country, teenagers are usually interested in going to the beach.
10. American students are accustomed to wearing jeans to school.
    Students in my country are accustomed to wearing uniforms to school.

Exercise 9

Answers will vary.

1. listening to native speakers.
2. sending out a resume.
3. having experience.
4. going "cold turkey."
5. looking in the newspaper.
6. translating into my native language first.
7. taking an eye exam.
8. taking the test.

Exercise 10

Answers will vary.

A. I need to find a job. I've had 10 interviews, but so far no job.
B. Have you thought about going to a job counselor?
A. No. Where can I find one?
B. Our school office has a counseling department. I suggest making an appointment with a counselor.
A. What can a job counselor do for me?
B. Do you know anything about interviewing skills?
A. No.
B. Well, with the job counselor, you can talk about making a good impression during an interview. You can practice asking questions that the interviewer might ask you.
A. Really? How does the counselor know what questions the interviewer will ask me?
B. Many interviewers ask the same general questions. For example, the interviewer might ask you, "Do you enjoy working with computers?" Or she might ask you, "Do

you mind working overtime and on weekends?" Or "Are you good atworking with other people?"

A. I dislike talking about myself.
B. That's what you have to do in the U.S.
A. What else can the counselor help me with?
B. If your skills are low, you can talk about improving your skills. If you don't know much about computers, for example, she can recommend taking more classes.
A. It feels like I'm never going to find a job. I'm tired of looking and not finding anything.
B. If you keep looking, you will succeed at finding a job. I'm sure. But it takes time and patience.
A. And job hunting skills.

Exercise 11

Answers will vary.

1. It's important to read the lease before you sign it.
2. It's impossible to find the perfect apartment.
3. It's possible to get your security deposit back.
4. It's necessary for me to take good care of my apartment.
5. It's dangerous to keep the doors unlocked at night.
6. It isn't good to rent an apartment without a lease.
7. It's expensive to take a taxi.
8. It's hard to understand some Americans.

Exercise 12

Answers will vary.

1. It's important for me to get a college degree.
2. It's important for me to find an interesting job.
3. It's not important for me to have a car.
4. It's important for me to speak English well.
5. It's important for me to read and write English well.
6. It's not important for me to study American history.
7. It's important for me to become an American citizen.
8. It's important for me to own a computer.
9. It's not important for me to have a cell phone.
10. It's not important for me to make a lot of money.

Exercise 13

Answers will vary.

1. It's important for us to learn English well.
2. It's difficult for Americans to understand customs of other countries.
3. It's easy for the teacher to like the students.
4. It's necessary for children to make friends.
5. It's difficult for a woman to travel alone.
6. It's difficult for a man to go shopping with his wife.

Exercise 14

Answers will vary.

1. Being well groomed is important.
2. Appearing confident is important.
3. It's important to explain your experience and skills.
4. It's important to send a thank you letter after an interview.

Exercise 15

Answers will vary.

1. Having a good English dictionary is important.
2. It is important to be open to other cultures.
3. Speaking English outside of class will help you progress faster.
4. It is possible to learn a lot about the culture if you ask questions.

Exercise 16

Answers will vary.

1. to have such a good teacher.
2. of being one of the best students in the class.
3. of walking home
4. of meeting new people.
5. of moving away from home.
6. of not making friends.
7. to start the next lesson?
8. to go to the party yet.

Exercise 17

1. A. Do you want to learn another language?
   B. Yes, I do. OR No, I don't.
2. A. Do you plan to take classes here next semester?
   B. Yes, I do. OR No, I don't.
3. A. Do you hope to speak English fluently?
   B. Yes, I do. OR No, I don't.
4. A. Do you like to write compositions?
   B. Yes, I do. OR No, I don't.
5. A. Do you continue to speak your native language at home?
   B. Yes, I do. OR No, I don't.
6. A. Do you try to read novels in English?
   B. Yes, I do. OR No, I don't.
7. A. Do you plan to move this year?
   B. Yes, I do. OR No, I don't.
8. A. Do you need your own fax machine?
   B. Yes, I do. OR No, I don't.
9. A. Do you expect to return to your country?
   B. Yes, I do. OR No, I don't.
10. A. Do you need to use a dictionary when you read the newspaper?
    B. Yes, I do. OR No, I don't.

Exercise 18

Answers will vary.

1. I like to read mysteries.
2. I don't like to eat late at night.
3. I want to visit Canada.
4. I decided to go to the movies.
5. I tried to learn the piano.
6. I'll begin to study Spanish after I learn English.

Exercise 19

Answers will vary.

Exercise 20

Answers will vary.

1. coming; February.
2. studying; five years ago.
3. to watch the news
4. living in the city.
5. wearing baggy clothes.
6. to wear suits.
7. I love eating ice cream.

Exercise 21

1. The teacher doesn't want us to talk to another student during a test.
2. The teacher wants us to study before a test.
3. The teacher doesn't want us to copy another student's homework.
4. The teacher wants us to learn English.
5. The teacher doesn't wants us to speak our native languages in class.
6. The teacher wants us to improve our pronunciation.

Exercise 22

1. I expect him to correct the homework.
2. I expect her to give tests.
3. I don't expect him to speak my language.
4. I don't expect her to help me after class.
5. I expect him to come to class on time.
6. I don't expect her to pass all the students.
7. I (don't) expect him to know a lot about my country.
8. I expect her to answer all my questions in class.
9. I don't expect him to teach us American history.
10. I (don't) expect her to pronounce my name correctly.

Exercise 23

Answers will vary.

1. me to work on Sundays.
2. us to attend a meeting once a week.
3. us to talk to each other while we're working.
4. him to give me a raise.
5. him to treat us with respect.
6. me to wear a suit and tie every day.
7. us to go on strike.
8. us to eat lunch in 20 minutes.
9. him to give me a compliment or a word of praise.
10. to quit this job.

Exercise 24

Answers will vary.

1. I don't want her to raise the rent.
2. I want them to lower the volume of their TV at night.
3. I want him to paint my walls.
4. I want them to close the front door securely.
5. She wants them to be quiet.

Exercise 25

Answers will vary.

1. My mother wants me to get a haircut.
2. My father doesn't want me to get my ears pierced.
3. I don't want my sister to borrow my clothes.
4. I want my sister to be quiet when I'm studying.

Exercise 26

Answers will vary.

1. to make
2. to earn more money
3. to look for
4. to improve
5. to drive to
6. to send packages
7. to get a job; to get experience
8. to speak; to access
9. to make calls
10. to mail
11. to get
12. to tell him

Exercise 27

Answers will vary.

1. Now I do it as soon as it is assigned.
2. Now I try to work out my problems on my own.
3. Now I hardly ever ask them for money.
4. Now I save my money.
5. Now I do my laundry myself.

Exercise 28

Answers will vary.

1. I used to be very lazy. Now I exercise three times a week.
2. I used to eat fattening foods. Now I am careful about what I eat.
3. I used to be nervous about speaking in public. Now I am comfortable speaking in public.
4. I used to speak only my native language at home. Now I speak my native language and English at home.

Exercise 29

Answers will vary.

1. I used to live with my family. Now I live with my friend.
2. I used to live in the country. Now I live in the city.
3. I used to have a lot of friends. Now I have only a few friends.
4. I used to spend my free time at the beach. Now I spend my free time studying.

Exercise 30

1. sitting
2. calling
3. writing
4. wearing
5. working
6. spending
7. sitting

Exercise 31

Answers will vary.

1. taking public transportation
2. being in a muti-cultural environment
3. American customs
4. calling before visiting friends

Exercise 32

Answers will vary.

1. I'm used to eating a lot of fruits and vegetables.
2. I'm used to sunny weather.
3. I'm used to getting up at 7:30.
4. I'm used to wearing jeans to class.
5. I'm used to drinking coffee every day.
6. I'm used to doing group work in class.
7. I'm used to taking walks alone.

LESSON TEN TEST / REVIEW

Part 1

1. C	12. C
2. seeing	13. C
3. C	14. C
4. Saving	15. to find
5. C	16. C
6. for her	17. of spending
7. go fishing	18. C
8. C	19. I'm used to living
9. C; C	20. get used to driving
10. tried to explain	21. wants me to call
11. it is	22. loosing

Part 2

Answers will vary.

A. Hi, Molly. I haven't seen you in ages. What's going on in your life?

B. I've made many changes. First, I quit working in a factory. I disliked doing the same thing every day. And I'm not used to standing on my feet all day. My boss often wanted me to work overtime on Saturdays. I need to spend time with my children on Saturdays. Sometimes they want me to take them to the zoo or to the museum. And I need to help them with their homework.

A. So what do you plan on doing?

B. I've started going to college to take some general courses.

A. What career are you planning?

B. I'm not sure. I'm interested in working with children. Maybe I'll become a teacher's aide. I've also thought about working in a day-care center. I care about helping people.

A. Yes, it's wonderful to help other people, especially children. It's important to find a job that you like. So you're starting a whole new career.

B. It's not new, really. Before I came to the U.S., I used to be a kindergarten teacher in my country. But my English wasn't so good when I came here, so I found a job in a factory. I look forward to returning to my former profession or doing something similar.

A. How did you learn English so fast?

B. By speaking with people at work, by watching TV, and by reading the newspaper. It hasn't been easy for me to learn American English. I studied British English in my country, but here I have to get used to hearing things like "gonna" and "wanna". At first I didn't understand Americans, but now I'm used to their pronunciation. I have to make a lot of changes.

A. You should be proud of making so many changes in your life so quickly.

B. I am.

A. Let's get together some time and talk some more.

B. I'd love to. I love to dance. Maybe we can go dancing together sometime.

A. That would be great. And I love to dance. Maybe we can go shopping together sometime.

LESSON ELEVEN

Exercise 1

1. T	4. F	7. T
2. F	5. T	8. T
3. T	6. F	

Exercise 2

1. who wrote the ad
2. that he placed in the newspaper
3. who is under 5'5" tall
4. who has been married before
5. who has the same interests as he does
6. who answers this ad
7. who writes SWM
8. that have abbreviations

Exercise 3

Answers will vary.

1. who are romantic.
2. who explains confusing material well.
3. who work hard.
4. who are single parents.
5. who have never visited the U.S.

Exercise 4

Answers will vary.

1. who have a kind heart
2. who lie
3. who are never satisfied with anything
4. who spend a lot of time with their children
5. who have little time for their children

Exercise 5

Answers will vary.

1. don't have many friends.
2. can't find good jobs.
3. must work hard to find new ones.
4. feel good.

5. have trouble catching up with the class work.
6. don't develop good interpersonal skills.
7. become heavy.
8. can make calls from almost anywhere.
9. put themselves and others in danger.
10. don't have a lot of energy.
11. get take out food often.
12. must schedule their time very carefully.

Exercise 6

1. he put in the paper
2. whom he met through his ads
3. I want to marry
4. he doesn't like
5. she met in her biology class
6. I'd like you to meet
7. we are using
8. we find

Exercise 7

Answers will vary.

1. gave.
2. trust.
3. really liked.
4. don't understand.
5. can't get used to.
6. gave you?

Exercise 8

Answers will vary.

1. I bought
2. is wearing
3. I had OR you gave me
4. saw
5. borrowed
6. she made. OR she makes.
7. I learned OR I studied
8. said. OR are saying

Exercise 9

Answers will vary.

A. I don't have enough friends in this country.
B. Haven't you met any people here?
A. Of course. But the people I've met here don't have my interests.
B. What are you interested in?
A. I like reading, meditating, going for quiet walks. Americans seem to like parties, TV, sports, movies, going to restaurants. The interests they have are so different from mine.
B. You're never going to meet people with the interests you have. Your interests don't include other people. You should find some interests that involve other people, like tennis or dancing, to mention only a few.
A. The activities that involve other people cost money, and I don't have a lot of money.
B. There are many parks in this city that have free tennis courts. If you like to dance, I know of a park district near here that offers free dance classes. In fact, there are a lot of things that are free or very low cost in the U.S. I can give you a list of free activities, if you want.

A. Thanks. I'd love to have the list. Thanks for all the suggestions you've given me.
B. I'd be happy to give you more, but I don't have time now. Tomorrow I'll bring you a list of activities from the parks in this city. I'm sure you'll find something that you're interested in on that list.
A. Thanks.

Exercise 10

Answers will vary.

1. A babysitter is a person who takes care of children.
2. An immigrant is a person who has moved to another country.
3. An adjective is a word that describes a noun.
4. A verb is a word that tells what someone or something is or does.
5. A fax machine is a device that sends and receives documents through the phone lines.
6. A dictionary is a reference book that explains the meaning of words.
7. A mouse is a device that allows the user to move a cursor around on a computer screen.
8. A coupon is a piece of paper that can be used to get discounts on goods and services.

Exercise 11

1. whose attendance is bad
2. whose explanations are clear
3. whose compositions were good
4. whose class I took last semester
5. whose names I can't pronounce
6. whose husband has died
7. whose ad we read
8. whose story we read

Exercise 12

1. whose family incomes are low
2. whose children are in college
3. whose children graduate from college
4. whose hobbies are the same as his
5. whose names I don't remember
6. whose language I speak
7. whose class I took last semester
8. whose book I bought

Exercise 13

1. (whom) I can trust.
2. who doesn't put his family first.
3. who makes a good living.
4. whose family I like.
5. who's older than I am.
6. who wants to have children.

1. who has a sense of humor.
2. whose wisdom I can admire.
3. whose manners are good.
4. whose mother doesn't interfere.
5. who I have known for a long time.
6. who wants to have a lot of kids.

Exercise 14

1. who won the lottery.
2. that is very difficult to program.
3. who has a lot of patience.
4. who has a lot of friends.
5. that has low mileage.
6. who makes always has parties on Saturday nights.
7. who don't use their brains.
8. who you can trust.

Exercise 15

A. I'm getting married next month.
B. Congratulations. Are you marrying the woman you met at Mark's party last year?
A. Oh, no. I broke up with that woman a long time ago. The woman I'm marrying is a person I met in my biology class.
B. What's her name? I know some of the people who are in your biology class.
A. Lisa Martin.
B. I think I know her. Is she the young woman who got the highest mark on the mid term test?
A. Yes. She always gets an A on every test. She's very intelligent.

B. Well, you're a lucky man. Lisa is smart and pretty too. Are you getting married in church?
A. No. We're going to get married in a house.
B. I didn't know you have a house.
A. We don't. We're going to use a friend's house. The person whose house we're going to use is an old friend of Lisa's mother. She has a very big house. If the weather is nice, the wedding is going to be outside.
B. My wife and I made plans to get married outside too, but we had to change the plans that we made because it rained that day.
A. That's OK. The woman I marry is more important than the place where we get married. And the life that we'll have together is more important than the wedding day.
B. You're right about that!

Exercise 16

1. I see
2. who would lend me money
3. who knows everything about me
4. who has different political opinions
5. who doesn't speak my language
6. whose religious beliefs are different from mine
7. who lives far away
8. I have

LESSON ELEVEN TEST / REVIEW

Part 1

1. which my husband found
2. C
3. that live
4. C
5. who make
6. C
7. friend who lives
8. A person who
9. C
10. who speaks
11. C
12. anyone who
13. C
14. whose
15. whose
16. whose dictionary I borrowed never came back

Part 2

1. who play their stereo music every night.
2. you had?
3. who speaks French
4. I met
5. whose name begins with A
6. whose house I bought
7. who doesn't
8. whose wallet I found

LESSON TWELVE

Exercise 1

Comparative	Superlative
1. more interesting	the most interesting
2. younger	the youngest
3. more beautiful	the most beautiful
4. better	the best
5. more common OR commoner	most common OR the commonest
6. thinner	the thinnest
7. more carefully	the most carefully
8. prettier	the prettiest
9. worse	the worst
10. more famous	the most famous
11. luckier	the luckiest
12. simple OR more simple	the simplest OR the most simple
13. higher	the highest
14. more delicious	the most delicious
15. farther OR further	the farthest OR the furthest
16. more foolishly	the most foolishly

Exercise 2

1. the most popular
2. the greatest
3. the most powerful
4. the most graceful
5. the best
6. the most valuable
7. the richest
8. the best

Exercise 3

1. the highest
2. the smallest
3. the commonest OR the most common
4. the most interesting
5. the most populated
6. the most popular

Exercise 4

Answers will vary.

1. Moscow is the biggest city.
2. St. Petersburg is the most beautiful city.
3. Technology is the most important industry.
4. Soccer is the most popular sport.
5. Oksana Baiul is the most famous athlete.
6. Honda is the most popular car.
7. Patel is the most common last name.
8. January is the coldest month.
9. The Amazon is the longest river.
10. Lake Baikal is the largest lake.

Exercise 5

Answers will vary.

1. In my opinion, an engineer has the most interesting job.
2. In my opinion, a firefighter has the most dangerous job.
3. In my opinion, a politician has the easiest job.
4. In my opinion, a high school teacher has the most tiring job.
5. In my opinion, a factory worker has the dirtiest job.
6. In my opinion, a bus driver has the most boring job.
7. In my opinion, a photojournalist has the most exciting job.
8. In my opinion, a doctor has the most important job.
9. In my opinion, a high school teacher has the most challenging job.
10. In my opinion, a social worker has a difficult job.

Exercise 6

Answers will vary.

1. Getting involved in a lot of activities is the best way to meet a spouse.
2. Living in the country is the quickest way to learn a language.
3. Seeing all the beautiful sights is one of the best things about living in the U.S.
4. Not having a good job is the worst thing about living in the U.S.
5. Hunger is one of the most terrible world tragedies.

Exercise 7

Answers will vary.

1. The Sears Tower is the tallest building I have ever visited.
2. Julia Roberts is the most beautiful actress I have ever seen.
3. Physics is the most difficult subject I have ever studied.
4. Four thousand miles is the furthest distance I have ever traveled.

5. My wife is the most interesting person I have ever met.
6. Hot dogs are the worst American food I have ever eaten.
7. My $15,000 car is the most money I have ever spent on one thing.
8. My honeymoon in Venice was the best vacation I have ever had.
9. Michael Jordon is the best athlete I have ever seen.
10. *Crime and Punishment* is the most interesting book I have ever read.
11. My mother is the best friend I have ever had.
12. The apartment I had last year was the worst apartment I have ever had.
13. Last New Year's Eve was the best time I have ever had.
14. London is the biggest city I have ever visited.
15. Working as a waitress was the hardest job I have ever had.

Exercise 8

Answers will vary.

1. Walking around Times Square alone at midnight
2. Deciding to move to the U.S.

Exercise 9

Answers will vary.

1. My brother drives the best.
2. My aunt and uncle live the farthest from me.
3. My sister speaks English the most confidently.
4. I spend the most money.
5. My brother is the best dressed.
6. My son watches the most TV.
7. My mother worries the most.
8. My parents live the best.
9. My husband works the hardest.
10. My daughter is the most athletic.
11. My daughter is the biggest sports fan.
12. My sister is learning English most quickly.

Exercise 10

Answers will vary.

1. more
2. faster
3. more
4. less
5. less

Exercise 11

1. smaller than
2. more responsible than
3. more expensive
4. bigger
5. more carefully than
6. better than
7. more dangerous than
8. more easily than

Exercise 12

Answers will vary.

1. Japanese people are more polite than Americans.
2. Americans are friendlier than Japanese people.
3. Japanese people are more formal than Americans.
4. Americans are taller than Japanese people.
5. Japanese people are thinner than Americans.

6. Japanese people are more serious than Americans.
7. Americans are wealthier than Japanese people.
8. Japanese people are more educated than Americans.

Exercise 13

Answers will vary.

1. Rents are cheaper in my country. Rents are very expensive in the U.S.
2. Housing is better in the U.S. The quality of the houses is better here than in my country.
3. Cars are better in my country. I don't like American cars.
4. Education is better in my country. Our government spends more money on education.
5. Medical care is better in the U.S. The U.S. has all of the latest medical technology. But medical care is much cheaper in my country.
6. Food is better in the U.S. There is a better variety of food here than in my country.
7. Gasoline is cheaper in the U.S. Gasoline is very expensive in my country.
8. The government is better in the U.S. The people are more involved in the government in the U.S. than in my country.
9. Clothes are better in the U.S. People spend more money on clothes in the U.S. than in my country.
10. People are more relaxed in my country. They spend less time working.

Exercise 14

1. A turtle moves more slowly than a rabbit.
2. An elephant is bigger than a cow.
3. An elephant lives longer than a dog.
4. A whale stays under water longer than a dolphin.
5. A shark has a better sense of smell than a dolphin.
6. A bear runs faster than a person.

Exercise 15

Answers will vary.

1. Spanish people dress more stylishly.
2. Americans work harder.
3. Americans spend more.
4. Americans drive better.
5. Spanish people live longer.
6. Spanish people worry less.
7. Americans live more comfortably.
8. Americans have more freedom.
9. Americans drive more skillfully.
10. Spanish people have a better life.

Exercise 16

Answers will vary.

1. This class has fewer students than a class in my country.
2. This school has more courses than a school in my country.
3. The teachers in this school have less experience than teachers in a school in my country.

4. The library in this school has more books than a library in a school in my country.
5. This school has more facilities than a school in my country.
6. This school has fewer teachers than a school in my country.

Exercise 17

1. shorter than
2. the shortest; the fewest
3. the most common OR the commonest
4. more economical than
5. The most economical
6. the most popular
7. more popular than
8. the cheapest
9. farther
10. more beautiful than

Exercise 18

Answers will vary.

1. I'm not as old as my husband.
2. My mother-in-law is not as educated as I am.
3. I'm as intelligent as my brother.
4. My mother is not as patient as my father.
5. I am not as lazy as my sister.
6. My mother is as tall as my father.
7. I am not as religious as my mother.
8. I am as friendly as my brother.
9. I am not as strong as my brother.
10. I am as talkative as my mother.
11. My brother is not as athletic as my sister.
12. My brother is as interested in sports as my sister.

Exercise 19

Answers will vary.

1. I don't arrive at class as promptly as the teacher.
2. I work as hard in class as the teacher.
3. I don't understand American customs as well as the teacher.
4. I speak more quietly than the teacher.
5. I don't speak as fluently as the teacher.
6. I understand a foreigner's problems as well as the teacher.
7. I don't write as neatly as the teacher.
8. I don't speak as quickly as the teacher.

Exercises 20

Answers will vary.

1. Women don't earn as much money as men.
2. Women spend more money than men.
3. Women talk as much as men.
4. Men don't gossip as much as women.
5. Women don't use as many bad words as men.
6. Men have as many responsibilities as women.
7. Women don't have as much freedom as men.
8. Women don't have as much free time as men.

Exercise 21

Answers will vary.

1. This school doesn't have as many teachers as Teachers College.
2. Teachers College doesn't have as many classrooms as this school.
3. This school has as many floors as Teachers College.
4. Teachers College doesn't have as many English courses as this school.
5. This school has as many exams as Teachers College.
6. This school has as many students as Teachers College.

Exercise 22

Part A

Answers will vary.

Part B

Answers will vary.

1. I'm not as tall as Lisa.
2. Lisa doesn't have as much education as I do.
3. I don't work as many hours as Lisa.
4. I study more hours a day than Lisa.
5. I drive as carefully as Lisa.
6. I exercise more frequently than Lisa.
7. Lisa isn't taking as many courses as I am.
8. I have as many siblings as Lisa.
9. I live as far from school as Lisa.

Exercise 23

1. A motorcycle doesn't cost as much as a car.
2. Milk doesn't have as much fat as cream.
3. Men don't live as long as women.
4. I don't speak English as well as the teacher.
5. Miami doesn't have as many people as Chicago.
6. Los Angeles isn't as crowded as Tokyo.
7. Soccer isn't as popular as baseball in the U.S.
8. Soccer players don't have as many injuries as soccer players.

Exercise 24

Answers will vary.

1. Women in my country don't have as much freedom as American women.
2. Medial care in my country is cheaper than medial care in the U.S.
3. American teachers are less formal than teachers in my country.
4. Learning English in the U.S. is not as difficult as learning English in my country.

Exercise 25

Answers will vary.

1. My boyfriend is not as old as I am.
2. My son and daughter aren't the same height.
3. My friend and I are the same weight.
4. My two friends are the same nationality.

5. My parents aren't the same religion.
6. My parents have the same level of education.

Exercise 26

Answers will vary.

1. My bag and yours are the same color. They're both black.
2. My house and yours don't have the same value. Your house is much more valuable.
3. My feet aren't the same size as yours. I'm a size 7, and you're a size 6.
4. Our mirrors are the same shape. They're both round.
5. This subway token and this cup of coffee are the same price. They both cost $1.00.
6. She speaks the same language as you. Both of you speak Russian.

Exercise 27

Answers will vary.

1. taller
2. older
3. taller
4. larger
5. heavier

Exercise 28

Answers will vary.

1. Diet cola doesn't taste like regular cola to me.
2. Milk in the U.S. and milk in my country taste alike.
3. An American classroom doesn't look like a classroom in my country.
4. Asian music sounds like American music.
5. Polyester doesn't feel like silk.
6. Cologne and perfume smell alike.
7. Salt looks like sugar.
8. Salt doesn't taste like sugar.
9. Michael Jordan and Dennis Rodman don't act alike.
10. Michael Jordan and Dennis Rodman don't dress alike.
11. American teachers act like teachers in my country.
12. American teenagers dress like teenagers in my country.

Exercise 29

Answers will vary.

1. look
2. sound
3. acts like
4. looks like
5. dress alike
6. like
7. sound like
8. look
9. sound
10. act like

Exercise 30

Answers will vary.

1. A. Is an English class in the U.S. like an English class in your country?
   B. Yes, they are very similar.
2. A. Is your house in the U.S. like your house in your country?
   B. No, my house here in not like my house in my country. My house here is much smaller.
3. A. Is the weather in this city like the weather in your hometown?

B. Yes, the weather is alike. It is warm here and in my hometown.
4. A. Is American food like food in your country?
   B. No, American food isn't like food in my country. Food in my country has more spices.
5. A. Are women's clothes in the U.S. like women's clothes in your country?
   B. Yes, they are similar.
6. A. Is a college in the U.S. like a college in your country?
   B. No, a college in the U.S. isn't like a college in my country. There are many differences.
7. A. Are American teachers like teachers in your country?
   B. No, teachers in America aren't like teachers in my country. Teachers in America are less formal.
8. A. Are American athletes like athletes in your country?
   B. No, American athletes aren't like athletes in my country. American athletes make more money and are treated like celebrities.

Exercise 31

Answers will vary.

1. Borrow and lend are different.
2. Big and large are the same.
3. My book is the same as the teacher's book.
4. My last name is different from my mother's last name.
5. Washington, D.C. and Washington state are different.
6. L.A. is the same as Los Angeles.
7. 2+5 and 5+2 are the same.
8. A mile is different from a kilometer.
9. A half gallon is the same as two quarts.
10. An ESL course is different from a regular English course.
11. The Chicago Bulls are different from the Chicago Bears.
12. Football and rugby are different.

Exercise 32

A. I heard that you have a twin brother.
B. Yes, I do.
A. Do you look alike?
B. No he doesn't look like me at all.
A. But you're twins.
B. We're fraternal twins. That's different from identical twins who have the same genetic code. We're just brothers who were born at the same time. I'm much taller than his is.
A. But you're similar in many ways, aren't you?
B. No. We're completely different. I'm athletic, and David is not interested in sports at all. He's a much better student than I am. He's much more like our mother, who loves to read and learn new things, and I am like our father, who's athletic and loves to build things.
A. What about your character?
B. I'm outgoing and he's very shy. Also we don't dress alike at all. He likes to wear neat, conservative clothes, but I prefer torn jeans and T-shirts.
A. From your description, it sounds like you're not even from the same family.
B. We have one thing in common. We're both interested in the same girl at school.
A. What happened?
B. She didn't want to go out with either one of us!

Exercise 33

1. as much energy as
2. more mature than
3. more responsible
4. the best
5. older than
6. longer than
7. oldest
8. younger than
9. the same age
10. the most handsome
11. the same eyes
12. the same smile
13. as curly as
14. the most beautiful

LESSON TWELVE TEST / REVIEW

Part 1

1. as
2. largest
3. than
4. better
5. more crime
6. C
7. most
8. cities
9. C
10. types faster
11. states
12. drives more carefully
13. C
14. than she is
15. Your
16. doesn't look

1. the same
2. much as
3. looks
4. the same
5. from
6. size as
7. height.
8. tastes
9. is
10. alike
11. as soon as
12. the same
13. like
14. alike

Part 2

LESSON THIRTEEN

Exercise 1

1. A
2. A
3. P
4. P
5. P
6. A
7. P
8. P
9. A
10. A
11. A
12. P
13. P
14. A

Exercise 2

1. He will be chosen.
2. He is always chosen.
3. He can't be chosen.
4. He has been chosen.
5. She wasn't chosen.

6. Was she chosen?
7. She shouldn't be chosen.
8. Why was I chosen?

Exercise 3

1. The jury has made a decision.
2. The jury usually makes a decision.
3. The jury must make a decision.
4. The jury made a decision.
5. The jury can't make a decision.
6. He doesn't make a decision.
7. Did she make a decision?
8. When will they make a decision?
9. He probably made a decision.
10. How did we make a decision?

Exercise 4

1. are selected
2. are sent
3. are filled; (are) returned
4. are called
5. is chosen
6. are asked
7. are not permitted
8. are given

Exercise 5

1. was told
2. was called
3. was given
4. was shown
5. were taken
6. was asked
7. was not chosen
8. was sent

Exercise 6

1. has been repeated
2. have been written
3. have been chosen
4. have been paid
5. has been left
6. has been put
7. has been called
8. has been found

Exercise 7

1. will be given
2. should be written
3. must be used; it will be scored
4. can be used
5. will be graded
6. will not be permitted
7. will be collected
8. will be sent

Exercise 8

1. were asked
2. will be paid
3. were told
4. were given
5. are paid
6. should be used
7. were shown
8. Was; sent
9. Are; allowed
10. wasn't chosen

Exercise 9

1. The U.S. Constitution was signed by John Hancock.
2. Many mystery novels have been written by Steven King.
3. The telephone was invented by Alexander Graham Bell.
4. America was discovered by Columbus.

5. The airplane was invented by the Wright Brothers.
6. A bus boycott was led by Martin Luther King.
7. The laws are made by Congress.
8. A new law is signed by the president.
9. Microsoft was created by Bill Gates.
10. A decision will be made by the judge.

Exercise 10

1. I was sent a questionnaire.
2. We have been taken to a separate room.
3. We were told not to discuss the case.
4. Twelve people will be chosen.
5. Your name has been selected.
6. We weren't permitted to read any newspapers.
7. He will not be selected for jury duty again.
8. You will be paid.
9. We are not allowed to eat in the classroom.
10. My name has been called.

Exercise 11

1. Everyone had a good time.
2. I need you.
3. The dog ate my homework.
4. She will help you.
5. My classmates have seen the photo.
6. You should help your mother.
7. He spends a lot of money.
8. We see movies every week.
9. I wrote the paper.
10. The teacher explained the grammar.

Exercise 12

A. Why weren't you at work last week? Were you sick?
B. No. I was chosen to be on a jury.
A. How was it?
B. It was very interesting. A man was arrested for fighting with a police officer.
A. It sounds like an interesting case.
B. The jury selection was interesting too. But it took half a day to choose 12 people.
A. Why?
B. The judge and lawyers interviewed more than 50 people.
A. Why so many people?
B. Well, several people didn't understand the judge's questions. They didn't speak English very well. And a woman told the judge that she was very sick. The judge gave her permission to leave. I don't know why the other people weren't chosen.
A. What kind of questions were you asked by the judge and lawyers?
B. First the lawyers wanted to see if we could be fair to the police officer. Some jurors said that they had a bad experience with a police officer. Those jurors weren't selected.
A. Why not?
B. Because the judge probably thought they couldn't be fair in this case.
A. How long did the trial last?
B. Only two days.
A. Did you talk about the case with your family when you got home the first night?

B. Oh, no. We were told not to talk to anyone about the case. When it was over, I told my wife and kids about it. It was so interesting.

A. How long did it take the jurors to make a decision?

B. About two hours. One of the jurors didn't agree with the other eleven. We talked about the evidence until she changed her mind.

A. Did your boss pay you for the days you missed work?

B. Of course. He had to pay me. That's the law.

A. Now that you've done it once, you won't have to do it again. Right?

B. That's not true. This was the second time I was chosen.

Exercise 13

1. happened	7. worked
2. fell	8. was paid
3. did you sleep	9. went
4. was awakened	10. was chosen
5. lived	11. stayed
6. was raised	12. killed

LESSON THIRTEEN TEST / REVIEW

Part 1

1. should be taught	6. were; found
2. C	7. were found
3. was never given	8. happened
4. have had	9. C
5. C	10. aren't written

Part 2

1. English is spoken in the U.S.
2. A dictionary can be used during the test.
3. The criminal was taken to jail.
4. The President has been seen on TV many times.
5. You will be taken to the courtroom.
6. The mirror was broken into small pieces.
7. You are expected to learn English in the U.S.
8. Cameras aren't allowed in the courtroom.

Part 3

1. Paul McCartney wrote and sang the song *Yesterday*.
2. The teacher has told you to write a composition.

3. You must pay your phone bill.
4. The teacher does not allow you to use your books during a test.
5. The teacher will return the test.
6. Fleming discovered penicillin.
7. When do the bride and groom open wedding gifts?
8. The police didn't find your missing car.

Part 4

1. was taken
2. will visit
3. have seen
4. was seen
5. have
6. have been helped
7. died
8. were rescued
9. comes
10. was driven
11. wasn't known OR isn't known
12. didn't know OR doesn't know

LESSON FOURTEEN

Exercise 1

1. is a mineral. OR is an element.
2. is a continent.
3. is a vegetable.
4. is a country. ·
5. is a city.
6. are languages.
7. are countries.
8. are sports.
9. are animals.
10. are cities.

5. are baseball players.
6. were U.S. presidents.
7. John Kennedy was a U.S. president.
8. Oprah Winfrey is a TV talk show hostess.

Exercise 2

Answers will vary.

1. was a scientist.
2. was a baseball player.
3. is a singer.
4. was a boxer.

Exercise 3

1. an	5. some
2. any	6. some
3. a	7. a
4. an	8. any

Exercise 4
Conversation 1

1. a	6. some
2. The	7. the
3. an	8. an
4. a	9. the
5. the	

Conversation 2
1. a
2. the
3. a
4. the
5. a
6. some
7. a
8. the

Conversation 3
1. the
2. the
3. a
4. the
5. the
6. the
7. a
8. the
9. the
10. the
11. a

Exercise 5
1. ∅
2. The
3. The
4. A
5. The
6. ∅
7. The
8. ∅
9. The
10. ∅
11. ∅
12. The
13. ∅
14. The
15. ∅: ∅
16. The

Exercise 6
Answers will vary.

1. I don't like tea.
2. I like corn.
3. I like peaches.
4. I like potato chips.
5. I don't like milk.
6. I don't like oranges.
7. I like cookies.
8. I like pizza.
9. I don't like potatoes.
10. I don't like eggs.

Exercise 7
1. some
2. a
3. the
4. ∅ OR Some
5. a
6. some OR ∅
7. ∅
8. the
9. a
10. a
11. the
12. an
13. the
14. the
15. ∅
16. some OR ∅
17. the
18. the

Exercise 8
1. the
2. Some OR ∅
3. ∅ OR some
4. an
5. some OR ∅
6. The
7. ∅
8. some OR ∅
9. ∅
10. ∅

Exercise 9
Answers will vary.

1. All
2. Most
3. Very few
4. Some
5. Most
6. Most
7. Some
8. All
9. Few
10. All

Exercise 10
Answers will vary.

1. Some of the
2. All of the
3. None of the students is absent today.
4. Most of the
5. Very few of the
6. None of the students is married.
7. Some of the
8. All of the
9. Very few
10. Some

Exercise 11
1. Other
2. the other
3. Other
4. Another
5. The other
6. Other
7. The other
8. The other
9. Other
10. Another
11. the other
12. Other
13. Other; Others
14. Others
15. Other
16. The other
17. Others
18. other

Exercise 12
Answers will vary. See example.

Exercise 13
Answers will vary. See example.

Exercise 14
Answers will vary. See example.

Exercise 15
A. Can I have fifteen dollars?
B. What for?
A. I have to buy a poster of my favorite singer.
B. I gave you some (OR ∅) money last week. What did you do with it?
A. I spent it on a CD.
B. No, you can't have any more money until next week.
A. Please, please, please. All of my friends have it. I'll die if I don't get it.
B. What happened to all the money Grandpa gave you for your birthday?
A. I spent it.
B. What about the money you put in the bank after your graduatio?
A. I don't have any more money in the bank.
B. You have to learn that (∅) money doesn't grow on trees. If you want it, you'll have to work for it. You can start by cleaning your room.
A. But I cleaned it two weeks ago.
B. Two weeks ago was two weeks ago. It's dirty again.
A. I don't have any time. I have to meet my friends.
B. You can't go out. You need to do your homework.
A. I don't have any. Please let me have fifteen dollars.
B. When I was your age, I had a job. And I gave my parents

half of the money I earned. You kids today have an easy life.

A. Why do (∅) parents always say that to (∅) kids?

B. Because it's true. It's time you learn that (∅) life is hard.
A. I bet Grandpa said that to you when you were a child.
B. And I bet you'll say it to your kids when you're an adult.

LESSON FOURTEEN TEST / REVIEW

Part 1
1. All (of the) teachers
2. Some animals
3. Other
4. The other
5. C
6. C
7. C
8. one
9. C
10. is a country
11. C
12. C
13. C
14. The other brother OR My other brother
15. Most of OR Almost all of
16. The Golden Gate Bridge is

Part 2
1. some OR ∅
2.
12. a
13.

   the
3. a
4. the
5. the
6. some OR ∅
7. ∅
8. ∅
9. ∅
10. the
11. a

   a
14. some OR ∅
15. some OR ∅
16. ∅
17. ∅ OR a
18. a
19. a
20. the
21. the
22. the

Part 3
1. other
2. others
3. the other
4. another
5. the other (one)
6. the other
7. another

Part 4
1. it
2. them
3. any
4. any?
5. them
6. some.
7. it?
8. some
9. any.

LESSON FIFTEEN

Exercise 1
1. are you doing
2. 'm studying
3. Do you want
4. am trying
5. do you have
6. Do you mean
7. gives
8. think
9. seems
10. learn
11. review
12. take
13. is improving
14. do you learn
15. write
16. study
17. have
18. gives

Exercise 2
1. study
2. will buy
3. C
4. I'm
5. takes
6. have
7. C
8. are going to OR will
9. C
10. Will you be angry
11. 'll cook
12. C
13. has
14. C

Exercise 3
1. am writing
2. am waiting
3. am taking
4. like
5. will have OR are going to have

6. arrives
7. we'll study OR we are going to study
8. knows
9. don't understand
10. explains
11. study
12. are going to study
13. is going to show
14. see
15. is walking
16. will write
17. have

Exercise 4
1. started
2. was studying
3. broke
4. had
5. went
6. lived
7. wanted
8. studied
9. got
10. arrived
11. was waiting
12. took
13. were driving
14. was looking
15. seemed
16. was thinking
17. said
18. started

Exercise 5
1. have been working OR have worked
2. have been trying

3. have had
4. haven't found
5. haven't lost
6. worked
7. haven't learned
8. are talking
9. have always wanted

Exercise 6
1. broke
2. lived
3. have worked OR have been working
4. have been watching
5. have been studying
6. C
7. was sleeping
8. know
9. eat
10. C

Exercise 7
1. were eating
2. came
3. followed
4. said
5. have been
6. have decided
7. left
8. went
9. felt
10. am looking
11. buy
12. look
13. haven't found
14. suggested
15. went
16. was waiting
17. noticed
18. saw
19. was writing
20. came
21. introduced
22. took
23. gave
24. will start OR am going to start
25. am going to call OR will call
26. hope
27. need
28. find
29. am going to save

Exercise 8
1. I was waiting; were you
2. C
3. seen
4. is
5. There are
6. Were
7. been
8. were
9. She is talking
10. My sister is in
11. C
12. was stolen

Exercise 9
1. to learn
2. able to find
3. to see
4. C
5. C
6. to talk
7. Mr. Jackson to fix
8. to pay
9. C
10. C
11. like to write
12. want him to go
13. important to explain
14. C
15. sorry to keep
16. C
17. to drive
18. able to help

Exercise 10
1. talk
2. can't
3. talk
4. write
5. C
6. shouldn't
7. shouldn't
8. C
9. C
10. couldn't

Exercise 11
1. C
2. Did she buy
3. Did she drive
4. When did your father come
5. were you doing
6. C
7. did the airplane arrive?
8. C
9. C
10. were you doing
11. TK
12. does he go
13. will you do
14. knows
15. will your father arrive
16. do you spell
17. does "bug" mean?
18. is he speaking
19. C
20. C
21. C
22. can't you
23. C
24. How old are you?
25. C

Exercise 12
1. happened
2. moved
3. were carrying
4. dropped
5. broke
6. pointed
7. said
8. have lived OR have been living
9. haven't heard
10. am getting
11. is
12. want
13. to come
14. come
15. will see
16. want
17. to take
18. can pay
19. receive
20. know
21. have
22. have used
23. have recommended
24. do not fix
25. will never use
26. will tell
27. don't take

Exercise 13

1. hasn't been living
2. won't receive
3. didn't break
4. doesn't write
5. wasn't living
6. doesn't need to fix
7. isn't going to tell
8. can't ignore

Exercise 14

1. When did she move?
2. How long has she lived (OR has she been living) in her new apartment?
3. Why is she complaining?
4. When will he receive her letter?
5. Why won't she use the company again?
6. Who broke the table?
7. How much should he pay her?
8. When does she want him to look at the table?
9. Why hasn't Mr. Jackson called her?
10. Whom is Margaret going to tell her problem to?
11. How many times has she used the company?
12. What does she want Mr. Jackson to do?
13. Where were they carrying it when they dropped it?
14. How much did the table cost?

Exercise 15

1. My sister and I went to the movies.
2. Before his father arrived, he was very unhappy.
3. She read the letter very quickly.

4. We go to a baseball game from time to time. OR From time to time, we go to a baseball game.
5. She is 25 years old.
6. She can't understand the lesson.
7. C
8. Their house is very expensive.
9. The car that my brother bought cost $5000.
10. Your composition is very interesting.
11. There are a lot of new books in the library.
12. London is a very beautiful city.
13. He didn't go skiing yesterday because it was too cold.
14. C
15. My wife made dinner when she came home from work.
16. It is important to speak English well.
17. I didn't understand anything the teacher said.
18. I usually go to bed at 11:30.
19. C
20. You should always bring your dictionary to class.
21. C
22. My wife is very intelligent.
23. He doesn't have any money for college.

LESSON ONE

Exercise 1
1. has been
2. have seen
3. has had
4. has got
5. have been
6. have always been
7. has recently graduated
8. have read
9. has never worked
10. has written
11. has sent
12. has interviewed

Exercise 2
1. have
2. had
3. ve
4. have
5. have
6. had/owned
7. Have
8. have
9. has
10. been
11. has
12. been
13. told
14. Have
15. ve
16. interviewed

Exercise 3
1. in Chicago
2. two years
3. three
4. a large hotel
5. the hotel business
6. his phone number
7. four
8. found

Exercise 4
1. since
2. long
3. since
4. graduated
5. [correct as is]
6. past
7. Have
8. How long
9. s / since
10. ve

Exercise 5
Answers will vary.

1. I've always disliked loud music.
2. I've always liked good food.
3. I've always wanted to own my own house.
4. I've always wanted to travel around the world.
5. I've always believed in freedom and justice.

Exercise 6
Answers will vary.

1. I've always lived in the same city.
2. I've always been very shy.
3. I've always had lots of friends.
4. I've always liked to read.

Exercise 7
Answers will vary.

1. I've never tried sushi.
2. I've never drunk coffee.
3. I've never owned a car.
4. I've never gone to Europe.
5. The teacher has never been late.

Exercise 8
Answers will vary.

1. I've never learned to play an instrument, but I'd like to.
2. I've never been on a long vacation, but I'd like to.
3. I've never been to a concert, but I'd like to.
4. I've never tried Vietnamese food, but I'd like to.

Exercise 9
Answers will vary.

1. I haven't seen my sister in a long time.
2. I haven't visited my hometown in a long time.
3. I haven't had fish soup for a long time.
4. I haven't studied algebra since high school.
5. I haven't played soccer since I was a child.
6. I haven't had time to read a book since I started to study English.

Exercise 10
1. A: have you had
   B: have had
2. A: have you been
   B: have been married
3. B: do
   A: have you had
   B: have had / for / [nine months]
4. A: How long / have you wanted
   B: have wanted / moved
5. B: does
   A: long has she had
   B: has had / [she was a teenager]
6. A: Is
   A: has she been
   B: [the last nine months]
7. B: does
   A: How / has it had
   B: has had / [last year]
8. B: do
   A: have you known
   B: have known / since / were
9. A: Does / have
   B: does
   A: has he had a cell phone
   B: has had
10. B: do
    A: Have / liked
    B: has / liked

Exercise 11

1. always taught adults?
2. always taught ESL?
3. always been a teacher at this college?
4. always thought about grammar?
5. always been easy for you?
6. [Smith] / always been [Smith]?
7. always lived in this city?
8. always liked teaching?

Exercise 12

Answers will vary.

1. A: Are you a good student?
   B: Yes, I am.
   A: Have you always been a good student?
   B: Yes. I've been a good student ever since I was a little kid.
2. A: Do you wear glasses?
   B: No, I don't.
   A: Have you ever worn glasses?
   B: No, I've never worn glasses.
3. A: Do you like to travel?
   B: Yes, I do?
   A: have you always liked to travel?
   B: Yes, I've liked to travel since my first trip to the west coast.
4. A: Are you interested in politics?
   B: Yes, I am.
   A: Have you always been interested in politics?
   B: Yes, I've been interested in politics ever since I can remember.
5. A: Do you like movies?
   B: No, I don't.
   A: Have you always been like that?
   B: Yes, I've never liked movies.
6. A: Are you an optimist?
   B: Yes, I am.
   A: Have you always been an optimist?
   B: Yes, I've been an optimist ever since I can remember.
7. A: Do you think about your future?
   B: Yes, I do.
   A: Have you always thought about your future?
   B: No, I've just started thinking about my future recently.
8. A: Do you live in an apartment?
   B: Yes, I do.
   A: Have you always lived in an apartment?
   B: Yes, I've lived in an apartment ever since I moved out of my parents' house.
9. A: Are you a friendly person?
   B: Yes, I am.
   A: Have you always been a friendly person?
   B: Yes, I've always been friendly.
10. A: Do you use credit cards?
    B: No, I don't.
    A: Have you ever used credit cards?
    B: No, I've never owned one.

Exercise 13

1. A: have / worked
   B: have worked

2. A: Does
   A: has / studying English
   B: has been studying / [retired]
3. B: does
   A: has she been
   B: has been teaching
4. B: do
   A: long have you been wearing
   B: have been wearing / was
5. A: Do
   B: do
   A: long have they lived
   B: [about three years]
6. B: is
   A: has he been preparing
   B: [February]
7. A: Are
   B: am
   A: long have been studying
   B: have been studying
8. A: Is
   B: is
   A: has he been using
   B: he has been using / since
9. A: Is
   B: is
   A: has it been raining
   B: has been raining / [this morning]
10. A: Is
    B: is
    A: has she been talking
    B: [hours]

Exercise 14

Answers will vary.

1. as a legal secretary.
2. in New York.
3. college.
4. get a degree in legal studies.
5. casual clothes.
6. a grammar point.
7. the chores I need to do when I get home.
8. a pen to write these answers.

Exercise 15

1. was
2. was
3. has Bill Clinton been
4. has been / 1993.
5. have been studying
6. studied
7. lived
8. have lived / [three]
9. did you buy
10. bought
11. have you had
12. have had
13. have you known
14. have known
15. did you meet
16. met
17. did you study English
18. have you studied

Exercise 16

1. I have had three jobs.
2. I have had a lot of job interviews.
3. I haven't had any traffic tickets.
4. I have bought one car.
5. I have attended two schools.

6. I have lived in one apartment.
7. I have gone downtown countless times.

Exercise 17

1. A: How much tea have you had today?
   B: I haven't had any tea today.
2. A: How many glasses of water have you had today?
   B: I've had about two glasses of water.
3. A: How many cookies have you eaten today?
   B: I haven't eaten any cookies today.
4. A: How many glasses of cola have you had today?
   B: I've had one glass of cola.
5. A: How many e-mails have you sent today?
   B: I've sent a lot of e-mails.
6. A: How many miles have you walked today?
   B: I've walked about five miles today.
7. A: How much money have you spent today?
   B: I've spent about ten dollars so far.
8. A: How much coffee have you had?
   B: I've had about three cups of coffee.

Exercise 18

1. have made	11. haven't had
2. had	12. Was it
3. had	13. never had
4. has offered	14. graduated
5. have been	15. found
6. have seen	16. worked
7. given	17. have had
8. gave	18. had
9. haven't had	19. lived
10. have talked	20. lived

Exercise 19

The following verb phrases should be underlined in the passage:

I've been going	I've realized
I've been looking	I've talked
I've just rewritten	I've taken
I haven't found	I've also taken
I've already given	Have you decided
I've worked	I've decided
I haven't had	

Exercise 20

Answers will vary.

1. A: Have you ever found money on the street?
   B: Yes, I found money on the street once.
2. A: Have you ever gone to a garage sale?
   B: Yes, I've been to garage sales many times.
3. A: Have you ever met a famous person?
   B: No, I've never met a famous person.
4. A: Have you ever studied art history?
   B: Yes, I studied art history when I was a freshman.
5. A: Have you ever got a ticket for speeding?
   B: No, I've never got a speeding ticket.
6. A: Have you ever been on television?
   B: No, I've never been on television.
7. A: Have you ever won a contest?
   B: Yes, I won a contest last year.

8. A: Have you ever loaned money to a friend?
   B: Yes, I've loaned money to friends many times.
9. A: Have you ever lost your keys?
   B: Yes, I've lost my keys several times.
10. A: Have you broke an arm or a leg?
    B: Yes, I broke my arm when I was a little kid.
11. A: Have you ever got lost in this city?
    B: Yes, I got lost a few times when I first moved here.
12. A: Have you ever gone to court?
    B: No, I've never been to court.
13. A: Have you ever heard of Martin Luther King, Jr.?
    B: Yes, I have.
14. A: Have you ever eaten in a Vietnamese restaurant?
    B: Yes, I've eaten in a Vietnamese restaurant a few times.
15. A: Have you ever ordered products over the Internet?
    B: Yes, I ordered something over the Internet last month.

Exercise 21

Answers will vary.

1. A: Have you ever gone to a football game?
   B: Yes, I have.
   A: When did you go to a football game?
   B: I went to one last year.
2. A: Have you ever told a lie.
   B: No, I haven't.
3. A: Have you ever gone to Canada.
   B: Yes, I have.
   A: When did you go to Canada?
   B: I went there last summer.
4. A: Have you ever traveled by train.
   B: Yes, I have.
   A: When did you travel by train?
   B: I traveled by train on my last vacation.
5. A: Have you ever eaten pizza?
   B: Yes, I have.
   A: When did you eat pizza?
   B: I eat pizza all the time.
6. A: Have you ever been to Disneyworld?
   B: Yes, I have.
   A: When did you go to Disneyworld.
   B: I used to go to Disneyworld a lot when I was a kid.
7. A: Have you ever been on a roller coaster.
   B: No, I haven't.
8. A: Have you ever seen a play in this city?
   B: Yes, I have.
   A: When did you see a play here?
   B: I saw Shakespeare In the Park last spring.
9. A: Have you ever eaten Chinese food?
   B: Yes, I have.
   A: When did you eat Chinese food?
   A: I used to eat Chinese food a lot when I lived in San Francisco.
10. A: Have you ever used a fax machine?
    B: Yes, I have.
    A: When did you use a fax machine?
    B. I have to use a fax machine every day at work.
11. A: Have you ever bought a lottery ticket?
    B: No, I haven't.
12. A: Have you ever gone camping?
    B: Yes, I have.

A: When did you go camping?
B: I go camping every summer with my family.

Exercise 22

Answers will vary.

1. Have you ever learned another language?
2. Have you ever been to Cape Verde?
3. Have you ever taught at another school?
4. Have you ever studied in another country?

Exercise 23

1. B: have / liked
2. A: been
   A: Have
   B: went
3. B: broke / fell
   A: did / break
4. A: Have
   B: have / came
5. A: Have / seen
   B: have
   A: have / seen
6. A: Have / been
   B: have / went / read
   A: Have / read
   B: read

Exercise 24

Answers will vary.

1. A: Have you ever filled out a job application?
   B: Yes, I've filled out many applications.
2. A: Have you ever had an interview?
   B: Yes, I've had several interviews.
3. A: Have you ever used the Occupational Outlook Handbook?
   B: No, I never have.
4. A: Have you ever seen a job counselor?
   B: Yes, I saw a counselor last week.
5. A: Have you ever attended a job fair?
   B: No, I never have.
6. A: Have you ever used a résumé writing service?
   B: Yes, I used one once.
7. A: Have you ever taken courses to train for a job?
   B: Yes, I took a job-training course last year.
8. A: Have you ever used the Internet to find a job?
   B: Yes, I've used the Internet many times to look for jobs.
9. A: Have you ever gone to a state employment office.
   B: No, I never have.
10. A: Have you ever read a book about finding a job?
    B: Yes, I've read a few.
11. A: Have you ever quit a job?
    B: Yes, I quit my last job.
12. A: Have you ever had your own business?
    B: Yes, I have my own business at home.

Exercise 25

Answers will vary.

1. A: Have you bought all your books yet.
   B: Yes, I've bought all the books I need for all my classes.

2. A: Have you decided what you want to major in yet?
   B: Yes, I want to major in Political Science.
3. A: Have you registered for all your classes yet?
   B: No, I haven't.
4. A: Have you paid your tuition yet?
   B: Yes, I paid it last week.
5. A: Have you visited the school library yet?
   B: Yes, I went there last night.
6. A: Have you finished all the class assignments yet?
   B: No, I haven't.

Exercise 26

1. A: Have we had an exam yet?
   B: Yes, we have. We had a midterm exam last week.
2. A: Have we studied modals yet?
   B: No, we haven't.
3. A: Have you learned the irregular past tenses yet?
   B: No, not yet.
4. A: Has the teacher learned the students' names yet?
   B: Yes, he has. He learned everybody's names quickly.
5. A: Have you learned the other students' names yet?
   B: No, I haven't.
6. A: Has the teacher taught the past perfect yet?
   B: Yes, he has. He started teaching it last week.

Exercise 27

1. He has already bought a new tie.
2. He has already washed his white shirt.
3. He hasn't ironed his white shirt yet.
4. He has already got a haircut.
5. He has already rewritten his résumé.
6. He hasn't taken his resume to the copy center yet.
7. He has already seen a job counselor.
8. He hasn't put his papers in his briefcase yet.
9. He hasn't sent for transcripts yet.
10. He has already got his letters of recommendation.

Exercise 28

1. A: eaten
   B: ate
2. A: Has
   B: got / had
   A: got
   B: got
3. A: found
   B: haven't
4. A: seen
   B: saw
5. B: thought
   A: made / bought
6. A: started
   B: started
7. B: Have / made
8. A: Has / arrived
9. B: left
   B: left
10. B: finished

Exercise 29

1. A: Have you written to your family lately?
   B: Yes, I have. I wrote them a letter last week.

2. A: Have you gone to the library recently?
   B: Yes, I have. I went to the library yesterday.
3. A: Have you gone to the zoo lately?
   B: No, I haven't.
4. A: Have you seen any good movies lately?
   B: Yes, I have. I saw a good movie last week.
5. A: Have you received any letters lately?
   B: Yes, I have. I got a letter from my boyfriend yesterday.
6. A: Have you been absent lately?
   B: Yes, I have. I was absent last week.
7. A: have you had a job interview lately?
   B: No, I haven't.
8. A: have you read any good books recently?
   B: No, I haven't. I never have enough time.
9. A: Have you made any long-distance calls lately?
   B: Yes, I have. I called my mother in California last week.
10. A: Have you taken any tests recently?
    B: Yes, I have. I had a test in my other class on Monday.

Exercise 30

Answers will vary.

1. Have you taken a day off lately?
2. Have you read any good books lately?
3. Have you been on a trip recently?
4. Have you enjoyed the weather lately?

Exercise 31
1. A: taken
   B: haven't
2. A: seen
   B: saw
3. A: gone
   B: went
4. A: bought
   B: bought
5. A: had
   B: haven't had
6. A: had
   B: have / had
7. A: done
   B: did
8. A: gone
   B: haven't

Exercise 32

Answers will vary.

Exercise 33

Answers will vary. The following are samples.

1. My reading comprehension has been improving.
2. My hearing has been getting worse.
3. My reading speed has been increasing.
4. My friend has been helping me with my studies.

Exercise 34

Answers will vary.

Exercise 35

Answers will vary.

Exercise 36
1. have tried
2. have eaten
3. tried
4. have met
5. have seen
6. saw
7. asked
8. have visited
9. have gone
10. have taken
11. have even gone
12. have learned
13. have written
14. have had
15. have gone
16. have even used
17. went
18. gave

Exercise 37
1. He's been staying in bed.
2. She has just lost her job.
3. She has been looking for a new job.
4. I have been writing compositions.
5. She has changed her mind.
6. I have been meeting new people.
7. I have received a check from my insurance company.
8. I have been saving my money.
9. I have made my decision.
10. I have been working on my composition.

Exercise 38
1. has had
2. took
3. fell
4. hurt
5. didn't / go
6. happened
7. thought
8. has been getting

Exercise 39
1. have worked
2. became / took
3. have never thought
4. have been cutting
5. have never had
6. worked
7. have been / have had / have not had
8. have been thinking
9. was /
10. have often asked
11. have been using
12. have had / have not found
13. have never wanted to be
14. have always wanted to
15. have been looking
16. started
17. have been driving
18. Have you ever sold
19. have always liked
20. was

LESSON ONE TEST / REVIEW

Part 1
1. How long have you known
2. C
3. for five months
4. ever gone
5. has our teacher worked
6. I've been studying English for three years.
7. have you been living
8. since he came
9. have you called
10. did you come
11. C
12. given
13. C
14. has had

Part 2
1. have lived
2. has changed
3. came
4. worked
5. don't have
6. have been looking
7. haven't found
8. had
9. have met
10. have not known
11. have always wanted
12. got
13. have not bought
14. came
15. has not been easy

LESSON TWO

Exercise 1
1. (A)
2. (P)
3. (A)
4. (P)
5. (P)
6. (P)
7. (A)
8. (P)
9. (P)
10. (P)
11. (A)
12. (P)
13. (P)
14. (P)
15. (A)

Exercise 2
1. is seen
2. will be chosen
3. can be seen
4. have been made
5. is printed
6. was given
7. is being shown
8. was made
9. has been shown
10. were given
11. was given
12. was added
13. are often made
14. was / chosen / was

Exercise 3
1. Tom Sawyer was written by Mark Twain.
2. Huckleberry Finn was written by him, too.
3. Moon River was composed by Henry Mancini.
4. The light bulb was invented by Thomas Edison.
5. Mona Lisa was painted by Leonardo DaVinci.
6. The Old Man and the Sea was written by Ernest Hemingway.
7. The airplane was invented by the Wright brothers.
8. The theory of relativity was developed by Albert Einstein.
9. Star Wars was directed by George Lucas.
10. People was sung by Barbara Streisand.
11. Porgy and Bess was composed by George Gershwin.
12. President Nixon was played by Anthony Hopkins in a 1995 movie.

Exercise 4
1. Steven Spielberg made E.T.
2. He directed Jurassic Park, too.
3. Joseph Fiennes played Shakespeare in a 1998 movie.
4. Stephen King has written many novels.
5. Screenwriters rewrite many novels to make them into movies.
6. Steven Spielberg has made many great movies.
7. The Academy gave Spielberg an award for Schindler's List.
8. Calvin Klein will design the costumes.
9. Robin Williams presented the Oscar.
10. Spielberg is making a new movie.

Exercise 5
1. Many movies are made in Hollywood.
2. Parental guidance is suggested for many movies.
3. The popcorn is fresh. It is being made now.
4. Some old movies have been colorized.
5. Movie ratings can be found in the newspaper.
6. Children aren't allowed to see some movies.
7. Most older movies can be rented at a video store.
8. The winners will be announced soon.
9. In 1927, only 15 Oscars were presented.
10. Who was invited to the Oscar presentation?
11. The Academy Awards weren't seen on TV until 1952.
12. A new theater is being built near my house.
13. The movie was filmed in Canada.
14. A new movie is being filmed now.
15. All the tickets have been sold.
16. The video can be found in the sci-fi section of the video store.
17. I went to buy popcorn and my seat was taken.
18. A videocassette recorder is called a "VCR."
19. Videos should be returned before midnight.
20. Old movies can be seen on TV.
21. Rain Man was chosen as the best film of 1988.
22. Awards are given every year for the best movies.
23. The Oscar ceremony is televised each year.
24. In a movie theater, "coming attractions" are shown before the main movie.
25. An accident happened while the movie was being filmed.
26. The passive voice is used in technical writing.
27. Sound was added to movies in 1927.
28. English isn't spoken in Cuba.

Exercise 6

1. is known
2. was made
3. did not see
4. is being shown
5. was it filmed
6. are made
7. were probably done
8. have been made
9. were sold
10. was told
11. should be seen
12. were made
13. is being used
14. were filmed

Exercise 7

1. was called
2. were given
3. be driven / was towed
4. is repaired
5. were ordered
6. will be paid

Exercise 8

1. My brother will rent a video.
2. He should return the video.
3. The reviewer predicted the winner.
4. Steven Spielberg is announcing the winner's name.
5. I was watching the Oscar presentation when the phone rang.
6. The viewers are discussing the movie.
7. George Lucas has made good movies.
8. Calvin Klein designs many beautiful dresses.
9. Dustin Hoffman won an Academy Award.
10. The actress did not wear a black dress.
11. Did Randy Newman write the music?
12. Everyone at the Oscar presentations had a good time.
13. The winner usually thanks relatives.
14. Did your brother buy the tickets?
15. The teacher will show the children a movie.

Exercise 9

1. No change
2. Reagan was shot.
3. No change
4. Brady was changed by his experience in 1981.
5. The assassin was stopped before he could run away.
6. No change
7. No change
8. No change
9. The video store is opened at 9 a.m.
10. It is closed at 11 p.m.
11. No change
12. After hours, videos can be returned through the slot.

Exercise 10

1. invited
2. went
3. saw
4. was directed
5. happened
6. were eating
7. are sold
8. buy
9. are shown
10. were talking
11. started
12. became
13. applauded
14. were being shown
15. was reading
16. were left
17. was told
18. was divided
19. can be shown
20. make
21. enjoyed

Exercise 11

1. got elected
2. did not get reelected
3. got shot
4. got wounded
5. got killed
6. get hired
7. get paid
8. got stolen
9. got punished
10. get done
11. get sent
12. got taken
13. got caught
14. get towed

Exercise 12

1. The movie is frightening. / The children are frightened.
2. The book is interesting. / The children are interested.
3. The children are amusing. / The adults are amused.
4. The trip was tiring. / The children were tired.
5. The game was exciting. / The children were excited.
6. The vacation was exhausting. / The adults were exhausted.
7. The movie was boring. / The adults were bored.
8. Chaplin is interesting. / I am interested.

Exercise 13

1. tired
2. interesting
3. embarrassed
4. frightening
5. frightened
6. annoying
7. frustrating
8. disappointed
9. amused
10. exciting
11. exciting
12. excited

Exercise 14

1. closed
2. located
3. married
4. allowed
5. made
6. involved
7. paid
8. born
9. known
10. involved

Exercise 15

Answers will vary. The following are samples.

1. Julia Roberts
2. foreign
3. theater
4. crime
5. finding a job
6. Denzel Washington / actor
7. Yo Yo Ma
8. are more settled
9. see violent films
10. in the center of town

Exercise 16

1. tired
2. born
3. air conditioned
4. located
5. married
6. allowed
7. known
8. done
9. lost
10. made

Exercise 17

1. am confused
2. got confused
3. got married
4. is married
5. is well
6. gets well
7. got upset
8. is upset
9. is old
10. get old
11. is rich
12. got rich

Part 1

1. wasn't written
2. was taken
3. was found
4. C
5. did the accident happen
6. C
7. C
8. can be found
9. C
10. C
11. was Gone With the Wind made
12. C
13. C
14. didn't get killed
15. C
16. C
17. C / he became
18. C / him

Part 2

1. Whoopi Goldberg was given an Oscar for her performance in Ghost.
2. Which actor will be chosen next year?
3. Julia Roberts has been seen in many movies.
4. Star Wars should be seen on a big screen.
5. Star Wars can be found in the sci-fi section of the video store.
6. Gone With the Wind wasn't filmed in black and white.
7. A new movie is being filmed in New York.
8. Children under 17 aren't permitted to see some movies.
9. John Travolta is known for his performance in Saturday Night Fever.
10. When was Saturday Night Fever made?

Part 3

1. I did not see Star Wars.
2. George Lucas is directing the movie.
3. He is taking her to the movies.
4. Children shouldn't see some movies.
5. Jodie Foster won an Oscar.
6. Dustin Hoffman played Tootsie.
7. The audience was watching a movie.
8. When did George Lucas make Star Wars?
9. We will buy popcorn.
10. She doesn't eat popcorn during a movie.

Part 4

1. were made
2. are collected
3. always returns
4. usually write
5. be written
6. are not permitted
7. always watches
8. be returned
9. study
10. is always spoken
11. are not usually used
12. be sent

Part 5

1. confused
2. I am very tired
3. C
4. C
5. C
6. C
7. C / married
8. C
9. I'm not satisfied
10. is located
11. isn't crowded
12. Are you disappointed

Part 6

1. interesting
2. interested
3. known
4. allowed
5. married
6. entertaining
7. bored
8. exciting
9. interested
10. crowded
11. frightened
12. frightening
13. disappointed
14. exciting

LESSON THREE

Exercise 1

1. had left
2. had already made
3. had originally had
4. had received
5. had been
6. had broken
7. had happened
8. had been found
9. had already been invented
10. had ever been built

Exercise 2

1. had had
2. had been absent
3. had expired
4. had learned
5. had never spoken
6. had always had
7. had seen
8. had cut

Exercise 3

1. In 1912, the Wright brothers had already flown the first airplane.
2. In 1912, Henry Ford had not yet mass-produced cars.
3. In 1912, the radio had already been invented.
4. In 1912, President McKinley had been assassinated.
5. In 1912, the U.S. had not yet declared war on Germany.
6. In 1912, San Francisco had already been destroyed by an earthquake.
7. In 1912, the U.S. government had not yet started to collect income tax.

Exercise 4

1. By the time he left work, he had finished all his reports.
2. By the time she saw the movie, her husband had already seen it.
3. By the time the late movie was over, he had already fallen asleep.

4. By the time my parents got married, they had already known each other for ten years.
5. By the time the fire department arrived, the building had already burned down.
6. By the time I started college, I had already studied English in high school.
7. By the time I read about the Titanic in my grammar book, I had already seen the movie Titanic.
8. By the time he graduated from college, he had already found a job.

Exercise 5

Answers will vary.

1. By the time I got to class, the teacher had already arrived.
2. By the time I got to class, most of the students had already arrived.
3. When I got to class, the class hadn't begun yet.
4. By the time I got to class, the teacher had already taken attendance.
5. By the time I got to class, I had already done the homework.
6. When I got to class, the teacher hadn't handed back the homework yet.
7. By the time I got to class, the teacher had already explained the past perfect.

Exercise 6

Answers will vary.

1. When I got my first job, I hadn't bought a car yet.
2. By the time I got my first job, I had already finished high school.
3. When I got my first job, I hadn't started college yet.
4. By the time I got my first job, I had already studied English.
5. By the time I got my first job, I had already moved out of my parents' house.
6. When I got my first job, I hadn't lived by myself yet.
7. By the time I got my first job, I had already turned 18.

Exercise 7

1. I realized I had left my umbrella at work.
2. The captain realized that the Titanic had come close to the iceberg.
3. I didn't know you had lost your job.
4. I didn't know you had lived in Japan when you were a child.
5. I didn't know you had watered the plants.
6. I realized I had locked the keys in the car.
7. He thought he had lost his wallet.
8. The captain realized he had made a big mistake.

Exercise 8

1. had ever seen
2. had ever taken
3. had ever bought
4. had ever done
5. had ever made
6. had ever met
7. had ever seen

Exercise 9

1. got up / had already risen
2. noticed / had already made
3. made / had left
4. had to / had taken
5. got / had not arrived yet
6. went / had spoken
7. had
8. had already gone / got
9. fell / had had

Exercise 10

1. 1 / 2
2. 2 / 1
3. 1 / 2
4. 2 / 1
5. 2 / 1
6. 1 / 2
7. 2 / 1
8. 1 / 2

Exercise 11

1. came
2. had received
3. bought
4. had been removed
5. ran
6. broke
7. had never seen
8. had already died

Exercise 12

1. had waited / got
2. had been living / left
3. felt / had worked
4. had studied / broke out
5. left / had gone on
6. waited / had gotten
7. had gotten / traveled

Exercise 13

1. had been working
2. have been working
3. had spent
4. have spent
5. has never seen
6. had never seen
7. had never eaten
8. has eaten

Exercise 14

1. were dancing
2. was taking
3. were playing
4. was reading
5. was serving
6. was trying

Exercise 15

1. traveled / was traveling
2. was emigrating / happened
3. were eating / dancing / hit
4. was sleeping / heard
5. were being lowered / was sinking
6. jumped / was being lowered
7. were rowing / carried
8. was living / died

Exercise 16

1. was working
2. called
3. was watching
4. saw
5. thought
6. did not understand
12. found out
13. got
14. came
15. was doing
16. arrived
17. did you do

7. did not know
8. was talking
9. was working
10. was doing
11. did you find out

18. found out
19. was going
20. realized
21. explained
22. promised

Exercise 17
1. saw / tried
2. had been
3. was traveling / hit
4. were sleeping / heard
5. heard / woke
6. went / had already left
7. arrived / had already sunk
8. picked
9. made
10. was making / sank
11. was finally found
12. have been
13. have been written
14. have been made
15. had ever occurred
16. had already seen

Exercise 18
1. have rented
2. Have you ever seen
3. have never seen
4. saw

12. died
13. was planning
14. met
15. fell

5. rented
6. was watching
7. went
8. had to
9. have forgotten
10. ended
11. sank

16. was traveling
17. felt
18. she had ever felt
19. found out
20. became
21. have already seen

Exercise 19
1. lived
2. fell
3. took
4. was studying
5. was taking
6. came
7. had fallen
8. became
9. stopped
10. told
11. got
12. had already made
13. were
14. had been working
15. left
16. had
17. took
18. left
19. had taken
20. left
21. went
22. stayed

23. were waiting
24. studied
25. wanted
26. was helping
27. ran
28. had given
29. were
30. told
31. arrived
32. was waiting
33. was holding
34. were
35. started
36. have been
37. finished
38. has not taken
39. has been studying
40. has been working
41. have had
42. had taken
43. had given

LESSON THREE TEST / REVIEW

Part 1
1. was working / C
2. have you been living / have you lived
3. got
4. C
5. Have you ever seen
6. C
7. C
8. came / had never studied
9. C / was
10. C
11. have been working
12. has been
13. had finished / C
14. happened
15. C
16. was wearing
17. C
18. C
19. C
20. C
21. C
22. C

Part 2
1. had already had / registered
2. wanted / had never gone

3. got / had already explained
4. realized / had left
5. was / had never driven
6. started / had already studied
7. died / jumped
8. had already died / was found
9. called / started
10. had already burned

Part 3
1. had
2. did it happen
3. was driving
4. ran
5. stopped
6. hit
7. was following
8. Did you get
9. hit
10. got
11. gave

12. had only had
13. have been driving
14. got
15. had had
16. moved
17. Have you ever gotten
18. was driving
19. stopped
20. gave
21. wasn't wearing

LESSON FOUR

Exercise 1
1. have
2. put
3. take
4. be
5. put/install
6. buy
7. wear

Exercise 2
Answers will vary.

1. study
2. teach
3. rest
4. practice
5. go on a diet
6. check the dictionary
7. exercise

Exercise 3
Answers will vary.

Exercise 4
Answers will vary.

Exercise 5
1. am supposed to do
2. am not supposed to talk
3. am supposed to clean
4. am supposed to tell my parents
5. am supposed to help / am supposed to wash / am supposed to take out
6. am supposed to put / am not supposed to spend
7. is supposed to put
8. is not supposed to turn on
9. is not supposed to watch
10. is supposed to go

Exercise 6
Answers will vary.

Exercise 7
1. don't have to
2. must not
3. don't have to
4. must not
5. don't have to
6. must not
7. must not
8. don't have to
9. must not
10. don't have to
11. don't have to
12. must not

Exercise 8
Answers will vary.

1. don't have to
2. must not
3. don't have to
4. don't have to
5. must not
6. must not

Exercise 9
Answers will vary.

1. I have to turn in my work on time.
2. I have to study English.
3. I don't have to get up early on Sundays.
4. I don't have to cook every day.
5. I don't have to wear formal clothes to school.
6. I don't have to come to school on Saturdays.

Exercise 10
Answers will vary.

1. Students in my school don't have to stand up to answer a question.
2. Students in my school don't have to got to the blackboard to answer a question.
3. Students in my school don't have to call the teacher by his or her title.
4. Students in my school have to buy their own textbooks.
5. Students in my school have to pay tuition.
6. Students in my school have to attend classes every day.
7. Students in my school don't have to have a written excuse for an absence.
8. Students in my school don't have to get permission to leave the classroom.

Exercise 11
1. People can own a gun.
2. People under 18 can get married.
3. Children can work.
4. Children aren't permitted to see any movie they want.
5. A man isn't permitted to have more than one wife.
6. A married woman can get a passport without her husband's permission.
7. Teachers aren't permitted to talk about religion in public schools.
8. Teachers aren't permitted to hit children.
9. People can travel freely.
10. People can live anywhere they want.

Exercise 12
Answers will vary.

1. You should take some aspirin.
2. You should ask the teacher to read it for you.
3. You should talk to the teacher about how you can improve your compositions.
4. You should call and get more details.
5. You should buy one that isn't very expensive.
6. You should take the new job.
7. You should take into a garage.
8. You should exercise and go on a diet.
9. You should stop telling him your secrets.
10. You should look at some samples.

Exercise 13
Answers will vary.

1. you should pay.
2. you should excuse yourself.
3. you should ask the person to repeat the statement.
4. you should answer and then ask that person how he or she is.
5. you should excuse yourself.

6. you should give her your seat.
7. you should bring a small gift.
8. you should introduce yourself.

Exercise 14

Answers will vary.

1. You'd better come back on time
2. You'd better work faster
3. You'd better
4. You'd better wear formal clothes
5. You'd better not
6. You'd better not tell him anything secret

Exercise 15

Answers will vary.

Exercise 16

Answers will vary. The following are samples.

1. You must not speed.
2. You must not go through a red light.
3. You must not leave the scene of an accident.

Exercise 17

1. can't	8. may not
2. don't have to	9. don't have to
3. can't	10. don't have to
4. don't have to	11. shouldn't
5. shouldn't	12. must not
6. don't have to	13. 'd better not
7. shouldn't	14. must not

Exercise 18

Answers will vary.

Exercise 19

1. You could watch the weather channel. You could also check the Internet.
2. You could go on a diet. You could also start an exercise program.
3. You could ask the landlord to not raise the rent. Or, you could look for a new place.
4. You could study more. You could also watch English-language programs on TV.
5. You could call a travel agency. You could also check the Internet.
6. You could go to a computer store. You could also call computer dealers.
7. You could take salad or you could take a dessert.
8. You could practice more. You could also take a typing class.

Exercise 20

1. Do you have to work during the summer?
2. Do you have to give a final exam?
3. Do you have teach reading?
4. Do you have to take more courses in the teaching of English?
5. Do you call the school when you're going to be absent?

6. Do you work in the evenings?
7. Do you have to have office hours?
8. Do you have to write lesson plans?
9. Do you have to take attendance?
10. Do you have to call students by their last names?
11. Do you have to know another language to teach English?
12. Do you have to attend teachers' meetings?

Exercise 21

1. It's supposed to make your hair grow.
2. It's supposed to make you look stronger.
3. It's supposed to increase your memory power.
4. It's supposed to improve your English.
5. It's supposed to whiten your teeth.
6. It's supposed to help you make money.
7. It's supposed to help you lose weight.
8. It's supposed to help you chop vegetables.

Exercise 22

1. is supposed to rain
2. is supposed to be good
3. is supposed to arrive
4. is supposed to call
5. is supposed to give me
6. are we supposed to write
7. are we supposed to get
8. is registration for next semester supposed to be paid
9. am supposed to take
10. are supposed to help me

Exercise 23

Answers will vary.

Exercise 24

Answers will vary.

Exercise 25

1. It may give out prizes.
2. They could be cheap.
3. You might be chosen as a winner.
4. They might not give you anything.
5. You could win a cheap prize.

Exercise 26

Answers will vary. The following are samples.

1. I might get evicted.
2. I might be able to take a trip.
3. I might not be able to sleep.
4. I might ruin my teeth.
5. I might get into an accident.
6. I might lose shape.
7. I might be able to get a job as a computer programmer.
8. they may not be able to get good jobs.
9. they could get fined.
10. I may buy a house.
11. they may have problems later on.

12. you might get fired.
13. you may not pass the course.
14. I might win a lot of money.

Exercise 27

1. find
2. go
3. work
4. come
5. travel
6. buy
7. be
8. know
9. think
10. cause

Exercise 28

1. A: know
   B: be
2. S: like
   S: be
3. T: have
4. S: be
   S: be
   N: know
5. A: know
   B: believe

Exercise 29

1. must be
2. must not be
3. must have
4. must be
5. must know
6. must not be

7. must be / must not have
8. must like
9. must have
10. must be
11. must be
12. must like
13. must be
14. must have

Exercise 30

1. A: might
2. B: must be
3. B: must
4. B: may
5. B: may / could
6. A: must
7. B: might
8. B: might
9. B: must
10. B: must
11. B: could / might not
12. B: must
13. B: must

Exercise 31

1. He may be sitting at the desk now.
2. He must be doing the exercises now.
3. She should be explaining the grammar now.
4. He must be helping the students now.
5. He might be reviewing now.
6. They are supposed to pay attention.
7. They must be wondering where I am.
8. He might be passing back papers now.

LESSON FOUR TEST / REVIEW

Part 1

1. must
2. We are not allowed
3. C
4. C
5. You'd better
6. You'd better not
7. can type
8. can I
9. C
10. C
11. C
12. I've got to
13. C
14. supposed to rain

7. must
8. must
9. are supposed to
10. might
11. aren't supposed to
12. don't have to / cannot
13. may not
14. must not
15. must

Part 2

1. have to / must / 'd better not / might not could / might
2. are supposed to
3. are supposed
4. don't have to
5. are supposed to
6. should / can

Part 3

1. S	7. S	13. S
2. D	8. D	14. S
3. D	9. S	15. S
4. D	10. D	16. S
5. D	11. D	17. S
6. S	12. S	18. S

LESSON FIVE

Exercise 1

1. had
2. been
3. prevented
4. been
5. been
6. paid
7. been
8. given

Exercise 2

1. He could have preferred an earlier class.
2. He might have wanted to be in his friend's class.

3. The class may have been too hard for him.
4. He could have gotten sick.
5. He may have not liked the teacher.
6. He might have found a full-time job.
7. He could have had a lot of problems at home.
8. He might have left town.

Exercise 3

1. been / been / heard / turned
2. been / been gone / had

3. forgotten
4. been / gotten / had
5. put / fallen / lost
6. given / lost / thought

Exercise 4
1. B: have seen
2. B: have dialed
3. B: have had
4. B: have met
5. B: have been
6. have gone
7. have paid
8. have had
9. have taken
10. have failed
11. have been accepted
12. have dropped out
13. have gotten the money
14. have thought

Exercise 5
1. have been
2. have had
3. had to take
4. had to walk
5. had to cancel
6. must have been
7. must have felt
8. must have died
9. had to identify
10. must have cried

Exercise 6
1. have left
2. have bought
3. have chosen
4. have paid
5. have had
6. have waited

Exercise 7
1. have shown
2. have come
3. have listened
4. have given
5. have said
6. have helped
7. have been
8. have given
9. have paid
10. have been

Exercise 8
Answers will vary.

1. He should have made more food.
2. He should have invited all of his coworkers.
3. He should have invited other children.
4. He should have asked people to be quiet.
5. He should have made sure she knew what time the party was starting.
6. He should have given better directions.

Exercise 9
1. They should have brought a map.
2. They should have put air in the tires.
3. The should have checked the oil.
4. They shouldn't have drove so fast.
5. They shouldn't have taken so much cash.
6. They should have taken a spare tire.
7. They should have packed warm clothes.

Exercise 10
1. pay
2. bring
3. make
4. do
5. wash
6. do
7. buy
8. get

Exercise 11
1. able to get to
2. walk
3. see
4. understand
5. believe
6. find

Exercise 12
1. have slept
2. have killed
3. have had
4. have kissed
5. have watched
6. have eaten
7. have danced
8. have been

Exercise 13
1. have had
2. have spent
3. have bought
4. have lived
5. have got married
6. have had
7. have been
8. have gone

Exercise 14
Answers will vary.

Exercise 15
Answers will vary.

Exercise 16
1. couldn't have won.
2. couldn't have had a test.
3. couldn't have run.
4. couldn't have gone to prison.
5. couldn't have met last year.
6. couldn't have got
7. couldn't have been
8. couldn't have written
9. couldn't have been
10. couldn't have failed
11. couldn't have left
12. couldn't have done it
13. couldn't have come
14. couldn't have caught
15. couldn't have learned

Exercise 17
1. have made
2. have asked
3. have left
4. have charged
5. have charged
6. have brought
7. have hit
8. have gone
9. have gone
10. have stayed
11. have watched

LESSON FIVE TEST / REVIEW

Part 1
1. C
2. C
3. must have been
4. C
5. must have had
6. could have gone
7. should have called
8. had to work
9. should have told
10. C
11. C
12. should have studied
13. couldn't have gone
14. C
15. should have brought
16. couldn't call

Part 2
1. have been killed
2. have been
3. have flown
4. find
5. have been
6. have gone
7. have been
8. have flown
9. find
10. have had
11. have survived / have died
12. cancel

Part 3
1. print in black ink or type
2. have written
3. have included it
4. include that
5. write / have understood
6. have written the month before the day
7. have graduated / have graduated
8. have attended
9. have left / have left
10. have filled it in
11. write in the shaded box / have read
12. include his religion / not have read
13. sign it
14. have mailed it sooner / arrive

Part 4
1. couldn't
2. should have taken
3. couldn't read
4. must have taken
5. couldn't have gotten
6. must have been
7. couldn't call
8. might have taken
9. had to go
10. should have called
11. couldn't find
12. must have lost
13. couldn't wait

LESSON SIX

Exercise 1
Answers will vary.

Exercise 2
1. who don't watch a lot of TV / who watch a lot of TV
2. their children watch
3. who watch a lot of TV
4. they watch
5. who see violence
6. who see violence
7. for food and candy that they see on TV
8. whose parents read to them when they're small
9. no clause
10. that their child watches TV
11. no clause
12. their parents give them

Exercise 3
Answers will vary. The following are samples.

1. are very busy.
2. are likely to get in trouble.
3. will watch too much TV.
4. will have less problems with them when they are in their teens.
5. have a lot of good stimulation.
6. become more passive.
7. are a bad influence on children.
8. are annoying.
9. are lively and active.
10. have a lot of channels to choose from.

Exercise 4
Answers will vary. The following are samples.

1. that show a lot of violence.
2. that are rated for adults.
3. that have cartoon characters
4. that encourage violence.
5. who are very young.
6. who spends a lot of time with his or child.
7. who cares about her students.
8. that are full of fantasy and adventure.

Exercise 5
Answers will vary. The following are samples.

1. who say one thing but do something else.
2. that are small and expensive.
3. that don't have good endings.
4. that tell good stories.
5. who talk too much.
6. who encourage discussion in class.
7. who are rude.
8. who are considerate and clean.
9. who are noisy and inconsiderate.
10. that contain good news.
11. who is famous.
12. who are cruel to animals.
13. that are interesting.

14. who are positive and friendly.
15. who are negative and mean.
16. who you can trust.
17. who is always there for me.
18. that always broke down.

Exercise 6

Answers will vary.

1. Teachers who speak another language are good at teaching ESL.
2. Colleges that have big libraries are good schools to attend.
3. I like textbooks that you can write in.
4. Classes that have fewer than 20 students are better than large classes.
5. I don't like classrooms that don't have windows.

Exercise 7

1. I had
2. I am studying
3. she gave.
4. don't understand
5. I have
6. you found
7. I wrote
8. I read
9. I see/watch
10. she meets

Exercise 8

Answers will vary.

Exercise 9

Answers will vary.

Exercise 10

1. I ate
2. I met
3. I was traveling with
4. s/he is interested in
5. I am interested in
6. It took
7. I found
8. they speak
9. I spent
10. I bought
11. It take

Exercise 11

1. when some students were celebrating a religious holiday.
2. when the house is quiet.
3. I am busiest.
4. where I bought my books
5. where I cash my checks
6. where I study

Exercise 12

Answers will vary.

Exercise 13

1. where
2. that
3. that
4. that
5. which
6. where
7. where
8. that
9. where
10. which

Exercise 14

1. that (or nothing)
2. that
3. when
4. when
5. that
6. that (or nothing)
7. when
8. that (or nothing)

Exercise 15

1. whose native language isn't English
2. whose homework has a lot of mistakes
3. whose homework is always late
4. whose wallet I found and returned
5. whose car she bought

Exercise 16

1. whose mothers work.
2. whose children are small
3. whose incomes are below a certain level
4. whose husband has died
5. whose compositions the teacher loves to read
6. whose book I borrowed
7. whose names I can't remember
8. whose class you are taking

Exercise 17

1. that
2. that
3. who
4. where
5. that
6. whose
7. that
8. who
9. who

Exercise 18

1. you said
2. you did
3. you want
4. you gave me
5. you want to go
6. I've said

Exercise 19

Answers will vary.

1. you've written
2. that is private
3. I got
4. they get
5. on the list
6. you don't know

Exercise 20

Answers will vary.

1. who is famous
2. who can help
3. who passes
4. who is confused
5. that you read in this book

Exercise 21

1. you recommended
2. I had to move
3. whose name I found in the yellow pages
4. I moved
5. that were their fault
6. I had just bought
7. I had just cleaned
8. they sent to my home

9. they had given me
10. I talked to
11. they broke or ruined
12. that doesn't have insurance
13. I've talked to
14. we make
15. I know
16. I was renting from
17. where my sister works
18. I'm free

Exercise 22

1. The abacus, which was created about 2000 years ago, helped people solve arithmetic problems.
2. The first modern computer, which was called ENIAC, took up a lot of space.
3. ENIAC was created in 1942, when the U.S. was involved in WWII.
4. ENIAC, which helped the government keep important data, was built at the University of Pennsylvania.
5. Personal computers, which were introduced in the 1970s, are much smaller and faster than previous computers.
6. Bill Gates went to Harvard University, where he developed the programming language BASIC.
7. Bill Gates dropped out of Harvard to work with Paul Allen, who was his old high school friend.
8. Together, Bill Gates and Allen founded Microsoft, which has made both of them very rich.
9. In 1984, Apple produced the first Macintosh computer, which as easier to use than earlier computers.
10. In 1990, Bill Gates introduced Windows, which was Microsoft's version of the popular Macintosh.

Exercise 23

1. NC
2. My grammar teacher, who has been teaching here for 20 years, knows a lot about the problems of foreign students.
3. NC
4. NC
5. Berners-Lee, whose parents were very educated, gave him a love of learning.
6. Marc Andresson created Netscape, which is a popular Web browser.
7. Berners-Lee worked in Switzerland, where the CERN physics laboratory is located.
8. The Instant Message, which was a creation of America Online, is available to many e-mail users.
9. NC
10. NC
11. The computer, which is one of the most important inventions of the twentieth century, has changed the way people process information.
12. Bill Gates, who created Microsoft with his friend, became a billionaire.

Exercise 24

1. John Kennedy, whom we read about earlier, was the 35th president of the U.S.
2. The Kennedys, who were of Irish descent, were very powerful in Boston.

3. Jacqueline Bouvier, whom John Kennedy married in 1953, was a young and beautiful first lady.
4. John Kennedy, who was only three years old when his father died, could hardly remember his father.
5. John Kennedy Jr., who had only had a pilot's license for a short time, died when his plane crashed.
6. Kennedy's wife Carolyn, who was only 33 years old, died in the plane crash too.
7. John and Carolyn, who did not have any children, died in 1999.
8. John Kennedy, who was only 39 years old when he died, was seven years younger than his father when he died.
9. John and Carolyn, who were going to attend a cousin's wedding, were on their way to Massachusetts.
10. John's cousin's wedding, which was supposed to take place on July 17, was postponed.

Exercise 25

1. Television popular in the 1950s changed the way people get information.
2. The foods advertised during Saturday morning TV programs are not usually healthy.
3. Some parents don't know how to use the controls provided by their Internet service.
4. TV programs directed to children have a lot of commercials.
5. Tim Berners-Lee, born in England, now works at M.I.T.
6. M.I.T., located in Cambridge, Massachusetts, is an excellent university.
7. Berners-Lee developed the idea for the Web when he was working at CERN, a physics lab in Switzerland.
8. Berners-Lee's parents worked on the first computer sold commercially.
9. People using the Web can shop from their homes.
10. People interested in reading newspapers from other cities can find them on the Web.
11. The World Wide Web, abbreviated WWW, was first introduced on the Internet in 1991.
12. Computers sold today have much more memory and speed than computers sold ten years ago.
13. Marc Andreesen, creator of Netscape, quickly became a millionaire.
14. You can download Netscape, a popular Internet browser.

Exercise 26

1. Alaska, the largest state, is separate from the other states.
2. Rhode Island, on the east coast, is the smallest state.
3. Arizona, in the Southwest, has a dry climate.
4. The White House, the home of the President, in Washington, D.C.
5. Puerto Rico, a Caribbean Island, is a U.S. territory.
6. Hawaii, located in the Pacific Ocean, is a group of islands.

Part 1

1. that we have
2. the TOEFL test was given
3. C
4. Whoever
5. who know
6. C
7. who helps students
8. C
9. sitting
10. A teacher who speaks Haitian Creole helped me at registration.
11. that had 25 questions
12. who
13. C
14. C
15. C

Part 2

1. car I hit
2. we use
3. where we buy our books
4. mother interfered in my life
5. who has a black-and-white TV
6. she said
7. we met
8. she is talking about
9. I already have
10. whose names I can't remember

Part 3

Answers will vary.

1. who taught that class
2. my parents say
3. who can't explain things clearly
4. work is incomplete
5. that is in the country
6. at the end of the hall
7. I met you
8. I asked
9. who came to the party
10. I have
11. that were made
12. experiments are conducted
13. where I can rest
14. parents read to them

Part 4

1. In 1963, President Kennedy, whose son was only three years old, was killed.
2. The television, which became popular in the 1950s, changed the way Americans got their information.
3. Berners-Lee, whose parents were programmers, studied physics in college.
4. Berners-Lee, whom we read about in this lesson, is not a well know person.
5. Berners-Lee, who has a small office at M.I.T, works at M.I.T.
6. The V-chip, which has been installed in all new TVs, allows parents to control their children's viewing.

Part 5

The following are words that should be crossed out.

1. that is
2. which is
3. who are
4. who are
5. that
6. that
7.
8. whom
9.
10. that
11.
12. which was

Part 6

1. Ms. Thomson, who was my English teacher last semester, retired last year.
2. no commas
3. I studied engineering at the University of Michigan, which is located in Ann Arbor, Michigan.
4. no commas
5. The computer, which is one of the most important inventions of the twentieth century, can be found in many American homes.
6. no commas
7. My mother, who lives in Miami, has a degree in engineering.
8. no commas
9. Our parents, who live with us now, are beginning to study English.
10. The American flag, which has 13 stripes and 50 stars, is red, white, and blue.
11. no commas
12. St. Petersburg, where I was born, has beautiful museums.

LESSON SEVEN

Exercise 1

Answers will vary.

1. to work
2. to buy a car
3. to learn Russian
4. to see a movie
5. to write my paper
6. to feed my cat
7. to eat and sleep
8. to brush my teeth
9. to speak Chinese
10. to meet Charlie Chaplin

Exercise 2

Answers will vary.

Exercise 3

1. to be told
2. to be taken
3. to be given
4. to be respected
5. to be seen
6. to be loved
7. to be told
8. to be taught
9. to be permitted
10. to be given

Exercise 4

Answers will vary.

1. I want the teacher to explain the grammar.
2. I want the teacher to review modals.
3. I don't want the teacher to give us a lot of homework.
4. I don't want the teacher to give us a test on gerunds and infinitives.
5. I want the teacher to give a lot of examples.
6. I want the teacher to speak slowly.
7. I want the teacher to correct my pronunciation.
8. I want the teacher to teach us idioms.

Exercise 5

Answers will vary.

1. The teacher doesn't expect us to write perfect compositions.
2. The teacher doesn't expect us to learn English in six months.
3. The teacher expects us to do the homework.
4. The teacher doesn't expect us to stand up to answer a question.
5. The teacher doesn't expect us to raise our hands to answer a question.
6. The teacher expects us to ask questions.
7. The teacher doesn't expect us to study on Saturdays.
8. The teacher expects us to practice every day.
9. The teacher doesn't expect us to speak English without an accent.
10. The teacher doesn't expect us to use the Internet.

Exercise 6

1. them to write a composition
2. them to run off the TV
3. him to come home late
4. his children to study hard
5. her to dance
6. her to go to college
7. the teacher to repeat the word
8. his wife to pick up the kids after school
9. my brother to help me on Saturday
10. rich people to give away their money

Exercise 7

Answers will vary.

1. My parents expected me to respect older people.
2. My parents didn't allow me to stay out late at night.
3. My parents didn't want me to move away.
4. My parents expected me to get good grades in school.
5. My parents encouraged me to have a lot of friends.
6. My parents wanted me to be obedient.
7. My parents wanted me to be independent.
8. My parents permitted me to choose my own friends.
9. My parents didn't expect me to get married.
10. My parents encouraged me to save money.
11. My parents advised me to be honest.
12. My parents encouraged me to go to college.

Exercise 8

Answers will vary.

1. stay out after 10 p.m.
2. clean my room every week.
3. learn responsibility.
4. do exercises.
5. talk.
6. choose between public and private schools.
7. study.
8. go out without her.
9. be unhappy.
10. do things I don't want to do.
11. correct papers for her.
12. pick up trash.

Exercise 9

1. set
2. prepare
3. clean
4. to rake
5. to buy
6. to study
7. do
8. turn
9. to relax
10. do

Exercise 10

Answers will vary.

1. to live on my own.
2. to find out how hard it was.
3. to walk in the dark.
4. to be at this school.
5. to skydive.
6. to help others.
7. to be able to study.
8. seventeen / to start driving.

Exercise 11

Answers will vary.

1. help my children do their schoolwork.
2. get a degree in law.
3. learn about infinitives.
4. verify the spelling of new words.
5. check spelling before they print the document.
6. keep in touch with their friends.
7. meditate
8. read
9. avoid late charges.
10. help with tuition.

Exercise 12

Answers will vary.

1. to drive when you're tired.
2. to eat a lot of sugar.
3. to stare at people.
4. to drive through a red light.
5. to check the spelling of new words.

6. to tell us about our assignments.
7. to buy a house.
8. to get an education.
9. to study without a break.
10. to play.
11. to waste time.
12. to get a good job.
13. to buy a computer.
14. to figure out what I want to do.

Exercise 13

Answers will vary.

1. It's fun for children to play games and tell jokes.
2. It's necessary for children to have discipline.
3. It's important for a family to spend together.
4. It's difficult for a large family to schedule activities.
5. It's necessary for working parents to get good childcare.
6. It's difficult for women to be treated fairly in the workplace.
7. It's hard for single parents to spend as much time with their kids as they'd like.
8. It's difficult for the teacher to explain some grammar points in simple terms.

Exercise 14

Answers will vary.

1. It's tiring
2. It's easy
3. It's exciting
4. It's easy
5. It's sad
6. It's important
7. It costs a lot
8. It's cheap
9. It's expensive
10. It's expensive
11. It's hard
12. It's a nice gesture
13. It's entertaining
14. It's interesting

Exercise 15

1. It's time-consuming to find a job.
2. It's my goal to graduate from school.
3. It takes a lot of patience to raise children.
4. It's the responsibility of rich people to give away money.
5. It's natural to make mistakes in English.
6. It's boring to do the same thing every day.

Exercise 16

1. too long
2. too noisy
3. too quickly
4. too crowded
5. too cold
6. too hard
7. too much money
8. too many things to do

Exercise 17

1. short enough
2. fast enough
3. enough time
4. old enough
5. hard enough
6. enough money

Exercise 18

Answers will vary.

1. Going to college was the best decision I ever made.
2. Making new friends makes me feel good.
3. Changing old habits is one of the hardest things to do.

4. Learning a new language is a good experience.
5. Finding an apartment is time-consuming.
6. Thinking about my future fills me with dreams and hopes.
7. Getting a job is something we all have to face.
8. Leaving home is a step toward becoming an adult.

Exercise 19

Answers will vary.

1. Getting an education
2. Understanding idioms
3. Deciding on a career
4. Stealing
5. Jogging
6. Interrupting people
7. Eating fattening foods
8. Learning how to play an instrument
9. Helping others
10. Doing something well

Exercise 20

Answers will vary.

1. studying English grammar?
2. taking the final exam?
3. having to do your assignments?
4. learning another language?
5. dropping out of school?
6. coming here?
7. doing the things you like to do?
8. becoming famous?

Exercise 21

Answers will vary.

1. getting a loan.
2. taking care of children.
3. doing physical labor.
4. shopping for my nephews and nieces.
5. watching TV.
6. playing sports.
7. staying at home.
8. helping other people.

Exercise 22

1. of getting
2. for being
3. about starting
4. studying
5. in becoming
6. at working
7. going
8. in finding

Exercise 23

1. Do you have trouble understanding spoken English?
2. Are you lazy about doing the homework?
3. Do you have a technique for learning new words?
4. Are you afraid of failing this course?
5. Are you good at spelling English words?
6. Are you interested in studying computer programming?
7. Do you have experience working with computers?
8. Have you thought about buying a house one day?

Exercise 24

Answers will vary.

1. eating in class.
2. giving my seat to mothers with children.
3. drinking coffee.
4. reading.
5. listening to classical music.
6. living somewhere else.
7. swimming in the ocean.
8. walking alone at night.
9. getting a compliment.
10. cleaning my house.

Exercise 25

1. being criticized
2. being given
3. being asked
4. being fired
5. being corrected
6. being caught
7. being injured
8. being cared for

Exercise 26

1. Do you prefer studying in the morning?
2. She hates to wash the dishes.
3. When did you begin to study English?
4. If you continue to talk about politics, I'm going to leave.
5. He can't stand watching violent movies.
6. I love getting letters, don't you?

Exercise 27

1. to study / studying
2. to speak / speaking
3. to study / studying
4. talking
5. to speak
6. making
7. to be
8. speaking
9. to communicate
10. doing
11. filling
12. writing
13. doing

Exercise 28

1. Meeting new people is fascinating.
2. Doing the same thing every day is boring.
3. Raising children is seldom easy.
4. Using the Internet takes practice.
5. Going to college costs a lot of money.

Exercise 29

1. talking
2. using
3. to take
4. to speak
5. speaking
6. to return
7. to use
8. to do
9. learning
10. to use
11. understanding
12. studying
13. to learn
14. living
15. calling / to use (or using) / to tell (or telling)
16. to find

Exercise 30

1. hearing
2. living
3. finding
4. meeting
5. to rest
6. to get
7. to pick up
8. to call
9. worrying
10. giving
11. to understand

Exercise 31

1. to be
2. used
3. I can't
4. I
5. live
6. used to
7. I'm
8. eating
9. used to
10. I'm
11. driving
12. use
13. living

Exercise 32

1. to be poor
2. drive
3. rent
4. have a pet
5. go out
6. spend
7. read
8. be called

Exercise 33

Answers will vary.

Exercise 34

1. living
2. cold weather
3. being
4. American English
5. doing chores
6. talking

Exercise 35

Answers will vary.

Exercise 36

1. go
2. hit
3. leave
4. arrive
5. take
6. put
7. drive
8. tow

Exercise 37

1. telling
2. playing
3. playing
4. having
5. waving
6. playing
7. eating/cooking
8. having

LESSON SEVEN TEST / REVIEW

Part 1

1. use
2. her to call
3. C
4. to get
5. C
6. C
7. to finish
8. to move
9. Living
10. C
11. me / C
12. needs to speak
13. C
14. C
15. for me to din
16. C
17. It costs
18. to watch
19. working
20. C
21. C / washing
22. C
23. shipping
24. to live
25. get used to living
26. C
27. fighting
28. C
29. for taking
30. finding
31. C
32. C
33. not coming
34. C
35. C
36. C

4. to donate / to give (giving)
5. buying
6. Telling / interrupt
7. listen
8. to tell (telling) / be bothered
9. getting
10. changing
11. Changing
12. to stop / calling
13. to get
14. to see
15. picking / not picking

Part 2

1. to eat / eating
2. to sell
3. being interrupted

Part 3

1. for
2. on
3. of (about)
4. on
5. for
6. in
7. about
8. to
9. in
10. of
11. about
12. to

Part 4

1. Different
2. Same
3. Same
4. Same
5. Different
6. Same

LESSON EIGHT

Exercise 1

1. for
2. During
3. When
4. for
5. since
6. while
7. Before
8. During
9. When
10. Whenever
11. for

Exercise 2

1. Whenever (When)
2. for
3. Whenever
4. When
5. During
6. When
7. While
8. until
9. since
10. While
11. for
12. While
13. during
14. until

Exercise 3

Answers will vary.

1. high school
2. the last two years
3. 1999
4. she was in college
5. she was a teenager
6. she graduated from high school
7. seven years
8. he was skiing
9. the whole evening
10. the wedding
11. she heard the joke
12. recently
13. she needs some fresh air
14. reads an unfamiliar word
15. a long time
16. he was 17
17. he was 20
18. the weekends
19. he had saved enough money
20. driving in the rain

Exercise 4

Answers will vary.

1. I've wanted to be an artist.
2. I never had a dull moment.
3. I'm always busy
4. I had a lot to learn
5. I had a lot less stress
6. I had to pay a lot of tuition
7. I've met a lot of people
8. He graduated from high school
9. He was in high school
10. He's been very curious about a lot of things
11. they change their lives dramatically.
12. I see her a lot less.
13. I thought she would be single forever.
14. I was so happy
15. I can afford to buy myself things

16. I was always broke
17. He had to start paying for insurance
18. he had to walk everywhere
19. he goes on trips every weekend.

Exercise 5

1. Before taking a test, I study.
2. Maria will go back to Arizona after graduating.
3. While traveling through Europe, Jack learned about Italian architecture.
4. After getting married, Susan moved to London.
5. After being at sea for many days, Columbus saw land.
6. She always makes a list before going shopping.

Exercise 6

1. because	7. Since (Because)
2. so	8. to
3. so	9. for
4. because	10. so (that)
5. because of	11. to
6. to	12. because

Exercise 7

Answers will vary.

1. they have family members here.
2. get an education.
3. political reasons.
4. economic conditions may be severe
5. racism and discrimination
6. I know it well.
7. it has a good reputation.
8. the educational opportunities.
9. check spellings.
10. I'll need it in the future.
11. I can buy a car if I need to.
12. any emergency that might come up.
13. buy a car.
14. cities have a lot of jobs

Exercise 8

1. because	4. since
2. because	5. because of
3. in order to	6. so that

Exercise 9

1. in spite of
2. In spite of the fact that
3. in spite of
4. in spite of the fact that
5. In spite of the fact that
6. In spite of
7. In spite of the fact that

Exercise 10

Answers will vary.

Exercise 11

Answers will vary.

Exercise 12

Answers will vary.

Exercise 13

1. You can't go fishing unless you have a license.
2. Children cannot see R-rated movies unless they are accompanied by an adult.
3. Children of immigrants will forget their language unless they use it.
4. Immigrants will continue to come to the U.S. unless conditions in their countries improve.
5. You cannot travel to most foreign countries unless you have a passport.
6. An American citizen can't be President unless he or she was born in the U.S.
7. You shouldn't give friends advice unless they ask for it.
8. You shouldn't dial 911 unless it's an emergency.

Exercise 14

Answers will vary.

Exercise 15

1. if it's cold.
2. you make mistakes.
3. you have an accent.
4. the weather is bad.
5. he takes the final exam
6. I am absent.
7. I move to a suburb.
8. their parents don't.

Exercise 16

1. if	5. if
2. even if	6. even if
3. unless	7. unless
4. If	

Exercise 17

1. As a result	10. In addition
2. Therefore	11. As a result
3. However	12. However
4. Furthermore	13. Nevertheless
5. In addition	14. As a result
6. As a result	15. However
7. As a result	16. However
8. However	17. Furthermore
9. Nevertheless	18. As a result

Exercise 18

Answers will vary.

Exercise 19

1. to
2. to
3. Because of
4. In spite of the fact that
5. so that
6. Although

7. since
8. Even though
9. In spite of
10. Because
11. However
12. Furthermore
13. However
14. Until
15. In spite of the fact that
16. because of
17. until
18. Although

Exercise 20

1. so many
2. such a
3. so
4. so
5. such a
6. so
7. so

Exercise 21

Answers will vary.

1. so / that I get an A on every test.
2. so many / that he doesn't have any time to go out.
3. so much / that there's never enough time to do it.
4. so / that I can't understand him.
5. so / that she's going to be an interpreter.
6. so / that I'm going to drop it.
7. such a / that everyone likes him.
8. so many / that it's hard to remember them all.
9. such a / that I was tired by the end of it.
10. so many / that I though I must have failed.
11. such a / that it was impossible to understand.
12. so / that I fell asleep.

LESSON EIGHT TEST / REVIEW

Part 1

1. Although
2. C
3. C
4. (delete so)
5. go
6. (delete but)
7. to buy
8. C
9. because of
10. In spite of the fact that
11. even if
12. preparing
13. C
14. C
15. so that she can
16. because
17. C
18. C
19. such a bad cook
20. C
21. to stay
22. I have to take the TOEFL

Part 2

1. C
2. C
3. Even though owning a dog has some disadvantages, there are more advantages.
4. Because he didn't study, he failed the test.
5. Before he got married, his friends had a party for him.
6. She did all the homework and wrote all the compositions. However, she didn't pass the course.
7. Although I didn't do the homework, I understood everything that the teacher said.
8. Even though he worked hard all weekend, he wasn't tired.

9. C
10. I am unhappy with my job because I don't get paid enough. Furthermore, my boss is an unpleasant person.
11. C
12. My boss never showed any respect for the workers. As a result, many people quit.

Part 3

1. whenever
2. while
3. when
4. for
5. until
6. When
7. since
8. during

Part 4

1. in order to
2. to
3. because of
4. in order to
5. for
6. Because
7. Therefore
8. since (because)

Part 5

1. In spite of
2. However
3. Even though
4. In spite of the fact (Even though)

Part 6

1. even if
2. even if
3. If
4. unless

Part 7

1. so many
2. so
3. such a
4. so
5. such a

Part 8

Answers will vary.

LESSON NINE

Exercise 1

Answers will vary.

1. I'm not surprised that only 26% of households are made up of a mother, father, and children.
2. I'm not surprised that about 7 million children are home alone after school.
3. I'm surprised that 12% of children don't have health insurance.
4. I'm surprised that 20% of children live in poverty.
5. I'm not surprised that 68% of married mothers work outside of the home.
6. I'm not surprised that, in families where both parents work, women do most of the housework and childcare.
7. I'm surprised that 31% of working wives earn more than their husbands.
8. I'm surprised that 56% of adults are married.
9. I'm not surprised that 10% of adults live alone.
10. I'm not surprised that 56% of families own their own homes.

Exercise 2

Answers will vary.

1. I think that all children should have health insurance.
2. I'm disappointed that so many children live in poverty.
3. I know that it can be hard to raise a child.
4. I'm afraid that there aren't enough qualified teachers.
5. It's unfortunate that so many people get divorced.
6. I'm surprised that so many people live alone.
7. I've noticed that many people prefer living in cities.
8. Many people think that it's better to own a home than to rent an apartment.

Exercise 3

Answers will vary.

Exercise 4

1. you eat a healthy diet.
2. you exercise regularly.
3. a child receive love.
4. students be quiet in the library.
5. students register early for classes.
6. foreign students take the TOEFL.
7. students do the homework.
8. be on time
9. the teacher review modals
10. her husband help with the children

Exercise 5

1. how many students in this class come from South America.
2. who read the article about working mothers.
3. what happened in the last class.
4. who brought a dictionary yesterday.
5. who failed the test.

Exercise 6

1. we will have the final exam.
2. how many lessons we are going to finish.
3. where the teacher is from.
4. where the final exam will be.
5. when the teacher can see me.

Exercise 7

1. when the semester ends?
2. what grade I got on the last test?
3. how many mistakes I made.
4. how many questions the test has.
5. how many compositions she wants.

Exercise 8

1. if the test is going to be hard.
2. if you are going to be our teacher next semester.
3. if you can help us with registration.
4. if you've been teaching here for a long time.
5. if the students are confused.

Exercise 9

1. if the school has a cafeteria.
2. if everyone passed the test.
3. if you bought a used book.
4. if the teacher speaks Spanish.
5. if I need to write a composition.

Exercise 10

1. if the caregivers have a lot of experience.
2. how the caregiver disciplines the children.
3. if the caregiver can handle problems without getting angry or impatient.
4. if the caregiver likes children.
5. if I am welcome to drop in and visit.
6. how the caregiver takes care of sick children.
7. if there is a nurse or doctor to help with medical care.
8. if the caregivers know first aid.
9. if there are smoke alarms in the building.
10. how many caregivers there are.
11. if the caregiver hugs the child.
12. if the caregiver talks with each child.
13. how many children there are for each caregiver.
14. if the place is clean and safe.
15. if there are enough toys.
16. if the toys are clean.
17. how long the caregivers have been working there.
18. if there is a high turnover of caregivers.
19. if the caregiver is patient.
20. if the care center is licensed by the state.
21. if the caregiver enjoys children.
22. if the child has stimulating activities.

Exercise 11

1. where to buy my textbooks.
2. which classes to register for.
3. whether to take morning classes or evening classes.
4. what else to do.

5. how to use the computer in the library.
6. what to do about closed classes.
7. who to ask about graduation.
8. to take biology or physics.
9. whether to buy new or used textbooks.

Exercise 12

Answers will vary.

1. what to major in.
2. what to write about.
3. what to study.
4. where to find the library.
5. what to buy.

Exercise 13

1. it is
2. to write about.
3. he died.
4. whether he died
5. to find it
6. to find it
7. to use it
8. it opens
9. I can
10. I will be finished
11. to use

Exercise 14

1. The woman asked, "How often should I feed my baby?"
2. She said, "The baby is hungry."
3. Dr. Spock said, "You know more than you think you do."
4. "Respect children," said Dr. Spock.
5. "Why did you write your book?" the interviewer asked Dr. Spock.
6. "I wanted to be supportive of parents," Spock answered.

Exercise 15

One day a neighbor passed Nasreddin's house and saw him outside his barn on his hands and knees. He appeared to be looking for something. "What are you doing" the neighbor asked.

"I'm looking for something," answered Nasreddin.

"What are you looking for?" the neighbor asked.

"I'm looking for my ring. It's very valuable," Nasreddin replied.

"I'll help you," said his neighbor. The neighbor got down on his hands and knees and started to help Nasreddin look for his ring. After searching for several hours, the neighbor finally asked, "Do you remember where you were when you lost it?"

"Of course," replied Nasreddin. "I was in the barn milking my cow."

"If you lost your ring inside the barn, then why are we looking for it outside the barn?" asked the neighbor.

"Don't be a fool," said Nasreddin. "It's too dark in the barn. But out here we have light."

Exercise 16

Last week my daughter's teacher called me at work and told me that my daughter had a fever and was resting in the nurse's office. I told my boss that I needed to leave work immediately. He said that it would be fine. As I was driving my car on the expressway to the school, a police officer stopped me and she said that I had been driving too fast. She said that I had been driving 10 mph over the speed limit. I told her that I was in a hurry because my daughter was sick. I said I needed to get to her school quickly. I told the police officer that I was sorry, that I hadn't realized I had been driving so fast. She said she wouldn't give me a ticket that time, but that I should be more careful in the future, whether my daughter was sick or not.

Exercise 17

1. My father said he hoped I would grow up to be President.
2. My mother said I had to make my own decision.
3. My grandmother said I could choose my own decision.
4. My grandmother said she had a difficult childhood.
5. My grandfather said he liked to see his grandchildren.
6. My grandparents said that their childhood had been very different from ours.
7. My grandmother said that she had been raised on a farm.
8. My grandfather said that he (had) worked on a farm when he was a child.
9. My grandfather said that his family (had) left Germany before the war.
10. My grandmother said that she was the oldest of 11 children.
11. My grandparents said that they wanted their children to be happy.
12. My grandparents said that we are living in a different world.
13. My grandparents said that they were glad that they could give me the opportunities that they never had.
14. My mother said that when I have children of my own, I would understand the difficulties of raising children.
15. My mother said that I would always be her baby.

Exercise 18

Answers will vary.

Police Officer: "You are driving too fast. You are driving 10 mph over the speed limit."

Driver: "I'm sorry, but I'm in a hurry because my daughter is sick. I need to get to her school quickly. I didn't realize I was driving so fast."

Police Officer: "I won't give you a ticket this time, but you should be more careful in the future, whether your daughter is sick or not."

Exercise 19

1. said
2. told
3. said
4. said
5. told
6. told
7. told
8. said

Exercise 20

Answers will vary.

Exercise 21

Answers will vary.

1. I could be whatever I wanted to be.
2. I would be happy in life.
3. I would grow up to be like them.
4. I would be famous.
5. life was all fun and games.

Exercise 22

1. The thief told the woman to give him her money.
2. The teacher told us to not be late for class.
3. The teacher told us to give her our tests.
4. The secretary asked the woman to please sit down.
5. The doctor told the man to take two aspirins and call him in the morning.
6. The man asked the doctor to call him when he had the lab results.
7. She asked her husband to help her clean the house.
8. The mother told her children to wash their hands before eating.
9. The girl asked her parents to take her to the zoo the next day.
10. The father told his son to not watch so much TV.
11. The dentist told me to brush my teeth after every meal.
12. The wife told her husband not to open her mail.
13. The father asked his son to bring him the newspaper.
14. The teacher told us to not use our books during the test.

Exercise 23

1. if they were bringing any fruit into the country.
2. if had my transcripts with me.
3. if I would visit her tomorrow.
4. if he could fix my car.
5. how much it would cost.
6. when the car would be ready.
7. if I could leave early tomorrow.
8. if I had seen the accident.
9. if she would return the final exam.
10. if he was lost.
11. if we wanted to have a party.
12. what I wanted to be when I grew up.

Exercise 24

1. he was looking for.
2. he was looking for his
3. would help
4. he had lost

5. had lost it
6. he was looking for it outside.
7. was foolish
8. was looking for / there was more light outside.

Exercise 25

1. she didn't want the bright light to hurt my eyes
2. that I could go into the dining room
3. not to go in the living room
4. that the brightness of the TV could hurt my eyes
5. if I knew why I couldn't go into the living room
6. I didn't understand
7. "dining" meant "eating," not "dying"
8. I would die

Exercise 26

Last January, I called my landlord and asked him if he could turn up the heat. I told him it was too cold in my apartment. He answered that none of the other tenants were complaining about the heat. He told me to put on a sweater and stop complaining. I called him many times after that, but I always got the same answer. I asked several other tenants if they were cold, and they all said they were. I asked them why they didn't complain to the landlord. They said that they had complained many times, but that he never did anything to solve the problem. Finally, I told the landlord that if he didn't turn up the heat, I would have to move. Of course, he didn't do anything, and I moved in March. But that wasn't the end of my problems with him.

Months went by and I still hadn't gotten back my security deposit. Finally I called him and asked why he hadn't returned my deposit. He said that the carpet wasn't clean, and that one of the windows was broken. I reminded him that the window was already broken when I moved in.

Yesterday I called the city and asked if the landlord could keep my deposit for a dirty carpet. The city worker told me that the landlord couldn't keep my deposit for normal wear and tear. I asked the woman what that expression meant. She explained that a landlord has to expect normal living to occur in the apartment and that he couldn't deduct money from my deposit for it. Then I told her about the broken window. She asked me if I had taken pictures of the window. I hadn't, but I told her that I had a copy of the letter that I had written to the landlord asking him to fix the broken window. The letter was dated May 10, 1998. She told me that that was good evidence. Then she asked me if the landlord had sent me a letter with the list of damages. I answered that he had told me about these problems by phone. She said that he had to put the damages in writing within 30 days after the move. She said that if he hadn't done that, I could take him to court.

LESSON NINE TEST / REVIEW

Part 1

1. C
2. that
3. C
4. told
5. what time it is
6. C
7. C
8. where I should go
9. C
10. would rain
11. that
12. C
13. I don't know whether

14. where I lived
15. He told me that he wanted
16. C
17. C
18. would find
19. C
20. C
21. told me
22. told me
23. that my friend visit
24. me to not take

Part 2

1. I don't know what time it is.
2. C
3. I'm sure that you'll find a job soon.
4. The teacher said, "I will return your tests on Monday."
5. I didn't realize that you had seen the movie already.
6. C
7. C
8. C
9. C
10. "Can you tell me where I can find the bookstore?"

Part 3

1. where Jack lives
2. whether she went home
3. why they were late
4. who ate the cake

5. what "liberty" means
6. if they are working now
7. whether I should buy the car
8. if she has ever gone to Paris
9. if we can use our books during the test
10. what to do

Part 4

1. He told me to give him the money.
2. She said that she could help me.
3. He told me not to go away.
4. He said that his mother had left yesterday.
5. She said that she was learning a lot.
6. He said that he had never heard of Dr. Spock.
7. They said that they had finished the job.
8. He said that they may need some help.
9. He told her that they were studying.
10. He told her that he had her book.
11. He told us that we should have called him.
12. He told his wife that he would call her.
13. He asked me if I had any children.
14. He asked me where I was from.
15. He asked me what time it was.
16. He asked me if my father had come home.
17. He asked me where I had been.
18. He asked me if I was going to leave tomorrow.
19. He asked me where I lived.
20. He asked me if I was a student.
21. He asked us if we needed help today.
22. He asked us who needed his help.

LESSON TEN

Exercise 1

1. were / would be
2. had / would be able
3. were / would look for
4. had / would read
5. knew / would have
6. could / studied
7. wouldn't bother / didn't need
8. would have / were
9. would be able to / had
10. didn't want / wouldn't have offered
11. would / didn't have to
12. were / would give
13. weren't / would move
14. wouldn't do / didn't love

Exercise 2

Answers will vary.

Exercise 3

Answers will vary.

Exercise 4

1. I would lower taxes.
2. I would give less homework.
3. I would have a lot of experience.

4. I would be able to give people a lot of advice.
5. I would buy my mother a house.
6. I would play more.
7. I would have more free time.
8. I would be so happy.
9. there would be a lot of ethical problems.
10. I would be you.

Exercise 5

Answers will vary.

1. I had more free time.
2. I could practice all the time.
3. I didn't have to work.
4. I had the time and money.
5. I lived alone.
6. I really needed to.

Exercise 6

Answers will vary.

1. Yes. If I didn't speak any other languages besides English, I wouldn't be in this class.
2. Yes. If I didn't know how to use computers, I wouldn't be able to do my research.
3. No. If I had to work on Sundays, I wouldn't be able to do my chores.

4. No. If everybody in this class spoke the same language, we could all understand each other.
5. Yes. If the teacher weren't bilingual, she wouldn't be able to talk to us in Spanish after class.
6. Yes. If I weren't taking other courses this semester, I wouldn't graduate on time.
7. Yes. If I didn't have a high school diploma, I couldn't attend college.
8. Yes. If I didn't have a car, I would have to take a bus everywhere.
9. No. If I lived in a dorm, I would always be on campus.
10. Yes. If I didn't have a job, I would have to get one.
11. Yes. If I didn't own a house, I would be saving to buy one.
12. No. If today were Saturday, we wouldn't be in class.
13. No. If I spoke English perfectly, I wouldn't have to study it.
14. Yes. If I didn't have a computer, I wouldn't be able to do my assignments.

Exercise 7
1. had / would buy
2. were / would find
3. made / wouldn't quit
4. had / wouldn't have to use
5. got / would be
6. were / wouldn't move
7. had / would be able to read
8. would have / didn't have children
9. weren't raining / would be playing
10. bought / would have to pay for
11. could travel / would visit
12. would take / had

Exercise 8
Answers will vary.

Exercise 9
Answers will vary.

Exercise 10
1. were / would be
2. wouldn't marry / were
3. comes / may be
4. would not / paid
5. calls
6. send / can
7. weren't / would drive
8. weren't raining / could go
9. wouldn't do / gave
10. were / would play
11. pass / will go
12. had / would take

Exercise 11
1. had / would have been
2. had been alive / wouldn't have used
3. had not done / would not have learned
4. would have studied / had known
5. had studied / would have been able to
6. would have called / had not lost
7. had found / would have returned
8. had known / would have apologized
9. had seen / would have enjoyed
10. had moved / would have told
11. had eaten / would have gotten
12. had stayed / would have finished
13. had known / he would have never trusted
14. hadn't been sleeping / she would have

Exercise 12
1. hadn't gone / wouldn't have met
2. had studied / would have passed
3. wouldn't have married / had known
4. wouldn't have told / had known
5. wouldn't have gotten / hadn't approved
6. had found / wouldn't have left
7. could have returned / had been
8. had known / would have prepared
9. wouldn't have punished / hadn't told
10. had known / would have
11. had got / could have paid
12. had asked / would have
13. hadn't sailed / would have
14. had known / have asked
15. not have crashed / had flown

Exercise 13
1. hadn't invested / wouldn't have become
2. had married / wouldn't be
3. had married / wouldn't be
3. wouldn't be / hadn't passed
4. were / wouldn't have bought
5. would be able to tell you / had seen
6. would be able to understand / had come
7. didn't have / would have stayed
8. would have graduated / had stayed
9. had a car / would have driven
10. had learned / wouldn't be having

Exercise 14
Answers will vary.

1. I wouldn't be learning about grammar.
2. I wouldn't be able to take this course.
3. I would have missed the assignment.
4. I wouldn't have passed it.
5. I would be in trouble with the landlord.
6. I wouldn't have met you.

Exercise 15
Answers will vary.

1. I had known the teacher needed help.
2. I had known class was canceled.
3. I had studied more for it.
4. she had known that we didn't understand it.
5. I had known how hard this one was going to be.
6. I had known it was your birthday.
7. I had known I was going to major in it.
8. I hadn't got an education.

Exercise 16

1. would have woke up / had set
2. had passed / would have passed
3. had seen / would be able to give
4. would have eaten / liked
5. hadn't loved / wouldn't have married
6. would have answered / had heard
7. hadn't left / would have been able to get
8. would have been able to buy / had had
9. had taken / would have
10. would have / had had

Exercise 17

Answers will vary.

1. they had healthier lifestyles.
2. I would have learned how to speak Italian.
3. we had already covered the material.
4. if I were rich.
5. I wouldn't have passed it.
6. I would go to Colombia.
7. the world would be very crowded.
8. I would have been able to predict the future.

Exercise 18

1. were
2. didn't have to
3. could
4. had
5. could go
6. were
7. didn't have
8. had
9. were 18 again
10. had
11. could grow
12. could speak

Exercise 19

Answers will vary.

1. able to speak Japanese.
2. cook French cuisine.
3. work every day.
4. more time and more money.
5. go around the world.

Exercise 20

1. had known
2. had gone
3. had seen
4. had studied
5. had seen
6. had left
7. I hadn't
8. had brought

Exercise 21

Answers will vary.

1. I wish I had learned how to play the guitar.
2. I wish I had studied English.

3. My family wishes I had never moved away.
4. I wish I had known the importance of saving money.
5. I wish I had traveled more.
6. I wish my parents had come to visit me last year.
7. I wish I had never sold my car.
8. I wish that there had never been any wars.

Exercise 22

1. had
2. didn't have to
3. had
4. were
5. could type
6. had
7. could have attended
8. had met
9. had studied
10. knew
11. could sing
12. had helped you

Exercise 23

1. would stay
2. would clean
3. would play
4. would pay for
5. they would be more quiet
6. would cut
7. wouldn't give
8. would go

Exercise 24

1. could spend more time together.
2. would give us less assignments.
3. were more quiet.
4. would provide free childcare.
5. were polite.
6. were bigger.

Exercise 25

1. would have
2. could
3. gave
4. had
5. were
6. had asked
7. would have told
8. had
9. wouldn't visit
10. had
11. would have
12. could
13. had known
14. wouldn't have

Exercise 26

1. had studied
2. had started
3. would be able
4. didn't have
5. spoke
6. were
7. would try
8. hadn't gotten
9. would be
10. had waited
11. had started going
12. could go
13. could
14. lived
15. would be
16. wouldn't be

LESSON TEN TEST / REVIEW

Part 1

1. had
2. would
3. C
4. C
5. would be
6. C
7. were
8. would have
9. didn't have
10. C
11. would have
12. C
13. C
14. were
15. would have called
16. would have known
17. C
18. C

19. found
20. C

Part 2

1. c.) would
2. d.) go
3. a.) were

11. d.) had
12. a.) could drive
13. d.) would have studied

21. could have gone
22. had been

4. b.) could
5. b.) won't
6. a.) knew
7. d.) didn't have
8. c.) weren't raining
9. b.) paid
10. c.) would live

14. c.) had taken
15. d.) had taken
16. c.) would have
17. a.) might not have had
18. b.) had told
19. a.) could have helped
20. c.) wouldn't talk